Making a Slave State

RYAN A. QUINTANA

Making a Slave State
Political Development in Early South Carolina

The University of North Carolina Press *Chapel Hill*

© 2018 The University of North Carolina Press
All rights reserved
Set in Arno Pro by Westchester Publishing Services
Manufactured in the United States of America

The University of North Carolina Press has been a member of the Green Press Initiative since 2003.

Library of Congress Cataloging-in-Publication Data
Names: Quintana, Ryan A. (Ryan Alexander), author.
Title: Making a slave state : political development in early South Carolina / Ryan A. Quintana.
Description: Chapel Hill : University of North Carolina Press, [2018] | Includes bibliographical references and index.
Identifiers: LCCN 2018001029| ISBN 9781469641065 (cloth : alk. paper) | ISBN 9781469642222 (pbk : alk. paper) | ISBN 9781469641072 (ebook)
Subjects: LCSH: Slavery—South Carolina—History—18th century. | Slavery—South Carolina—History—19th century. | Slaves—South Carolina—Social conditions. | Slaves—South Carolina—Economic conditions. | South Carolina—History. | South Carolina—Politics and government. | South Carolina—Race relations. | Human ecology. | Human geography.
Classification: LCC E445.S7 Q85 2018 | DDC 305.8009757—dc23
LC record available at https://lccn.loc.gov/2018001029

Jacket illustration: *Map of the Province of South Carolina* (1773) by James Cook. Courtesy of the David Rumsey Map Collection, http://www.davidrumsey.com.

Portions of chapter 5 were previously published as "Planners, Planters, and Slaves: Producing the State in Early National South Carolina," *Journal of Southern History* 81, no. 1 (February 2015): 79–116. Used here with permission.

For Rory, who's been there from the start

Contents

Acknowledgments xi

Introduction 1

CHAPTER ONE
The "Within Enemy": Slaves and the Production of
South Carolina's Early State 15

CHAPTER TWO
The Strength of This Country: Securing and Rebuilding the State
in the Revolutionary Era 48

CHAPTER THREE
Their Intentions Were to Ambuscade and Surround Me:
The Necessity of Slave Mobility 89

CHAPTER FOUR
This Negro Thoroughfare: The Meaning of Black Movement 116

CHAPTER FIVE
With the Labor of These Slaves: Producing the Modern State 149

Conclusion 183

Notes 187
Bibliography 211
Index 233

Illustrations

James Cook, *A Map of the Province of South Carolina*, 1773 67
Johann Christian Senf, *General Plan of the Canal*, 1800 69
John L. Wilson, *A Map of South Carolina*, 1822 156
Robert Mills, *Design for Kershaw County Courthouse*, 1825 163
Robert Mills, *Design for Lunatic Asylum, Columbia, SC*, 1822 166

Acknowledgments

Over the last decade, this book has come together in many places and a variety of circumstances. I began my research and writing in Madison, Wisconsin, and the book was completed in Wellesley, Massachusetts. In between, I've written in coffee shops, on mountain tops, tucked away in library carrels, and, distractedly, on the front porches of many a friend. At each stop, whether in Asheville, Franklin, Cambridge, Madison, or Columbia, the book's progress was continually sustained by the friendship, guidance, and support of a number of individuals and communities. I am grateful to them all.

I must express my gratitude for the generous support I've received for both research and writing from the University of Wisconsin History Department, the Colonial Dames, and Wellesley College. I've been fortunate to present portions of this book at various stages in a number of forums. I would like to thank all of the scholars who participated in the National Endowment of the Humanities Seminar "Intended Consequences: The Historical and Contemporary Problematics of Planning," hosted by the Jeanne and Dan Valente Center for Arts & Sciences at Bentley University, and in particular seminar organizers Cyrus Veeser and Sven Beckert. I'm grateful also to the participants at Brown University's 19th Century History Workshop, especially Seth Rockman, who not only invited me to present my work in this forum but has provided generous advice and encouragement over the last several years, without which this book would likely still be a work in progress. I'd also like to thank all of my fellow participants at the symposium "Taking Stock of the State in Nineteenth-Century America," hosted by the Yale Center for the Study of Representative Institutions, particularly Gautham Rao and Ariel Ron for organizing the event and inviting me to participate. I must also express my gratitude to the anonymous readers and the editorial staff at the *Journal of Southern History* who propelled my research and interest in slavery and space toward American political development. At the University of North Carolina Press, I've been fortunate to work closely with the editorial staff. I especially want to thank Chuck Grench and Jad Adkins for their unflagging patience and generosity.

I began my journey as a historian at the University of Wisconsin, where I benefited from working with a number of outstanding scholars who provided both mentorship and friendship along the way: Colleen Dunlavy, Susan

Johnson, Nan Enstad, Ned Blackhawk, Jim Sweet, Camille Guérin-Gonzalez, and Thongchai Winichakul. Jeanne Boydston provided unconditional support throughout my many years in Madison. She taught me not only how to think, teach, and write about the past but how to be a better person. She is and will always be greatly missed. It would be impossible to illuminate here all that Steve Kantrowitz has done for me in my years in Madison and those that have followed. Whether over beers at the Harmony, in his office, or on his front porch, Steve taught me how to be a scholar and how to be a mentor. I feel fortunate to have received his guidance and friendship.

Since I began teaching at Wellesley I've been privileged to have wonderful colleagues who have consistently encouraged the many turns my scholarship has taken. I'm grateful for the support offered me by Nina Tumarkin, Lidwien Kapteijns, Tak Matsusaka, Guy Rogers, Pat Giersch, Fran Molina, Simon Grote, and Valerie Ramseyer. Quinn Slobodian's friendship, insights, and knowledge of the best bars and restaurants in Cambridge have been invaluable to me in my years in New England. I have the good fortune of sharing a department with two of the best American historians I know, Brenna Greer and Katherine Grandjean. Their scholarly example and their kindness made this book possible. Finally, I cannot begin to fully convey my gratitude to Nikhil Rao and Alejandra Osorio. Dinners and drinks with them, which often lingered into the wee hours, transformed Wellesley from the place I work into the place I call home.

I have been fortunate to have close friends and colleagues who were willing to read the earliest drafts of this project, listen to my insistent monologues on the state and slavery (and whatever else was on my mind), and provide kindness and support as I labored (and sometimes struggled) to complete the book and who were always ready to share a beer and a laugh at the end of most days. I will be forever indebted to Zoë van Orsdol, Jerome Dotson, Tyina Steptoe, Charles Hughes, Scott Burkhardt, David Olsen, Kassie Teng, Brian Feltman, Mark Goldberg, Lisa Rakusin, Benjamin and Carrie Shepler, Tony Kaye, Thomas Buchanan, Jennifer Holland, Hannah Farber, Story Matkin-Rawn, Kori Graves, Constance Schulz, Lorri Glover, Thomas Kuehn, Paul Anderson, Matt Blanton, Kjerstin Moody, Scott Nelson, Erica Wojcik, and Eve Rabinoff. Keith Woodhouse and Tom Yoshikami welcomed me into their lives at a time when I needed it the most. Long bike rides, afternoons spent gardening, and evening discussions over cards and beers sustained and healed me, and for that I cannot thank them enough. Few people have had more influence over this book than Adam Malka. Whatever strengths this book may have are the product of his close edits, his erudite critiques, and our many conversations about the early republic. I am forever indebted to him for consistently reminding me why this book mattered and that I could finish it even when I had my own doubts. A good deal of this book was conceived and written in Asheville, North Carolina. There Jay Miller and Candace Reilly welcomed me into their lives and community, and in the process introduced me to my wife. For that and so much more I cannot thank them enough. I am also forever indebted to Dave Gilbert and Maia Surdam. Our bike rides, our late nights listening to music, our many meals, and our years of friendship made this book possible. Andrew Barrett is my oldest and closest friend. I could not have written this book without him; his wife, Amanda; and their two daughters, Cora and Adeline.

This book and my interest in the past have always been inspired by my family, who have been constant in their support. My paternal grandfather, Francisco Quintana de Hurtado, and grandmother, Rosa Quintana de Victoria, immigrated with my father and his siblings from Mexico City to tiny Robstown, a hardscrabble town in South Texas, in the 1950s. Before that, my grandfather, a child himself of a Chinese immigrant to Mexico, participated in the bracero program. Though he passed away when I was just a boy, it was my desire to understand and appreciate his experiences as a state-contracted worker that prompted my research and inspired this book. My maternal grandparents, Norman and Marie Cosby, motivated my particular interest in Southern History. For generations, they and their families have lived and worked in North Alabama as steelworkers and dance teachers. From them I learned the value of hard work, community, and family. Their lives and their example led me to search for and understand a Southern past that was not readily available to me in textbooks and monographs. It gives me great joy that my grandfather Norman, who just turned ninety, will be able to read this book.

My immediate family has supported me throughout this long and occasionally difficult process. My older brother Chris inspired my interest in academia at a very young age. His wife, Kim, and their children, Samuel and Chandler, have brought humor and encouragement throughout. My brother Jon's endless curiosity and sense of humor have continually inspired me. Trips to the West Coast to visit him and his partner, Cesar, were always a source of relief and rejuvenation. And I could not have written this book without the constant support and companionship of my twin brother, Rory. In the last years of writing, he inspired me with his hard work, his passion for justice, and his sense of humor. I cannot begin to adequately express my gratitude to my parents, Sharon and Alejandro Quintana. Their patience and generosity, love, and support have sustained me. From them I learned to follow my passions, to work hard, and to do everything with humility and kindness. I am forever grateful that my father has lived to see this project to its end. This book is for them.

As I write this, I'm sitting in the beautiful Kentucky home of my soon-to-be in-laws while my partner and our dog, Kino, nap beside me. Luiza Oliveira de Camargo came into my life in the last few years of writing this book. She's seen the highs (and occasional lows) of finishing a manuscript, and all the while she supported me, made me laugh, and always reminded me to not take myself too seriously. From her I've learned so much about beauty and thoughtfulness, patience and happiness. It is my greatest joy that I get to share my life with her.

Making a Slave State

Introduction

In an 1822 treatise on internal improvement in South Carolina's Lowcounty—the counties and parishes that bordered the ocean and made up South Carolina's coastal plain—renowned architect Robert Mills, then a superintendent for South Carolina's Board of Public Works, argued that "the time has now arrived when it is our best policy and true interest to begin a work with the labor of these slaves (for they only can effect it with any probability of success) that shall make it no longer necessary to retain them." Mills was advocating an improvement project that called for the state—already committed at that point to one of the nation's largest expenditures on infrastructural development—to transform the coastal plain from the deadly but lucrative site of plantation agriculture into a space for the exclusive "residence of a white population." As Mills made clear, the state's improvement agenda was focused on creating exclusive spaces of freedom, stability, and wealth for its white inhabitants; and yet, the only possible means by which he could imagine a space freed from slavery was through the unfree labor of black Carolinians.[1]

Making a Slave State uncovers the relationship that Mills highlighted in his treatise between state development and slavery, closely examining the important role that slaves played in the production of South Carolina's state space, governing policies and practices, and developmental agendas. As a state administrator, Mills's job was to contemplate, design, and oversee improvements to South Carolina's territory. He wrote this particular treatise in the shadow of two crises. The first, and best known, was the Denmark Vesey conspiracy, in which Vesey, a former slave who had purchased his freedom, reportedly organized a massive uprising in and around Charleston. The second was the 1820 census report, the results of which anticipated a diminution of South Carolina's political power at the national level. The census also strikingly revealed what many South Carolinians likely already knew: the majority of South Carolina's residents were enslaved. The reality of South Carolina's black majority was felt most pressingly in the Lowcountry, where in 1820 the state's 123,000 slaves outnumbered its white population by almost 90,000. Mills's proposal sought to address both issues at the same time: providing a safe, disease-free environment for increased white settlement and simultaneously diminishing the Lowcountry's dependence on slavery. Mills's farsighted proposal was swiftly rejected; removing slaves from the coastal plain simply was not feasible to most South Carolinians, particularly those whose wealth and power were born out of slave labor.[2]

Nevertheless, Mills's plan for internal improvement, despite its rejection, was revelatory. Mills could not envision the development of South Carolina's territory by any means other than the labor of slaves, even as the scheme he suggested called for the end of slavery itself. As this book makes clear, this unselfconscious reliance on enslaved labor was born out of a long history of slaves laboring for the state. For more than a century before Mills wrote his thesis, black Carolinians had worked for the province and state: building South Carolina's roads, canals, bridges, causeways, fortifications, and public buildings. As I'll make clear in what follows, however, slaves' state labor was not limited to physical work. Black Carolinians produced the state and shaped South Carolina's territory through their everyday labors; their daily movements—both in service of their owners and for their own purposes; and as the objects around and upon which South Carolinians crafted their governing discourse. Mills could not envision his ideas for South Carolina's improvement through any means other than the labor of slaves precisely because black Carolinians had long provided South Carolinians with the knowledge and material power necessary for the creation of the state and the production of its territory.

The History of State Space

This project began many years ago with the seemingly straightforward question, how do the enslaved produce space? As is most of the scholarship that concerns itself with the history of North American slavery, my initial focus was on the work slaves did in and around plantations. As I spent more time in the archives, however, what stood out to me was the amount of time slaves spent laboring for South Carolina's government. I observed black Carolinians at work building roads and bridges, digging canals and cuts (small canals), erecting public buildings and towering causeways. I could not help but see, alongside many of the runaway slave notices I found in Charleston's newspapers, the regular requests for slaves to labor on South Carolina's public works, and the reminders for owners to send their slaves to labor on local road maintenance. It also became increasingly clear that slaves did not simply build South Carolina's infrastructure but that they were also often the most frequent travelers on South Carolina's roads and rivers. Enslaved boatmen delivered goods to market, drivers and trusted slaves traveled down lonely roads to deliver information to their absentee masters, enslaved midwives traveled on local paths between plantations to provide their services, and entire groups of laborers moved, sometimes by water and sometimes by land, to augment labor forces on distant properties. Moreover, when closely examining the experiences of South Carolina's maroons, runaways, and rebels, it became obvious that many of their actions occurred not in the shelter of swamps and forests but rather along the roads, canals, and bridges that they and their peers had built and maintained. As I considered the Stono Rebellion's origins among slaves gathered for annual road work, and Forest Joe's long evasion from state authorities along the Santee-Cooper Canal, it seemed that there was a great deal more happening along South Carolina's roads and waterways than simply the delivery of commodity crops to market. As I increasingly understood, black Carolinians did not simply produce plantation space but more importantly created South Carolina's state space—its territory.[3]

But what exactly is state space? And how is it related to the production of the state? That there is state space is, of course, self-evident to most. One need only consider contemporary maps of the United States to recognize the centrality of space to our understanding of the modern state. Conceptually, Max Weber's classic formulation, which remains central to many scholarly and popular understandings of the state, argued that states are defined as "a human community that (successfully) claims the monopoly of the legitimate use of physical force *within a given territory*." While many theorists of the state and space have long ago moved away from Weber's model, avoiding what geographer John Agnew has termed the "territorial trap," as well as the ahistorical qualities of Weber's formulation, the notion of a bounded physical space remains a vital component of our everyday understanding of the state. For the most part, in fact, the predominant everyday experience of the state and governing practices occurs spatially: whether one is crossing or reinforcing the physical borders of nations (at landed checkpoints, or in the customs line of international terminals) or choosing a local school district.[4]

Space features so prominently in our daily experience and understanding of the state in part because the modern state was conceived in and of space. In other words, state space was a precondition for, as well as a consequence of, the emergence and evolution of the modern state. As noted earlier, the most recognizable features of the state are its territorial limits, its borders and boundaries. Securing and developing territory was and remains an essential aspect of statecraft and governing praxis. The modern state, however, is not simply a delimited territorial unit. Instead, the state is bound together with space. Physically, the state is mapped and more importantly transformed, unified, and brought into being materially through the construction of its infrastructure—its network of roads, canals, railroads, and information systems. Moreover, the institutional apparatuses and administrative hierarchies that animate the state and signal its presumed order are spatial units—local courthouses, jails, highway commissioners, and school districts—with jurisdictional limits defined by and through space. But the state is not simply the sum of its built environment, institutions, and administrative capacity. It is also the effect of social relations and practices that occur in space. The order that seems to cohere to the state is born not out of the will imposed on it by a powerful governing entity, but rather from the accumulation of everyday practices that occur in space, from travel on roads and highways to local and international border crossings.[5]

Importantly, this space—as well as the practices, institutions, physical landscape, and boundaries that all together constitute territory—has a history. Borders are negotiated, surveyed, and mapped numerous times over the course of a state's history, for a variety of reasons. Maps convey a sense of territorial timelessness, but close observation reveals the subtle shifts that regularly occur to political boundaries. Likewise, institutions and their administrative techniques change over time: organizational units are created and destroyed, jurisdictional limits redefined, and governing procedures regularly altered. The physical characteristics of state spaces shift through time as well: roads, bridges, canals, and public buildings are designed, built, and transformed. These changes are sometimes the consequence of political decision-making, but they often occur outside of the formal resolutions made by governing bodies. Such alterations to state space—be they the creation of new economic centers, the movement of local district boundaries, or the subtle shifts of natural landmarks—radically alter the meaning, experience, and practice of the state. In sum, the state is shaped by the historic production of space.

Despite the near ubiquity of space to our experience and understanding of the state, scholars of American political development have until recently largely avoided consideration of the historical production and maintenance of territory. To be sure, state space, even unexamined, plays a significant role in American historical analysis, whether that analysis is focused on the history of borderlands, expansionary policy, infrastructural development, Indian wars and removal, or land distribution. Often, however, both the state, as a discrete entity, and its territory, bounded and knowable, are taken as givens in most scholarship. This book, however, places the production and creation of state space at its center. In doing so, it does not simply ask the "what" of state space—the erection of its borders and boundaries, for example. Instead, it is concerned with *how* state space was produced. What were the technologies and techniques that political leaders and everyday South Carolinians deployed to create and maintain their security, to promote their economic wellbeing, and to unite their social lives? And in what ways did the everyday practices of South Carolinians—enslaved and free, black and white—create, sustain, and transform the state? In this way, this book looks beyond a close enumeration of state institutions and practices, and instead examines the everyday history of the early state.[6]

At least part of the reason historians have left the early production of state space unexamined is that it is only in the last few decades that scholars, especially historians, have brought the state back into their political analyses, and it is only recently that historians have reconsidered the presence and practice of the state in the early nation. Because scholarship for so long took for granted Weberian and liberal models of the state, many assumed that the early nation was bereft of state apparatuses, or presumed that if present, they were exceedingly weak. The recent pioneering works of William Novak, Brian Balogh, and others, following the lead of a generation of political scientists that reconsidered and reimagined American political development, have reframed our thinking on the early American state, making clear in their analysis of the law and police powers, frontier governance, and the assertion of war powers just some of the various ways that the early state shaped the first half of American history. They have been joined by historians who have recently begun to analyze the contingent processes through which the emergent ideas of jurisdiction, born out of the everyday practices of unlikely historical actors, gave rise to new governing techniques and ideas of sovereignty and territory at the beginning of the nineteenth century. Similarly, political scientists and historical sociologists have begun to excavate the important ways that race, gender, and sexuality were bound up with the early history of the American state, making clear that American governance was never idle, but instead that it was a focal point in the maintenance of societal norms and the racial and gender status quo.[7]

This book expands on these efforts. But rather than seek out the ways that the state participated in the maintenance of white supremacy and the institution of slavery, or how the familiar institutions and political practices of the state were shaped by the ideology and practice of race, I instead examine how the enslaved materially produced the early state and state space, and in doing so, how African Americans created and shaped the conditions of the modern state's possibility. Moreover, by focusing on the period between South Carolina's initial settlement and the early 1820s, this book moves our historical gaze from the familiar chronology and sites of state development. There is almost no discussion of traditional politics, and only a passing discussion of courts, legislative debates, and executive action. Instead, by turning to the production of space and the labor of slaves, this book focuses on the mundane practices of governance: the local road administrators, isolated contractors, and most importantly, the enslaved men and women who labored for the state.[8]

By placing the everyday activities of slaves at the center of this analysis of political development, this book reveals how the state was created not simply by planners, settlers, and the governing elite but also by a set of unlikely historical actors who were rarely self-consciously attempting to create the state of South Carolina. Moreover, by emphasizing the day-to-day activities of the enslaved—from their mundane labors in service to both the state and their masters, to their rebellious activities—the state's evolution and transformation are revealed as the consequence of an array of social practices. Importantly, this also makes clear that the enslaved, too often presumed to be impossible political actors, in fact often reoriented the infrastructure and practices of liberal governance toward a more egalitarian and emancipatory vision of freedom. In this way, black Carolinians not only created the conditions for the state's emergence but also established the basis of their own sustained challenge to modern, racial governance.[9]

I argue that black Carolinians produced the state in four distinct ways: through their physical labor; as the objects upon and around which governing discourse revolved; as a consequence of their daily movements delivering goods, supplies, and labor, which gave meaning to the state's planned infrastructure; and through the varied social and cultural meanings that slaves imposed on the landscape, which challenged the meaning and practice of liberal state space. At the core of this project, as is true of any work on slavery, are slaves' labors. Enslaved black Carolinians built South Carolina's earliest roads and bridges. They waded deep into murky swamps and marshes to carve out cuts and canals. They constructed South Carolina's fortifications during times of war and cooked, cleaned, and carried supplies for the state's army and navy. They erected local jails and courthouses during its moments of expansion. And they met regularly to maintain the infrastructure that they painstakingly built over generations. At almost every moment, and at nearly every site that marked the state's development and expansion, black Carolinians could be found, on the ground, working.

But this is not simply a story of slaves' labor. Black Carolinians were also the objects of informational exchanges between individual South Carolinians and provincial and later state administrators. The acquisition and allocation of slaves—for road work, as laborers for the state in times of war, and as confiscated property following the Revolution—led to the creation of new governing procedures, practices, and hierarchies, which, I argue, brought the nascent administrative state to life. Through this governing discourse, individual white men solidified their relationship to their government, while simultaneously crafting ideas of citizenship, duty, and the public good. In such exchanges, slaves were transformed from the private, protected property of individuals into the material strength of the state. Importantly, the knowledge created out of these interactions made the state, to borrow a phrase from Chandra Mukerji, an epistemological possibility, which I argue is most evident in the post-Revolutionary moment. The promise of state-owned slaves, acquired through the confiscation of loyalist property, permitted South Carolina's newly created government to envision the reconstruction, expansion, and unification of postwar South Carolina.[10]

Moreover, by examining enslaved mobility, I also argue that black Carolinians brought the state to life through their everyday movement. Peripatetic slaves—a necessity, I argue, brought on by the transformation of the plantation enterprise in the decades that surrounded the Revolution, were the circulating lifeblood of South Carolina's infrastructure. In the Lowcountry particularly but throughout South Carolina, slaves were often the primary occupants of the state's roads, canals, and bridges. They animated South Carolina's infrastructure, and in so doing fulfilled and shaped the modern state's promise of free economic exchange. When trusted drivers transported information to their owners, boatmen shipped commodities to market and supplies to scattered plantations, or field hands moved to new labor camps, their mobility sustained the plantation enterprise and made real the developmental aspirations of South Carolina's leaders.[11]

But as I also make clear, the meaningfulness of black movement was not limited to the whims and desires of their masters, and slaves were not simply the passive objects of state development. In the course of their everyday laboring movement, black Carolinians transformed the state's infrastructure to meet their own social, economic, and cultural needs. Black Carolinians used the state's built environment to create marketplaces, maintain spiritual and cultural practices, and preserve social ties. They used roads, rivers, and canals to run away from their masters, to plan insurrections, and to create their own independent communities. Such everyday activities not only motivated the creation of particular governing practices but also shaped and gave meaning to emergent ideas of sovereignty, authority, and surveillance. Importantly, in the course of these daily practices, the enslaved also produced an alternative politics of state space, one that offered a more sweeping vision of freedom, a vision that bent beyond the notion of racially limited economic opportunity and self-governance, toward survival, emancipation, and an end to white supremacy.

Producing the Modern State in South Carolina

South Carolina is an ideal setting to reconstruct the history of slavery and the early state. While scholarship on the American state primarily focuses on the nation and the institutions and practices of the federal government, throughout the eighteenth and early nineteenth centuries, most Americans primarily experienced governance at the local level. To be sure, the general government was a significant entity that affected people's everyday lives—from the postal service and Indian Removal to the construction of federal customhouses and land distribution. Nevertheless, to begin to grapple with the early state at the level of the everyday, it is necessary to consider local governing practices. And there is perhaps no better place to do so than South Carolina, where the rights and prerogatives of individual states were so jealously guarded.[12]

In fact, it was South Carolina's well-known commitment to states' rights that makes it such a compelling case study for the production of the modern state in North America. Numerous historians have examined the evolution of South Carolina's radical, proslavery states' rights position. They have taken note of local politics, the diminution of South Carolina's power in Congress in the face of rapid western expansion, South Carolinians' commitment to a notion of free trade, and of course, most importantly, their ideological defense of slavery in the face of the growing antislavery chorus. Still, while a great deal of ink has been spilled in an effort to understand South Carolina's political position at the start of the antebellum era, most of the scholarship produced over the last half century has focused on examining the rights and powers that South Carolinians sought to defend, rather than the *state*, which was the locus of their claims. This project argues that to fully understand South Carolina's antebellum politics, we must first acknowledge the concept of the state around which their ideas revolved. Doing so reveals that while South Carolinians were critics of governance at the national level, they remained committed to sweeping reform, modern development, and an active government within their own borders.[13]

Nullification was not the first time that South Carolinians sought to defend their claims to local governance. As numerous historians have argued,

South Carolina's colonial political history is, at least in part, defined by elite colonists' regular struggle in defense of their small measures of self-governance. Throughout the eighteenth century, South Carolina's provincial assembly passed laws in defiance of the crown, rejected royal governors, and sought to control the colony's treasury. Outside of Charlestown, middling planters and backcountry residents pressed for the expansion of South Carolina's government and regularly sought to affect the province's political development. To be sure, South Carolinians remained loyal to the crown until the Revolution, but as John Adams made clear in his Continental Congress diary, when he initially broached the subject of creating self-governed political entities (independent but united states) on the eve of declaring independence, his most exuberant audience was the South Carolinians in attendance. *Making a Slave State* suggests that South Carolinians' enthusiasm and confidence in their independent sovereignty was born out of the slow, material production of the state over the course of the eighteenth and early nineteenth centuries.[14]

Historians have long understood that the defining characteristic of South Carolina as a political entity—whether in fighting the Revolution or rejecting the federal government—was its commitment to and defense of the institution of slavery. This book argues, however, that the relationship between the state of South Carolina and slavery runs much deeper than the state's protection of individual rights of ownership. Enslaved Carolinians produced South Carolina's state space, and in doing so created and maintained the state, shaping its governing practices and animating its institutional life. Slaves' state labor secured the fragile claims of isolated colonists, provided the details to the independence that Revolutionary leadership declared, and gave meaning to the borders and powers that antebellum radicals sought to defend. South Carolina's political leaders defended the right of individuals to own slaves, but their perspective was shaped, at least in part, by the work the enslaved did for the state.[15]

Revealing the important role that black Carolinians played in the production of the state not only illuminates their significance to South Carolina but also uncovers the easy compatibility between unfreedom and modern governance. Historians of the state have avoided examination of South Carolina and the broader South for many of the same reasons that many historians of capitalism neglected the region until recently: a commitment to slavery seemed incongruous with the political economy of modernity. This perspective, however, has much more to do with the teleology of American historiography than with the region's actual import, which for so long held that the narrative arc of the nation's past bent toward freedom. This is especially true for the history of the state, where the focus was for so long on the role of the general government in the promotion and protection of individual freedom. Historians disagreed about and debated the degree, relative success, visibility, and utility of the state, but they all tacitly concurred, through the South's relative elision from the scholarship, that slavery and modernity were not simply incompatible but antagonistically opposed to modern developmental praxis. This book argues that such a perspective is incorrect. South Carolinians fully committed themselves and their property to the project of modern state governance. They were among the first in North America to embrace the techniques and procedures of statecraft: from cartographic surveys and the appointment of a civil engineer to the reform of their legal system and the establishment of asylums for the incapacitated. South Carolina was the first state to construct a long-distance summit canal, and in 1827 chartered a railroad company to construct what was then the longest route in North America. They accomplished these things not in spite of slavery but rather because of it.[16]

Making a Slave State reconstructs the central role that slaves played in the production of the state through an examination of a variety of sources, many of which have long been familiar to historians of colonial- and Revolutionary-era South Carolina. Evidence of slaves' state labor resides in the margins of numerous records that are often examined by South Carolina's historians, from the accounts of the colonial and General Assembly and advertisements in the *South-Carolina Gazette* to the reports made by the state comptroller, military commanders, and legislative committees. By closely reading petitions to the General Assembly, grand jury presentments, governor's messages, colonial correspondence, private planter diaries and letters, and newspaper reports, I uncovered slaves' daily efforts in service to the state. A close examination of the well-kept records of plantation owners and their correspondence with their overseers revealed the everyday movement that lay at the heart of the late colonial and early national plantation enterprise, while those same materials, alongside runaway notices, ex-slave narratives, militia reports, travel diaries, Courts of Magistrates and Freeholders records, and natural histories exposed just some of the numerous ways that black Carolinians imposed their own meaning onto the landscape.

This book begins by closely examining South Carolina's infrastructural and defensive policies and practices from its inception through the Revolutionary War and into the immediate postwar period. Chapter 1 illuminates colonial South Carolina's earliest developmental procedures: tracing their infrastructural agenda not only to the colonial assembly but also from the demands made by isolated, individual South Carolinians; exploring the growing power of local administrators; and uncovering the everyday labors of black Carolinians that made South Carolina's early expansion and security possible. Slaves' work on roads, canals, bridges, causeways, and fortifications produced South Carolina's territory, but slaves' centrality to the early state was not confined to their physical exertions. As chapter 1 also argues, black Carolinians were also the objects of informational exchanges between individual South Carolinians and provincial administrators. The outcomes of the subsequent developmental discourse were profound: South Carolinians solidified their relationship to the provincial government, which slowly accumulated infrastructural powers as a result; white Carolinians produced notions of citizenship and the public good in their discussions of slave labor; and slaves—their labors and their lives—were transformed from the private, protected property of individuals into the material strength of the state.

The knowledge generated by slaves' everyday labors and their role within governing discourse were essential not only for South Carolina's colonial development but also for their Revolutionary aspirations and post-Revolutionary reconstruction. As chapter 2 makes clear, the knowledge produced by slave-led development in the colonial era was quickly embraced by South Carolina's wartime government. Slaves hastily built South Carolina's fortifications, labored for the state's navy, and toiled in the state's ironworks; they accompanied state troops and the Continental army as pioneers, and by war's end became the promised payment to volunteer soldiers. All of this work for the Revolutionary government only solidified slaves as the primary material means of South Carolina's development. Thus, while the Revolution witnessed the radical emergence of South Carolina as an independent state, white Carolinians continued to rely upon unfree labor for the maintenance and development of their newly liberated polity. Embracing the governing techniques of their provincial forebears, South Carolinians brought their political visions to life through the labor of their slaves. For example, when South Carolinians punitively confiscated loyalists' property, the prospect of state-owned slaves fueled the nascent state's developmental fantasies. But more than simply stimulating state leaders' postwar aspirations, the acquisition and distribution of confiscated slaves forced the General Assembly to create new governing procedures and practices, which brought the nascent administrative state to life. Just as they had throughout the colonial era, black Carolinians' postwar work on the state's roads, canals, and government buildings materially produced South Carolina's postwar territory, making material what had long been imagined. While the labor seemed familiar, however, the work itself was altogether quite different, as black Carolinians labored no longer to support and secure England's most important North American colony but instead to create and maintain a nascent, self-governing state.

Of course, slaves were not simply the passive objects—the technology—of state development. As I argue in chapters 1 and 2, when black Carolinians ran away from their masters, when they rose up in rebellion, and when they created their own independent communities, they also produced the early state. Not only did their efforts force state leaders to craft governing practices that would secure the state from what white Carolinians believed to be their internal enemy, but out of slaves' everyday activities—the rebellious and the mundane—jurisdictional authority, local sovereignty, and state security derived their meaning.[17]

Paying particular attention to the Lowcountry, where the bulk of South Carolina's slaves resided in the colonial and early national eras, and where black Carolinians made up more than 80 percent of the total population, chapter 2 examines the sociospatial practices of the enslaved, making clear that black Carolinians' everyday activities produced and directly shaped early state space. In the late eighteenth and early nineteenth centuries, as the plantation complex expanded and changed, planters relied on the mobility of much of their labor force to maintain their investments. On the move and frequently unobserved by their masters, black Carolinians charted their own meanings onto the landscape—establishing economic entrepôts alongside rivers and at busy intersections, spiritual centers on or near the plantations where they labored, and safe havens in the swamps and forests of the coastal plain. And while their actions undermined and challenged the institution of slavery, slaves' sociospatial practices were about much more than resistance. In the swamps and forests of the coastal plain, they re-created older, seemingly distant cultural and spiritual networks, and established new socioeconomic connections for a variety of reasons that included, but were not limited to, responses to their brutal subjugation.[18]

Chapter 3 begins a more specific discussion of black spatial practices and their significance in the production of South Carolina's state space. In order to note the centrality of black Carolinians' role in the construction of the coastal plain, chapter 3 challenges two prevailing scholarly themes: first, the assumption that the defining characteristic of slaves' lives was captivity; and second, the tendency to cast black sociospatial practices as peripheral or invisible aspects of the broader production of space. Chapter 3 postulates instead that at the end of the colonial era, the shifting plantation enterprise required black Carolinians to remain highly mobile—transporting commodities and supplies, maintaining communication with their distant owners, and providing itinerant labor to dispersed holdings. By highlighting the necessity of slave movement in this era, the chapter problematizes the depiction of slaves as bound to a singular place and casts black movement as central to the maintenance of the plantation enterprise and subsequently the production of the state. Enslaved laboring movement shaped South Carolina's governing procedures—the slave pass and the slave patrol were born out of their necessary mobility. But more importantly, peripatetic slaves were the circulating lifeblood of South Carolina's infrastructure. A road without travelers, after all, is just a cleared piece of land. In the Lowcountry particularly but throughout South Carolina, slaves were often the primary occupants of the state's roads, canals, and bridges. They animated South Carolina's infrastructure. And their movement made real and lent significance to the developmental aspirations of South Carolina's leaders.

But as chapter 4 makes clear, the meaningfulness of black movement was not solely born out of service to their masters. Chapter 4 explains how black Carolinians understood the landscape through their religious and spiritual practices, marked certain sites as vital to their socioeconomic and physical survival, and rooted themselves to their specific interpretations of the coastal plain. This focus on the cultural and social practices of slaves both broadens our understanding of the ways that black Carolinians participated in the spatial production of the state and complicates our understanding of their everyday mobility by making clear that slavery was not the sole reason for black Carolinians' movement. As a close examination of the meaning of black movement reveals, black Carolinians took advantage of what state planners presumed were exclusively white (and male) spaces. In places well known and hidden, black Carolinians imposed their own meanings on the space, and in so doing directly dictated South Carolina's early national improvement agenda.

The final chapter of this book return to the topic of developmental policy in the years following the War of 1812, a moment long recognized by historians as transformative in the history of American state development and infrastructural improvement. South Carolinians led the nation in this movement. As chapter 5 makes clear, however, the drive for internal improvements that swept the nation and South Carolina following the War of 1812 was not simply a revolution in transportation or an update of their existing infrastructure, but rather was more broadly an effort to produce the early liberal state: political elites and private citizens alike pushed for legal and penal reforms, educational advances, poor relief, and asylums for the incapacitated. This was an altogether different project than earlier efforts at political development.

State leaders sought to not only transform the landscape but, more importantly, shape and discipline individual citizens as well. South Carolinians' experience of this moment was vastly different from that of most of their peers throughout the nation and around the world, not because their efforts were in any way muted but rather because their improvement agenda relied on the labor of enslaved black Carolinians. That labor and black Carolinians' everyday practices were deeply affected by the expansion and improvement of South Carolina's infrastructure. South Carolina's state planners and elite planters subsequently had to adapt their governing techniques and vision of the modern state to the reality of an unfree population whom they absolutely feared but could not be free without.

The results of their efforts were profound. In the face of an enslaved majority who were at one and the same time the source of all their wealth and all their fears, South Carolinians wed together the overt, and often violent, policing of African Americans—enslaved and free—with a reform-minded vision of the modern, liberal state. South Carolinians continued to promote education and economic opportunity, even as they jealously guarded their borders, barring the entry of free blacks, African American sailors, and some slaves. With the construction of an arsenal in Charleston, they armed their citizenry, who themselves more widely participated in vigilante police associations whose chief aim was to monitor and suppress the activities of the state's enslaved populace. South Carolina's government made it more onerous for slaves to become free, and made the lives of free blacks more difficult. The embrace of such policies and practices, however, did not signal South Carolina's abandonment of the modern state; instead, its new techniques of governance provided an alternative, almost prescient, model for liberal statecraft. In this new vision of the state, unfree black Carolinians, even as their own lives became more marginalized and circumscribed, were expected to sacrifice their lives and labor for the promotion of white Carolinians' self-government, territorial security, and economic opportunity.

CHAPTER ONE

The "Within Enemy"
Slaves and the Production of South Carolina's Early State

At the beginning of September 1739, dozens of slaves gathered in the swampy terrain of St. Paul's Parish along the Stono River to resume construction of a public road designed to transport goods from the expanding plantation complex to Charlestown. The road crew was composed of slaves from all the plantations within several miles of the building project. Gathered together for this annual rite, the enslaved men busily removed trees and undergrowth and leveled the path across the coastal plain. This backbreaking work was no reprieve from the endless tasks associated with plantation maintenance, but it did afford members of the workforce an opportunity to venture beyond the plantation and to interact with their fellow slaves from surrounding plantations. Like hundreds of other black Carolinians laboring on roads, bridges, cuts, and causeways across the coastal plain, those gathered to build the road between Willtown and Charlestown gained knowledge of the intricacies of the landscape. The black Carolinians who labored on the path along the river learned about the plantations that lined the road, who worked on them, who managed them, and what supplies they contained. For many of the recent African arrivals, road construction may have provided them with their first opportunity to reunite with their countrymen who labored on other plantations. As the enslaved laborers traveled through the interior carving out the highway, they encountered white Carolinians—merchants and farmers—and determined who would trade with them, and who would not; what supplies each maintained in their storehouse; and their hours of operation. They also became privy to the traffic on the highway, committing to memory the busiest times for travel and the number of white Carolinians they met upon the road. And while the road led to Charlestown, slaves may have pondered its opposite direction, away from the center of the colony and southward, toward Spanish Florida and, perhaps, freedom.[1]

With this information in hand, the slaves who labored on the road along the Stono River led the bloodiest attack against slavery in South Carolina's history. When remembering the Stono Rebellion in 1770, Lieutenant Governor William Bull, whose father happened upon the rebels in their march south along the road, noted that it "took its rise from the wantonness, and not oppression of our slaves, for too great a number had been very indiscreetly assembled and encamped together for several nights to do a large work on the public road with a slack inspection." The long days and nights spent laboring on South Carolina's infrastructure permitted the rebels to ascertain which slaves would join their ranks, which plantations to attack and ransack, where weapons and ammunition could be found, and the path that would perhaps lead them to their eventual freedom. The provincial report of the uprising stated that the rebels "got arms and ammunition out of a store [and] they bent their course to the Southward burning all the houses on the road." They turned south along a road that they constructed, past merchants from whom they regularly acquired goods for themselves and their masters, attacking plantations that they built, maintained, and lived upon.[2]

Both the provincial report and Bull's memory of the slave revolt bring to the surface an often-overlooked aspect of the Stono Rebellion: the men who fought against and killed their masters were gathered together to produce South Carolina's infrastructure. The Stono rebels, who were first gathered together as provincial laborers, simultaneously produced the early state and threatened its continued existence. The mundane activities that precipitated the insurgents' actions are often ignored or minimized for a variety of reasons, not least of which is the inattention paid to the everyday, material practices of infrastructural development in early South Carolina. This chapter refocuses attention on those activities, and in particular, illuminates the various ways that black Carolinians stood at the center of the early state-building process.[3]

Throughout the eighteenth century, South Carolina's provincial government passed numerous acts authorizing and directing the production and maintenance of roads, bridges, and cuts (small canals) to connect the expanding plantation complex to Charlestown. The Commons House created administrative bodies to oversee and direct this development, which over time accrued significant powers. And they tasked enslaved men with the construction of their expanding infrastructure. White Carolinians desired and demanded roads and causeways that could connect their increasingly lucrative plantations to the merchant ships that awaited their crops in Charlestown's bustling harbor, and provide individual Carolinians with access to their neighbors as well as local stores and churches. The roads and bridges that they built were also meant to provide security for one of Britain's most lucrative colonies, which rested dangerously on the edge of its North American empire. Slaves' labor on South Carolina's infrastructure simultaneously created, secured, and expanded South Carolina's territory, tethering distant places together with the colonial center.[4]

Black Carolinians' developmental labor, however, did much more than simply provide economic and social access to wealthy planters and distant farmers. To be sure, this work was vital to the early state. But so too were slaves' role as the objects of informational transactions between individual South Carolinians and their government. The colonial assembly granted local infrastructural administrators significant powers, including the ability to assess and call upon slave owners' property. When slave owners provided road commissioners with information regarding their labor force, or petitioned the assembly for compensation for their slaves' labors for the military or the commissioners of fortifications, dynamic exchanges occurred between South Carolina's citizen-subjects and their government. A great deal took place within these seemingly mundane interactions. The early state government's power was reified as white Carolinians acknowledged the assembly as the source of infrastructural development. Slaves were transformed from the private property of their owners into the material power of the state, and important bonds were created between individual subjects and the government, within which, on the eve of the Revolution, South Carolinians articulated their nascent ideas of citizenship and the common good. Slaves stood at the center of all of these exchanges.

But black Carolinians did more than simply facilitate the growth and development of the colony. As the Stono rebels made clear, just as slaves came to be seen as the strength of the state, they were also increasingly perceived as what provincial engineer William Gerard de Brahm described as South Carolina's "within enemy," an integral part of the colony that both promised and threatened its future. As white Carolinians quickly learned, the enslaved used the early state's infrastructure for their own ends, and often in direct conflict with South Carolina's developmental agenda. South Carolinians subsequently designed their infrastructure around this simultaneity: reorienting roads and river access to bar the economic lives of their slaves; reshaping their vision of the early state's territory to guard against internal threat; and inscribing the landscape with messages of terrible violence.[5]

South Carolina, like its neighboring colonies, was slow to create a developmental agenda. Nevertheless, by the end of the Yamasee War, as the plantation complex began its rapid expansion and proprietary rule was replaced by royal oversight, the provincial assembly—pressured by individual Carolinians—intensified its infrastructural agenda, granting local road commissioners more power and tasking slaves with the construction of a number of transportation and security improvements, the latter increasingly designed with slaves in mind. As South Carolina's development agenda expanded, so too did black

Carolinians' role as the objects around and upon which the provincial government solidified its relationship with South Carolina's citizen-subjects. By closely examining the work of the commissioners of roads, state engineers, and the compensatory demands made by South Carolinians, the chapter reveals how slaves stood at the center of early state production, both as the laboring power of the government and the consistent threat to its continued existence.

Developmental Powers

Throughout the eighteenth century, South Carolina's provincial government labored to manage the colony's steady growth. The incremental expansion of what would eventually become the wealthiest British colony in North America witnessed South Carolinians moving north, south, and west of Charlestown, building roads, clearing rivers, digging cuts and canals, and constructing bridges and causeways over and around the swamps, pine forests, savannas, and countless creeks that defined South Carolina's landscape. In doing so, white and black Carolinians simultaneously enlarged and created their colonial territory. Of course, both the crown and many settlers imagined South Carolina as an already geographically expansive territory, stretching at least as far as the Mississippi River: maps were drawn, property claims were asserted, and treaties were negotiated all with such a belief in mind. Nevertheless, movement and sustained settlement beyond the area nearest Charlestown only occurred in fits and starts, and only rapidly began following the Yamasee and Tuscarora Wars.[6]

In the first decades of the eighteenth century, then, Carolinians primarily moved by land along the paths burned and maintained by Native Americans. For example, when John Lawson first journeyed through South Carolina at the beginning of the eighteenth century, his overland travels were primarily dictated by his Indian chaperones. These guides, members of the various communities he encountered along his journey—Santees, Congarees, Waterees, Sugarees, Winyaws, Washaws, and Sewees—chaperoned him along well-worn paths that led from their towns to neighboring villages. Lawson noted only one provincial-built road during his journey, a thirty-six-mile path from Charlestown to the newly established French settlement on the Santee River. Lawson himself avoided this overland route in favor of the more dangerous coastal voyage from Charlestown to the Santee delta, despite noting that the colonial road was "a very good way by land."[7]

Like Lawson, the earliest successful settlers relied upon the numerous streams, creeks, and rivers carved into the coastal plains for their primary infrastructural needs. These waterways provided South Carolinians with a ready-made conveyance system, capable of delivering bulky commodities to market and supplies to their increasingly distant plantations. As the colony grew—geographically and commercially—the riverine system of transport remained important, but it also proved inadequate to the needs of the colony's flourishing population, not all of whom had easy access to South Carolina's waterways. The best riverside lands were claimed in South Carolina's earliest moments, which meant that later eighteenth-century settlers had no choice but to move into the interstitial spaces that lay between and beyond the Lowcountry's arterial waterways. Likewise, as both parishes and communities grew in size, the institutions that bound together white South Carolinians—churches, markets, race tracks, and public houses—were necessarily situated away from the valuable swamps and riversides where planters established their massive works. Travel to and from these sites, to their neighbors' plantations, and most importantly to Charlestown—the vibrant cultural and economic center of South Carolina, where the wealthiest South Carolinians increasingly spent the bulk of their time—was vital to South Carolina's aspiring planter class. Even more importantly, for those who settled on South Carolina's expanding periphery, access to Charlestown in times of threat was essential to their infrastructural needs, regardless of the source of that danger, be it from without—their Spanish, French, or Indian neighbors; or from within—the enslaved majority who made such growth possible.[8]

As the colony began to expand, South Carolina's provincial assembly slowly took steps to address the transportation dilemmas confronting the slowly sprawling colony. Political leaders began passing laws impelling the construction and maintenance of the colony's infrastructure. For the most part, both the proprietary and royal governments' earliest actions relied upon local residents—under the supervision of government-appointed commissioners—to construct and maintain roads, bridges, and cuts. These local administrators slowly accrued expansive powers as the transportation needs of their constituents grew. For example, in 1702, the proprietary government passed a law for "Making and Mending Highways," which granted local commissioners the power to lay out roads and highways "in their respective division, at the request and instance of any person which is already settled, or shall hereafter settle inland."[9]

This law provided the provincial government, through its local administrators, with the overall oversight of infrastructural improvement, but as the latter half of the law indicates, individual South Carolinians could, and often did, dictate the course of development in South Carolina, demanding—through petition and personal requests—the construction of roads, bridges, causeways, and river access from both the colonial assembly and their local road commissioners. For example, in 1712, local commissioners were appointed by the assembly and directed to construct a bridge and causeway for the convenience of "the inhabitants of St. John's Island, and the inhabitants of Wadmalaw, Bohickett, and other southern settlements." Residents of the coastal islands south of Charlestown had petitioned the assembly, complaining that lacking a proper bridge and causeway, they were "greatly interrupted in their communication with adjacent parts, and are kept from the worship of God, and attendance at musters and alarms." Colonial administrators often received such appeals, as settlers framed their developmental demands around their social and commercial needs as well as their duties to both God and crown. In 1725, settlers along the north branch of the Stono River complained that the only road available to them was neglected by local authorities, and as a consequence of poor management and frequent travel "was now stopped up, and the passage impeded." They were subsequently "twelve miles distance from any public established road, and that through deep and almost impassable swamps." The petitioners argued that they were consequently "rendered incapable of repairing to the service of God, and conveying their effects to markets."[10]

These settler petitions—along with the everyday activities that they sought to facilitate and ease—were essential for the implementation of early developmental policies. When South Carolinians traveled between the homes and plantations of their neighbors, journeyed to church, conveyed their produce to market, or traveled from Charlestown with needed supplies, they knit together the disparate places that made up colonial territory. Such excursions—be they social, commercial, or defensive—slowly but cumulatively expanded and produced South Carolina's early territory. By petitioning for aid in constructing roads, bridges, and canals, settlers themselves established the centrality of the provincial assembly in their everyday travels. In doing so, they legitimated the colonial government, acknowledging the assembly's ability to provide oversight in their everyday lives.

White Carolinians turned to their government with their developmental demands for a variety of reasons. Newly settled South Carolinians often lacked the financial reach to pay for costly bridges and causeways, were wanting for the legal power to construct roadways beyond their own property lines, and did not have the administrative ability to call upon and oversee the laborers needed for sizable infrastructural construction and maintenance. Nevertheless, despite requesting the aid and oversight of the colonial government, individual South Carolinians did not remove themselves from infrastructural decision-making; instead, they continued to make specific developmental demands, and provided the bulk of labor—in the form of their slaves' and their own labor—for the actual construction of infrastructural projects. In this way, individual South Carolinians shaped the contours of early governing practices, blurring the boundary between public and private necessity, and orienting developmental policies toward their own everyday social, spiritual, and commercial needs. As a consequence, in South Carolina, governing techniques were increasingly focused on the support of individuals and their everyday concerns.

While individual Carolinians pressed the Commons House and local administrators to improve and expand the colony's infrastructure, the colonial government primarily focused its overall developmental agenda on providing security to South Carolina, and more broadly the southern reach of Britain's North American empire, particularly during and after Queen Anne's War, the War of Jenkins' Ear, and the Seven Years' War. For example, in 1703, the assembly passed an act for the creation of the Willtown Road, which stretched along the coastal interior from Charlestown toward the Savannah River. As the colonial administrators noted, "the remoteness and great distances from Charlestowne of many of the southern inhabitants of this Colony, is a great hindrance to the speedy uniting our forces on any emergent occasion." Two years later, provincial leadership acknowledged, "The want of convenient ferries and roads upon all occasions, hath much prevented the uniting of her Majesties's [sic] forces in the defence of this colony." In 1711, the assembly ordered commissioners to continue the "High-Road from South Edisto River to Port Royal and the Island of Saint Helena" expressly "for the more easy conjunction of the forces of this colony in times of war and danger." Colonial administrators sought to ease the movement of troops and armed citizenry across the territory but also reassured their constituents that the creation of a well-maintained thoroughfare for security purposes would also ease the movement necessitated by "business and commerce."[11]

The fears that shaped and motivated South Carolina's security policies in the first decades of their settlement were validated during the Tuscarora War of 1711 and the Yamasee War of 1715. Both wars were primarily reactions to the thriving Indian slave and deerskin trades, commerce that radically altered the political dynamics and internal cohesion between and among various Native communities and polities. Colonial governments encouraged these conflicts, as violence between Indian communities resulted in an increase in Native American slaves. Subsequently, tensions and violence abounded between Carolinians and their Indian neighbors. Such strains were exacerbated by the steady encroachment of white settlers deeper and deeper into spaces claimed by Native communities, as well as the unchecked behavior of Euro-American traders. The resulting wars between allied Native communities and white Carolinians in both North and South Carolina were among the bloodiest in colonial North American history, devastating the lives of settlers and many of their closest indigenous neighbors.[12]

In South Carolina, the Yamasee War—perceived by many to be the consequence of official malfeasance—deepened settlers' disenchantment with the proprietary government, leading to the eventual establishment of South Carolina under a new royal charter just a few years later. In the years between the end of the war and the end of proprietary rule, South Carolina's developmental policy reflected the heightened concerns regarding possible Indian attack. In passing a law for the construction of a new bridge "near Childsbury Town," the assembly noted "the building of bridges over the creeks and rivers of this Province are of the greatest use, as well for the public security, in case of an Indian disturbance or other enemy." Ferries, though popular throughout the coastal colony, were unable to accommodate the increased traffic that war created, potentially stranding dozens of settlers on the wrong side of rivers in moments of crisis.[13]

In 1721, the provincial assembly, reflecting the newly established royal government's increased attention to the colony's well-being and the demands of settlers, granted "further powers to the commissioners" of roads, providing them with more influence and responsibility "than any heretofore have had." Commissioners were granted wide supervisory roles "in laying out both public and private paths, making causeys not exceeding twenty feet in width, building bridges not exceeding forty feet in length, clearing of water-courses and creeks, in order that the same may be made, altered and kept in repair, for the better communication of the inhabitants of this Province." The assembly named new commissioners for the respective districts and parishes within the growing colony and provided these officials with the power to "assess all the inhabitants of the said parish, according to their several estates within the same, in order to raise such sum and sums of money as will be necessary and wanting to mend and repair the public roads, creeks, bridges and passages in the said parish." This new authority not only aided South Carolina's developmental agenda but gave road administrators unique access to their neighbors, as tax assessments required that the commissioners be regularly provided with private information. Commissioners were also granted the ability to make contracts with "discreet and sober men" to build bridges, and more importantly were provided the power to demand the annual labor of all male residents between the ages of sixteen and sixty who resided near the public works. This further blurred the boundary between private and public development, as commissioners came to rely on a combination of contracted labor and the legislated mandatory road work of individual South Carolinians. Moreover, the commissioners' responsibilities and actions blurred the distinctions between private space and state space, as they were granted the power to reach within plantation borders to assess and call upon private labor forces to fulfill the early state's infrastructural needs.[14]

Infrastructural development, be it for security or individual need, was then one of the primary ways that the provincial government and British administrators augmented their overall control of the colony. The provincial assembly regularly passed new laws for specific projects and the overall upkeep of the colony's infrastructure. Importantly, developmental legislation did more than grant power to local road commissioners. To be sure, the colonial assembly had little day-to-day management of South Carolina's infrastructure; still, in passing laws that granted expansive powers to local administrators, the early state government sought to implement orderly growth through specific design proposals. For example, the same 1721 law that outlined road commissioners' powers and responsibilities also defined stringent guidelines for the overall upkeep of roads, including the strict protection of shade trees. Though such a restriction may seem inconsequential, in South Carolina, where the sweltering heat of the summer sun threatened travelers' lives, shade trees were more than just aesthetically pleasing; they were essential for safe movement throughout the colony. Likewise, the assembly established harsh penalties for anyone who disrupted or blocked commercial, social, or defensive traffic on any of the colony's thoroughfares, by land or by water.[15]

These governing procedures were more than simply the new government flexing its muscles; rather, these new regulations and developmental policies were responses to the tremendous growth South Carolina experienced beginning in the 1720s. Through immigration and natural increase, the white population grew exponentially throughout the eighteenth century: increasing from fewer than 7,000 in 1720 to approximately 15,000 in 1740, and steadily growing throughout the remainder of the century, nearing 50,000 on the eve of the Revolution. As numerous historians and contemporaries have made clear, the exact population of white Carolinians was difficult to assess, as an official census apparatus did not exist in South Carolina until after the

Revolution. Tax assessors, the militia, and local road commissioners kept track of adult white men, but even then, much of the growth in South Carolina's white population occurred in the backcountry, with white settlers from Pennsylvania, Virginia, and North Carolina migrating into the Upstate, often outside of the early state's official gaze. This explains in part how South Carolina's white population jumped from 50,000 in 1770 to an estimated 83,000 in just a decade. The number of slaves in South Carolina, however, was much more clear, as enslaved men, women, and children were considered taxable property and were thus regularly counted by local state administrators. In 1710, there were only 4,100 slaves in South Carolina. A decade later that number had sharply risen to approximately 12,000. The slave population steadily grew, as commodity production and slave importations escalated throughout the province: in 1730, the number of slaves jumped to 20,000, then 30,000 in 1740; again, nearly doubling by 1760 to 57,334 slaves, and as revolution came to South Carolina in 1780, the enslaved population neared 100,000 souls.[16]

This rapidly growing population, slave and free, spread across South Carolina beginning in the Lowcountry and then slowly moving into the colony's interior, expanding the plantation complex and settlement first south of Charlestown toward the Savannah River, then north toward Georgetown, and then slowly westward into the Piedmont and backcountry. Most of this growth was the consequence of the steady spread of plantation agriculture, as individual planters sought access to the fertile swamps and riversides where rice and then indigo thrived. The primary source of this territorial and commercial expansion was the explosive augmentation of the enslaved population, that steadily transformed former Native lands into thriving plantations and livestock ranges.[17]

Just as South Carolinians relied upon their slaves to construct the plantation complex, so too did they turn to black Carolinians to produce and maintain provincial infrastructure. As noted earlier, road commissioners were granted the power to call upon the labor of every male inhabitant between the ages of sixteen and sixty residing in their districts, distributing labor according to one's proximity to the roads, bridges, and causeways under construction. To be sure, white residents were called upon to work on the state's roads. Nevertheless, slaves provided the bulk of South Carolina's developmental labor force, particularly in the Lowcountry, where the enslaved were an overwhelming majority. For example, in September 1762, the commissioners for St. John's Berkley Parish reported just seventy-six white men available for road labor, alongside 1,064 slaves. When they reported for duty, white men rarely labored beside their slaves; instead, they oversaw the efforts of hundreds of slaves as they performed the dangerous and difficult work of infrastructural construction. For example, in March 1764, three hundred and twenty-two slaves, alongside just five white overseers, worked for more than a week on the Strawberry Causeway. Slaves cut timber for bridges and aided in their construction. They removed acres of forests and removed and smoothed miles of earth to create and maintain the state's roads. They dove deep into the murky waters of Lowcountry rivers to clear debris for water passage, heaped mountains of earth skyward to construct causeways for overland travel, and waded into mosquito-infested swamps and marshes to dig cuts for plantation irrigation and commercial traffic. Slaves, as would be expected, often died in the completion of these labors. Those who survived could expect to perform such labors annually, and even more frequently as infrastructural demands increased. Their labors and lives facilitated an explosion in settlement and economic growth for South Carolina. By the second half of the eighteenth century, the tiny province on the edge of Britain's North American empire surpassed all others in status and wealth.[18]

The boom in settlement and staple agriculture, however, was not an unqualified boon for white Carolinians; as the slave population grew and the Native population moved to the west, white Carolinians' fears of slave revolt, Indian war, and imperial invasion significantly magnified. Colonial leadership, from the beginning of the 1720s until the Revolution, continually sought to address two related concerns: facilitating economic growth and social and spatial cohesion through infrastructural development, and simultaneously providing security against the threats that seemed to loom in every direction. As colonial leaders argued in 1721, such dangers would, "if not timely prevented ... expose this frontier colony to the incursion of the Indians, insurrection of Negroes, and make the same easy prey to the invasion of any foreign enemy." Of course, as leadership learned during the Stono Rebellion, infrastructural development that relied upon the labor of the enslaved created as many dangers as it prevented. Following the 1739 slave revolt, South Carolina's Commons House created rigorous guidelines for the oversight of slaves on infrastructural projects; and yet, such regulations rang hollow in many coastal districts and parishes where the number of slaves dwarfed the white population. For provincial leaders, the best answer to such concerns was to increase South Carolina's white population. The assembly subsequently passed a law to prevent the desertion of "insolvent debtors," suspending legal action against white Carolinians for any noncriminal cases; another requiring planters to maintain "at least one white indented servant who can serve in the militia" on their property; and yet another that required slave owners to keep one white man on any plantation or cowpen with at least twenty slaves. The heart of the assembly's racialized defensive efforts, however, was the creation of the township system, which was meant to provide a buffer between South Carolina's core and the Indian-controlled backcountry, through the settlement of eleven communities arced across the coastal plain from the Savannah River through the Piedmont and on to the North Carolina border. The colonial government sought to provide these new communities with white residents and simultaneously offset the growing slave majority, by explicitly encouraging European immigration through the provision of subsidies, supplies, and lands free of quitrents. Such policies were oriented primarily toward securing the colony, and particularly coastal plantations, from what white Carolinians increasingly perceived as their internal enemies. In this way, provincial leaders began to reimagine the backcountry's relationship with the coastal plantation complex, reconfiguring South Carolina's early state space.[19]

Once settlement began, newly arrived Carolinians placed their own demands on the early state, increasingly clamoring for social access, economic thoroughfares, and bodily security. The upstart farmers, wealthy planters, slaves, and modest immigrant communities that migrated to various points throughout South Carolina, whether in the backcountry, near the townships, or along the coast, stretched and strained the early state's infrastructure, revealing the inadequacy and limited usefulness of the colony's early bridges, ferries, and roads. In 1743, inhabitants from St. James Santee Parish requested that the provincial assembly intercede on their behalf in replacing a road that stretched along the Santee River. The petitioners argued that the road "running parallel with Santee River" had "three large bridges" that crossed creeks often overflowed by the river. Subsequently, they noted, "travellers were obliged to shun several places along the said Road by heading the several Creeks when the said River was high." The bridges, in other words, were constructed below the high-water mark and were often washed out—a regular shortcoming in South Carolina and throughout the colonies, it seems, where road commissioners and bridge builders lacked the requisite knowledge to construct reliable river crossings. Even when the river was only slightly higher than normal, the petitioners complained, "Boats were often detained" by the low-lying bridges and subsequently "those who had Landings above the said Bridges sometimes lost the Advantage of the Market." As the petitioners made clear, when the road was originally created, it was for the benefit of landowners whose property abutted the Santee, meaning that the road was their secondary mode of transportation. "When the said Road was first laid out the Plantations were situated intirely [sic] on the said River," they argued, "but at present there were not near so many as on inland Swamps, who reaped no Advantage from the Said Road." Inland swamp planters did not benefit from the road, and its bridges often blocked their access to the Santee; but importantly, the petitioners complained, they were still liable for the road's maintenance. In other words, they and their slaves were required to maintain a road not only that they did not use but that actually limited their economic and social mobility. They thus demanded that local commissioners abolish the road and lay out a new thoroughfare that would be of greater benefit to residents on the north side of the Santee.[20]

Still, these inland swamp plantation owners had access to South Carolina's dense coastal riverine system; they simply needed to alter the state's existing infrastructure to suit their needs. The farther white Carolinians moved away from the coast, however, the more difficult transit became on those rivers and creeks. Bridges could be deconstructed easily enough, but upstream South Carolinians encountered falls, rapids, and debris, all of which disrupted river movement. For example, in 1753, residents "in and about the Township of Williamsburg" complained that they "for several Years suffered considerable loss in the Water Carriage of their Goods to Market down Black River by reason of the great Quantitys of Wood fallen in the same, which rendered Navigation both dangerous and often impracticable." The provincial government appointed commissioners for cleaning the river a decade earlier, but this was a problem that required substantial labor, particularly as Carolinians moved deeper and deeper into the backcountry, often discarding lumber and other waste from cleared fields into nearby streams that threatened to choke off access at places like the Black River's Narrows near Georgetown. The provincial assembly subsequently appointed new commissioners to the area, granted them further powers to draw upon the population within a larger area, and created new penalties for those who refused to provide labor as well as those who dumped waste into the river. Still, these were problems that many South Carolinians would have happily confronted. Proximity to South Carolina's waterways was a privilege often only the earliest and most successful settlers could claim, not to mention that in the coastal plain the backbreaking labor of infrastructural development and maintenance most often fell to the ever-increasing enslaved population.[21]

Those who came later or lacked the capital required to purchase South Carolina's best lands necessarily settled farther away from accessible rivers and creeks. For example, at midcentury many newly established residents of South Carolina's Piedmont settled between the Congaree and Wateree Rivers. While they were near two of South Carolina's major waterways, they still complained that they were "at a very great loss & inconvenience for want of good and convenient Roads and Ferries to travel from those Parts to Charles Town." As they argued in their petition to the provincial government, the lack of quality infrastructure was "a very great Discouragement to several of the said Inhabitants, in the raising of several Commodities that their Lands would plentifully produce." The petitioners requested the establishment of ferries along both the Congaree and Wateree Rivers, and the appointment of commissioners of roads, both of which they believed "would be very advantageous to the Petitioners, and likewise of great Benefit to the Market in Charles town." It is possible that petitioners highlighted the benefits Charlestown merchants might receive from increased commercial traffic with settlers in the backcountry in part because they believed that it would strengthen their request to the assembly.[22]

Regardless, their argument reveals an important aspect of infrastructural development in the later colonial era. Roads, cleared rivers, bridges, and canals promised to bind the distant parts of a nascent territory together. Of course, earlier developmental projects sought to do the same: roads were built to knit together the colony's early defenses, bridges were built to provide isolated South Carolinians with access to social and economic sites, and canals were cut to allow goods and supplies to flow between plantations and Charlestown. This request made by backcountry settlers is notable, however, for therein they articulated their desire to be bound together with the merchants and planters along the coast. In so doing, they illuminated, through their infrastructural demands, the slow unification of the early state's disparately settled populace. Regulators in the 1760s and backcountry loyalists during the Revolution would make similar requests for better access. Backcountry settlers routinely felt isolated from the colony's coastal core: socially, economically, and politically. As they argued in the petition mentioned earlier and others, not only would roads, bridges, and ferries provide them with access to the colonial center, but they believed that transportation improvements would tie their economic concerns together with those of the merchants and planters who resided in and around Charlestown.[23]

These petitions also reveal the important role individual South Carolinians would continue to play in the production of state space and the way that their demands morphed around the spatial practices of the enslaved. Provincial leaders encouraged the settlement of the backcountry in large part to guard against the rapid growth of the enslaved population but did little else to construct a unified provincial space. South Carolina's colonial leaders responded to individual demands to construct provincial infrastructure, but the basic contours of this process—through petition, grand jury presentment, or legislative action—often silenced the voices of those farthest from the colonial seat of power. As one backcountry resident argued, "the present Constitution of this Province is very defective, and [has] become a Burden rather than being beneficial to the Back-inhabitants." Still, despite systemic limitations, South Carolinians throughout the province continually communicated their developmental concerns and aspirations to the colonial assembly. Out of such discourse, individual South Carolinians, state leaders, and the slaves they often discussed produced a type of knowledge of the early state that would prove essential to its creation and maintenance.[24]

Producing Knowledge

Infrastructural development and early governing practices did much more than simply provide South Carolinians with community access and economic mobility. Commissioners of roads, as agents of the provincial government, were granted unique access to their neighbors, gathering information regarding who was responsible for labor within each road district. While this type of information gathering—oriented around the needs and demands of territorial governance—was still in its adolescence in colonial South Carolina, it nevertheless provided the provincial regime, local administrators, and individual South Carolinians with a type of knowledge vital to the production and maintenance of the nascent state, a manufactured knowledge that illuminated the material means by which South Carolina's state space would and could be created and maintained. Moreover, local commissioners, individual South Carolinians, and the slaves whom they discussed bound together the early state with its residents, demanding the attention, compliance, and labor of South Carolinians throughout any given year. Infrastructural development provided South Carolinians with important opportunities to interact and make demands on their state government, not only in the form of petitions and demands for road maintenance and infrastructural development but also as the providers of labor. In other words, the local administration of infrastructural developments and the discourse that underwrote such day-to-day governing practices—as much as the physical construction of roads, bridges, and canals—were essential to the development of the early state. The fact that slaves were the primary source of developmental labor meant that they were often the subjects around which this infrastructural discourse revolved.

In the eighteenth-century British Atlantic world, internal improvements were often the personal responsibility of the able-bodied men who resided in the immediate vicinity of the roads, canals, bridges, and causeways being constructed or repaired. While this governing technique was beginning to change in England, where infrastructural development was becoming centralized and professionalized, it remained policy in South Carolina and throughout much of North America well into the nineteenth century. Overall oversight of developmental projects, as noted earlier, was delegated to the commissioners of roads, who were appointed by the provincial assembly and acted as local agents of the colonial government. These local commissioners were typically chosen from among the most prominent members of South Carolina's planter elite and merchant class, and such positions were, at least until the Revolution, often maintained by commissioners' heirs following death or retirement. Divided by parish and project, the number of local commissioners assigned to particular places varied over time and space. Though records for colonial road commissions are sparse, in 1760 in St. John's Parish Berkley, for example, there were eleven commissioners in charge of all the roads in the parish, four causeways, four bridges, and the approaches to two ferries. Commissioners typically met twice a year at a site centrally located within each parish. In St. John's Parish, commissioners met at the parish church in Monck's Corner or at the Black Oak Club. There the commissioners discussed the work that needed to be done on parish infrastructure, tallied their assessments of available workers, issued warrants to residents for labor, and meted out punitive fines or labor for those who neglected their requisite annual service. While commissioners were granted the power to make contracts with builders for the completion of some projects, like bridge construction, they often did the work of design and oversight themselves.[25]

Distributing, defining, and sometimes overseeing the labor requirements of parish residents required commissioners to have an intimate knowledge of the landscape under their jurisdiction, as well as a specific understanding of the population under their command. In the absence of a centralized body of knowledge concerning the provincial population, commissioners had to acquire and process such information on their own. How they did so varied from parish to parish, but typically commissioners relied upon individual residents to willingly report the requisite information upon penalty of fine or additional labor. At one meeting in St. Stephen's Parish, for example, commissioners decided that "advertisements shall be put up in different parts of the parish requiring all persons possessing or having the management of slaves, to make a return (upon oath) of all the male slaves by them so possessed or managed." Such public announcements, placed in local newspapers, in public gathering spaces, and along roadsides extended and illuminated the power of commissioners, regularly reminding individual residents of their developmental duties. The extant commission records and newspaper advertisements indicate that residents sometimes failed or refused to provide local administrators with this information. In 1733, commissioners from St. James's Goose Creek Parish complained that many "inhabitants have neglected to come and return on Oath, to the commissioners, as the Law directs, the Number of their Males taxable to the highways." By and large, however, parish residents seemed to have acceded to this domestic intrusion, providing the colonial government with detailed information regarding the basic makeup of their households, and correspondingly the workforce and taxable property at the commissioners' disposal. So, for example, in 1762 in St. John's Parish, commissioners reported that there were 1,140 men between the ages of sixteen and sixty available to labor, with only four residents failing to report their household numbers. Of that available workforce, all but seventy-six were enslaved black Carolinians.[26]

This flow of information between individual households and local provincial agents not only provided administrators with an important view of South Carolina's overall population but also simultaneously modified that knowledge into a species of information oriented specifically toward the production and maintenance of the colony. In this way, the commissioners of the roads transformed South Carolinians, and specifically men, from individual subjects into extensions of early state power, reifying the gendered nature of the early state. Moreover, while commissioners were granted the power to assess the number of men between the ages of sixteen and sixty regardless of race, most of the men who became state laborers were enslaved, particularly in the Lowcountry. Subsequently, the commissioners of the roads' mundane administrative actions—in this instance, information gathering and labor assessments—transformed male, black Carolinians, at least temporarily, from the private property of individual planters into the servants and strength of the early state. The knowledge produced in such moments was vital to the maintenance of the early state. In order for South Carolina's territory to be produced, black Carolinians had to be first transformed from the personal property of individual slave owners into the material means—the technology—through which the landscape could be transformed into state space. Thus, black Carolinians did much more than simply work on developmental projects. Their role as the objects of informational transactions between individual white Carolinians and their government was a crucial element of the creation of the state, whereby the very idea of provincial infrastructural projects was rendered possible. In other words, before South Carolinians could plan provincial roads and canals, they required a sense of the proposed works' feasibility, and this hinged on an adequate understanding of the material and laboring strength of the state.[27]

Information gleaned by local road commissioners in this manner was not the only means by which South Carolinians produced such knowledge. Throughout the eighteenth century, white Carolinians volunteered or hired their slaves to the service of the colony, and in some instances had them impressed by order of the government, for the construction of defensive fortifications, to accompany military companies in campaigns against the Spanish to the south and the Cherokee to the west, and in the buildup to the Revolutionary War. In each instance, be it at the bequest of infrastructural commissioners, militia commanders, or treasury officials, the enslaved were similarly transformed from the private property of individual Carolinians into the very means by which the province was made secure. Eventually such knowledge, through repetition and practice, became commonsensically woven into the structure of day-to-day governing procedures. If a sizable number of black Carolinians resided within a parish or district, then they were assumed to be the primary labor force to whom infrastructural development fell. If white Carolinians needed fortifications erected in Charlestown or along the frontier amid the fear of war or insurrection, the enslaved were presumed essential to that process. Of course, the increased reliance on slave state labor was terribly complicated, given that the very black Carolinians who produced the early state's infrastructure and spaces of security were simultaneously the internal enemy white Carolinians feared the most.

South Carolinians and the provincial government were painfully aware of this incongruous reality, and throughout the eighteenth century devised a number of plans meant to alleviate the fears born out of their growing reliance on enslaved men and women. In the early 1740s, South Carolinians were still reeling from the effects of the Stono Rebellion. The colonial government passed a number of laws following the revolt that sought to dilute the threat of another insurrection. Some of the legislative reactions were specific to the Stono Rebellion itself, including a new law for the "better ordering and control of the slave population" and new rules for slaves' infrastructural labor. Colonial leaders, in the face of the rebellion, also reacted by attempting to reverse South Carolina's demographic trend, which veered toward an overwhelming enslaved majority. The colonial assembly passed a prohibitive duty on imported Africans, which effectively slowed the slave trade to a trickle for the years immediately following the revolt. They also created a bounty to encourage the immigration of poor, white Protestants, who, it was hoped, would settle along the fringes of the colony in one of the eleven townships the government created to provide a buffer against both Indian attack and slave insurrection. In the end, these measures had limited impact or only partially achieved their goals. Still, the passage of such laws reflects the growing power of the provincial government, and in particular how such power revolved around defining and controlling the enslaved population.[28]

Interestingly, while South Carolina's colonial leaders worked feverishly to craft new laws that would decrease the chances of another slave insurrection, they continued to rely on enslaved black Carolinians for the maintenance and even the security of the early state. This continued reliance is exemplified by two events in the early 1740s, both of which further illuminate how slaves stood at the center of early state knowledge production. In July 1742, South Carolina sent troops to aid the newly founded colony of Georgia against a Spanish invasion on nearby St. Simon's Island. The Spanish attack on the fledgling colony was part of the broader global conflict between the competing European powers. It was also likely a response to James Oglethorpe's failed 1740 invasion of St. Augustine—itself a response to the Stono Rebellion, believed by many South Carolinians to have been instigated by the Spanish. South Carolinians responded to the 1742 attack on Georgia by sending volunteers, supplies, and their slaves to aid in the successful repulsion of the Spanish. Two years earlier, during the invasion of St. Augustine, Oglethorpe requested similar aid from South Carolina. In his plea for assistance, Oglethorpe suggested that Georgia's northern neighbor send "600 men, 3 Troops of Rangers, 105 men, 800 Negroes for Pioneers, 160 white Men to guard and oversee them." South Carolinians did not fulfill Oglethorpe's 1740 request. Planters feared sending their slaves to a place that many assumed would offer them the promise of refuge and freedom, and many whites refused to accompany the expedition, out of fear that black Carolinians would take advantage of the absence of military-aged white men and again rise up in rebellion. In 1742, however, with a Spanish force at the very edge of their southern border, South Carolinians responded much more willingly, volunteering themselves and their slaves for the military effort.[29]

Such aid is remembered because at the end of 1742 and the beginning of 1743, dozens of individual slave owners demanded that the provincial assembly provide payment for the work their slaves did in service to colonial security—a demand that the assembly, despite some initial dissent, willingly met. The debates and considerations over payment hinged on the narration of slaves' contributions to South Carolina's military efforts. Such discourse and dialogue—between government officials, military leaders, the owners of slaves, and of course the silent, but essential, contribution of the slaves themselves—reinforced the same kind of knowledge produced by the commissioners of roads, wherein the enslaved were acknowledged as the material means by which the province could be secured from its external enemies. The dialogue was simple enough: individual South Carolinians petitioned the assembly for repayment of essential services, a process mirrored by individuals who had provided colonial leadership with horses, tools, and food to aid in the fight against the Spanish. Though seemingly mundane, like the communication between the commissioners of roads and parish residents, it was out of such everyday discourse that the subtle contours of early governance took shape—the government's relationship to individual subjects, the very meaning of citizenship, and the material means by which the state would be both imagined and maintained.[30]

Importantly, however, South Carolinians were quick to distinguish the varied efforts of black Carolinians who participated in South Carolina's expedition to Georgia. The Commons House of Assembly established a committee "to settle and adjust the Accounts of such persons as have Demands on the Public for Negro Hire and Provisions supplied the Militia during the late Alarm." The committee heard all of the demands for repayment, and settled with those whose claims were deemed appropriate. But, notably, the assembly sharply refused to financially reward the efforts of free blacks or slaves who had volunteered their own time and effort to South Carolina's cause. In the same session of the assembly, Lieutenant Governor William Bull sent the House "an Account of the Number of the Negroes who were inlisted and sent on the late Expedition for the Relief of the Colony of Georgia." Bull recounted that the men—seventy-three in all, who it seems were all sailors aboard the seven ships South Carolina sent to aid Georgia—"have applied to me for some small Reward for their Service on that Occasion." While the lieutenant governor lacked the fiscal power to personally grant their request, he recommended it to the assembly for consideration, as he believed that "a small Allowance, by Way of Reward, for what they have done, may be an Encouragement on future Occasions, wherein the Negroes may be of great service to the Province."

The assembly disagreed, and refused to provide the men with a financial reward, but not because they disagreed with the premise that "Negroes may be of great service to the Province." To the contrary, South Carolinians and the early state were becoming ever more reliant on enslaved labor; they simply did not feel compelled to reward black Carolinians for volunteering their own services to the state during a time of war. In part, it seems, this was because many white Carolinians believed black volunteerism unthinkable, refusing to acknowledge black Carolinians' individual will, much less the possibility that they would, or even could, choose to labor for the state. This was made more complicated by the fact that the provincial government did provide occasional rewards to enslaved men and women who provided information and aid to their owners and communities in the midst of insurrection scares. The debates and decisions then over how to provide recompense and who would receive rewards for enslaved labor for the state following the Stono Rebellion were filled with contradictions. Enslaved informants and volunteer sailors both seemingly were at work for the security of the state. But providing reward for the former, at least in the minds of white Carolinians, reinforced white power within the plantation system. Recompensing volunteer black labor, on the other hand, would have dangerously acknowledged the free will of black Carolinians, as well as the possibility that they were capable of civic duty.[31]

All the while that South Carolinians discussed and debated rewarding the labors of their slaves, the provincial government continued to rely on slave labor for the colony's everyday maintenance. For example, just a few months after their dismissal of the lieutenant governor's request and in the midst of their debate over repayment to the planters who offered their slaves' services to the fight against the Spanish, South Carolina confronted the very real possibility of further conflict. William Bull outlined all of the hazards threatening the colony in a letter to the assembly, citing first and foremost the menace of another slave insurrection, or as he described it, "the Dangers which lately threatened our Lives and Fortunes, to which we are still exposed." Beyond their internal enemy and the Spanish to the south, Bull urged the assembly to act "in case of a War with France," which seemed increasingly likely given escalating tensions between England and France over succession to the Spanish throne. Bull then remonstrated with the assembly, exclaiming, "I doubt not but you will readily agree in Opinion with me, that such are Matters where our present as well as future Safety are greatly concerned." To secure South Carolina and protect its white inhabitants, Bull urged the completion of Fort Johnson at the entrance to Charlestown's harbor, the completion of the city's defensive "curtain line" (a brick wall built to protect the city), and the appointment of a military engineer to oversee all of these projects. Bull recommended "Colonel [Othniel] Beale as a fit Person to erect several new Batteries and a Breast-work on Ashley River, in order to cover the South Part of the

Town." In addition to the suggestions made by Bull, the assembly pressed residents throughout the province to construct secure sites that they might use as places of retreat in the face of insurrection or invasion.[32]

The provincial government concurred with Bull and appointed Beale as the "principal Engineer and Chief Manager of all and singular the Batteries, Fortifications and Works erected, or to be erected, in Charles Town and Johnson's Fort in this Province for the Defence thereof." Beale was accordingly given the power to "agree with and employ such and so many Artificers and Workmen as shall be necessary for the raising, building, and carrying on all such Forts, Batteries, Fortifications and Works." To supplement this authority and ensure "the better and more expeditious carrying on the same," Beale was "authorized to impress any Negroes, Horses, Tools and other Implements whatsoever within the Limits of Saint Philip's Charles Town necessary to be used and employed in or about the same." The provincial assembly granted Beale the power to make contracts that the government would uphold, but more importantly, as an agent of the early state, he was given the ability to muster the material strength of South Carolina, its enslaved population, a power that further secured the relationship between the early state and slave labor.[33]

Despite being granted the broad authorities outlined earlier, Beale was not able to complete the projects as quickly as South Carolinians hoped. The newly appointed engineer made it clear to Lieutenant Governor Bull that "finishing of the Works for the Defence of Charles Town" with the "Dispatch that is apprehended to be necessary, requires the Assistance of a greater Number of Negroes that can be hired in or near the same." In other words, Beale needed more slaves than Charlestown's residents were willing to offer. While one possibility for overcoming such labor shortages would have been the impressment or demand for white labor, conceivable in the face of the very real prospect of war and possible invasion, provincial leaders instead sought ways to secure more enslaved labor. Lieutenant Governor Bull pushed the assembly to devise a means "to procure a sufficient Number of Negroes living near the Places where their Assistance is wanted." The Commons House considered Bull's request and responded in just two days. To complete the defensive works in Charlestown, Beale was given permission to "impress all those male Slaves who were usually hired out as Laborers or Porters in Charles Town." And to construct safe-havens throughout the province, the assembly agreed that Lieutenant Governor Bull could appoint persons to "direct the building of such Places of Security and Retreat" and that those local commissioners should be granted the power to "hire or impress every eighth male

Slave usually employed upon such Plantations as are within ten Miles of such Place of Security and Retreat, Tradesmen and Boatmen excepted." Without the least bit of irony, South Carolinians tasked slaves with the construction of the spaces wherein white Carolinians would seek shelter in the event of a slave insurrection. More importantly, by appointing local commissioners to oversee the construction of local sanctuaries, the provincial assembly continued to solidify its power throughout the colony, and did so by relying on its primary technology for development: enslaved men and women. Forts, curtain lines, and "places of security and retreat," like roads and cuts, marked the landscape as a provincial space, and the safety of the population as a central task overseen by a centralized governing body.[34]

Again and again, South Carolinians turned to their government, who then turned to slaves to produce their security and their economic infrastructure. By the time of the Revolution, the use of slaves for state labor had become so woven into South Carolinians' political reality that it was rarely even debated. Still, the incongruity of the potential enemies of the state providing the bulk of the provincial labor force did not go unnoticed. During the Seven Years' War, for example, South Carolinians again turned to their slaves to construct defensive structures, both along the coast and in the backcountry. William Gerard de Brahm, at the time a surveyor for Georgia's colonial government, was pressed into service as South Carolina's chief military engineer, tasked with planning and overseeing the construction of the colony's defenses under the watchful eye of the assembly-appointed commissioners of fortifications. His letters and the commissioners' journals highlight the continued centrality of slaves to South Carolina's war effort. Slaves dug out mud from Charlestown's marshes, loaded it on boats, delivered it to strategic locations, and then packed it into places for defensive breastworks. They secured the bridges around the city, cut lumber and transported it around the colony, and made "500 bricks" and laid them on a new platform "on the north part of the bay." Slaves cut trees and gathered wood from which they bundled together hundreds of fascines. They made thousands of wooden stakes, painstakingly dug trenches with spades and their hands, and then used wheelbarrows to remove the excess earth. At one point during the early part of 1756, de Brahm wrote the commissioners, imploring them to provide him not with more slaves—of those he seemed to have plenty—but rather with more white men, arguing that it was "impossible to carry on henceforth the works with advantage, by so few overseers." He argued, "Two gangs with two overseers are to be put on every task. One overseer is to be down to see the spadesmen speedily and sufficiently filling the wheelbarrows and the other is to be on the works to see them speedily and properly discharged." De Brahm made clear that the labor of the overseers was vital to the works, but given that "none is able to manage more than 20 hands" and there were then "never less than 200 working hands daily," he argued, "there are at present too few overseers." Black Carolinians worked to secure the city and the colony from the prospect of global war, but de Brahm worried that there were not enough white men laboring to protect the city and the colony from their slaves.[35]

As de Brahm argued, the circumstances of this particular construction effort were not ideal for guaranteeing the safety of South Carolina's residents. Laboring beside the colony's slaves were French Acadians, who had only recently arrived after their brutal expulsion from Nova Scotia, as well as some poor European immigrants who had arrived in South Carolina as part of the colonial government's aggressive effort to increase the province's white population. De Brahm warned the assembly that such a workforce represented a grave danger to the colony. He argued, "It proves not a sufficient carefulness when a body of men is in business [building defensive works] without being under guard; This is observed any where in Europe, tho' the employed people be subjects and friends, how much more are we to be carefull whilst our workmen are French and Negroes." Interestingly, de Brahm did not reject the use of such sources for labor—and if he did, he certainly did not say so—rather he feared relying on what he described as "our within enemies," without providing a proper security detail. Such a force was apparently never firmly established, initially because of an apparent "scarcity of soldiers" and later because the soldiers reported to de Brahm that they had heard a rumor that the commissioners "would not pay them."[36]

Samuel Prioleau was the apparent source of the soldiers' information. It is not entirely clear why Prioleau undermined the government's position with the soldiers, but he was privy to the status of South Carolina's treasury having entered into a dispute with the commissioners of fortifications over payment for his slaves' state labor. The treasurer ultimately awarded Prioleau £1,200, a substantial sum in 1755, "to apply towards payment of negro hire." Given that the commissioners of fortifications at one point agreed to pay "negroes five shillings for all the time they can work in the day," Prioleau's £1,200 reflects the sizable contribution to South Carolina's defensive efforts made by his enslaved laborers.[37]

Prioleau's disputed payment, alongside the reimbursement that slave owners demanded following the 1742 defense of Georgia, makes clear another important way that black Carolinians—as the transactional objects around and upon which individual white Carolinians and the provincial government forged their dynamic relationship—came to shape the contours of the early state. As noted earlier, slaves were the focal point of the early state's self-awareness. Through local administrators, the provincial government and individual citizens acquired and produced a type of knowledge oriented around the material and productive powers of the early state, a process that transmuted slaves into the material agents of the early state's development. Importantly, South Carolina's deployment of black Carolinians as state laborers also provided individual South Carolinians with an opportunity to shape the contours and shifting meaning of citizenship. More specifically, through their slaves' state labor, white South Carolinians discussed and debated the evolving significance of public service and sacrifice.

While slave owners like Samuel Prioleau demanded compensation for the emergency use of their slaves' labor, most white Carolinians perceived the early state's use of their slaves as their duty. This was most obvious in the case of infrastructural development. Twice a year, and sometimes more, planters were required to send their male slaves to labor on nearby roads, bridges, causeways, and canals. While they were surely the beneficiaries of these internal improvements, planters nevertheless often perceived the forfeiture of their adult male slaves' labor as an unwelcome inconvenience, particularly when it interrupted their plantation labors. Still, the commissioners of roads wielded a significant amount of power, both in their ability to punish individual slave owners for the dereliction of duty and also through their community and provincial stature. Henry Laurens experienced this firsthand in 1765 when he requested "an indulgence" from the St. John's Parish commissioners. Laurens explained to Commissioner James Cordes Jr., "The circumstances of my Indigo Plantation are such as will render it extremely detrimental to me to work on the High Road next week." Laurens was not asking to be excused from service; rather, he hoped the commissioners would "allot a reasonable proportion of work on the Road to be performed by my Male Slaves & to postpone the execution of it until I have got thro my first cutting of Indigo." While Cordes did not explicitly refuse Laurens's request, his response to Laurens's letter did manage to convince the wealthy merchant-planter to fulfill the demands of provincial service. Laurens, however, was arguably one of the most powerful individuals in all of South Carolina, so it should be noted that a few months later, the commissioners altered their rules for requisite service, accommodating the varied agricultural cycles of indigo and rice planting, a concession indicative of the back-and-forth between government administrators and individual subjects that reflected the dynamic process through which governing practices were shaped.[38]

Still, despite the commissioners' eventual concessions, in 1765 Laurens was pressed to comply with the commissioners' requests, and ultimately sent his slaves to labor on the parish roads. Nevertheless, in his letters to commissioners and associates discussing this matter, Laurens illuminated the centrality of slavery to his ideas of republican citizenship. When initially requesting the temporary reprieve from duty, Laurens wrote that he would never "otherwise apply for" such indulgences were it not for the needs of his indigo crop. He explained that "it is my inclination at all times to be obedient to Laws & to give those Gentlemen who are so good as to take the burthen of the executive part upon them, as little trouble as possible." He also acknowledged the importance of his slaves' service to St. John's Parish more broadly, but hoped that "no disadvantage will arise to the public from a few days forbearance." Cordes's response made clear to Laurens that the commissioners had resolved "to admit of no excuse." As Laurens explained to his Mepkin plantation overseer, "If every one (I plainly perceive now) was to be indulged to work upon the Road when it best suited him, all regularity & good order would be destroyed." In other words, the commissioners could not excuse Laurens, for if they did, they would be obligated to grant concessions to every planter and slave owner who presented them with similar hardships, a scenario that would have overwhelmed the commissioners, stretching their responsibilities throughout the year and making substantive road work an impossibility.[39]

While Cordes and the commissioners presented a practical argument for demanding the labor of Laurens's slaves, Laurens's correspondence reveals that his own consideration revolved around his ideas of public sacrifice and duty, an increasingly vital question in the years immediately preceding the Revolutionary War. What's striking about Laurens's language in his back-and-forth with the commissioners is the manner in which he perceived himself—and his relationship to the state—directly through the labor of his slaves. Cordes admonished Laurens for attempting to rearrange his slaves' compulsory labor, questioning how someone as wealthy as Laurens could find such an obligation so onerous or pressing—after all, Laurens was one of the most prominent slave dealers in Charlestown and was in the midst of a plantation-purchasing spree in the 1760s. Laurens responded to Cordes's letter pithily, "Money is not so very plenty nor ready with me as you seem to imagine," and continued, "but if I had as many pounds as there have been leaves before me I would not depart from an established maxim for the rule of my conduct as a Citizen & member of my community 'To do my Duty rather than to buy it off with a fine.'" Here, then, Laurens made clear precisely the value of his slaves' labor for his relationship to the early state: the fulfillment of his duty as a citizen. For Laurens, his obligations as a citizen revolved around submission to the early state's local administrators, which could only be facilitated through the labor of his slaves. In the conclusion to his second letter to Cordes, Laurens wrote, "Therefore, tho my present case is singularly hard, I have order'd Mr. Smith to attend Monday & Tuesday with my male slaves & faithfully to perform his duty with them accordingly to your legal commands."[40]

Laurens himself, of course, would not be participating in roadwork. But this did not matter, nor did it bar him from claiming membership in the broader community of South Carolina—a community he already represented as a member of the Provincial Assembly, and whom he would come to lead as a member of the Revolutionary Council of Safety, and then the young nation more broadly as the president of the Second Continental Congress. In fact, for Laurens, as for so many other South Carolinians, citizenship as often as not hinged not on his own industry but rather on the labor that his slaves fulfilled in the production of South Carolina's infrastructure and defensive works. As he made clear in a letter to James Marion regarding roadwork, "Obedience to Laws is the Duty of every Member of Community." That his slaves and his overseer were tasked with fulfilling Laurens's duty was insignificant in his understanding of the situation. For wealthy South Carolinians, the labor and lives of their slaves rightfully belonged to their owners. When slaves labored for the state, they worked not for themselves—as the 1742 decision to not reward black volunteers made clear—but for the fulfillment of their owners' responsibilities as citizens. Even more importantly, Laurens considered his slaves' state labor not as a benefit for him alone but rather as an activity specifically oriented toward the production and maintenance of what he termed the "public good," against which, he argued, "private Interest must not be set in competition." Laurens made this clear in his letter to Marion, asserting that he did not regard his slaves' parish work simply as the completion of an onerous, ill-timed obligation that threatened to ruin his indigo crop. Instead, he argued to Marion: "if we make a few pounds less Indigo it will be a good sacrifice to those Laws which will secure to us the property of what we do make." In Laurens's nascent republican formulation, private interest was best served by consideration of the broader public good. And the public good in South Carolina was facilitated, in this instance and many others, through the labor of black Carolinians. Slaves, then, did much more than simply improve the condition of local roads and river passages; their everyday laboring practices produced, strengthened, and secured the ties between subject and state.[41]

To be sure, not every South Carolinian felt as Laurens did, and his opinions on roadwork and state slave labor were surely shaped by his role as legislator and his slow embrace of revolutionary republican rhetoric. Still, Laurens was one of South Carolina's most prominent Revolutionary-era leaders, and his ideas surrounding duty and the sacrifice of his slaves seem to have taken hold during the war and in the years following its conclusion. Petitions following the Revolution demonstrate just how pervasive this perspective would become. For example, in 1802, Samuel Harris, "a citizen of the district [Abbeville] and state," petitioned the General Assembly for recompense for a slave who was killed while working on district roads. According to his petition, Harris was "summoned by the overseer of the road leading from Vienna to Abbeville Courthouse," a particularly important thoroughfare, as it connected isolated backcountry residents to both the Savannah River and the local site of state government. Harris echoed Laurens when he wrote that he considered "it his duty to yield obedience to the laws of this state" and subsequently sent his only slave, "a negro man named Harry," to work on the road. Again, like Laurens, Harris perceived Harry's sweat and toil to be his own, a fulfillment of Harris's obligation to the state as a citizen. But unlike Laurens, whose only sacrifice seemed to be the loss of valuable plantation labor, Harris lost Harry when on March 26 "he was accidentally killed by the fall of a tree."[42]

Slaves, it seems, were frequently killed while working for the public. Such events, mostly forgotten, illuminate the harsh reality slaves faced in completing state labor. Often called out to work in August, the interim period of crop production, black Carolinians faced unremitting heat and backbreaking labor. When slave owners and government administrators negotiated settlements for the deaths that occurred while slaves were laboring for the public, they were provided with an opportunity to define citizenship and shape the contours and meaning of governing practices. Samuel Harris sought recompense for the loss of Harry; he did so by first legitimating the state's authority, and then articulating the proper comportment of the dutiful citizen. But he also clarified the limits of the government's authority: road commissioners could claim the labor of his slave, but they could not completely usurp his rights as the owner of private property. Just like landowners who expected compensation when roads and canals altered their properties, slave owners demanded reparation when the public good cost them their slaves. These types of interactions were public rituals through which state and citizen were brought into being, and through which they forged the contours of their relationship in the early nation. William McCants petitioned the General Assembly for financial recompense for the loss of Daniel, who was considered "a good carter a cooper and every way a handy trusty and valuable negroe." According to testimony, Daniel "was killed by a tree whilst at work on the publick road." William Baker similarly lost "a negro man belonging to him while employed as a laborer on the building of the gaol of Marion District." The rapid expansion of South Carolina's government into the backcountry and the transformation of space into the state's territory through the construction of courthouses and jails provided some South Carolinians—carpenters, bricklayers, slave owners—with lucrative economic opportunities. But dangers lurked even among the most banal of projects. As Baker argued in his petition, he was "not aware of the danger to which he [his slave] might be exposed on works of that kind and calculating only on a moderate hire for him" he instead had "sustained an unlooked for and entire loss." Still, Baker argued what all of these petitioners believed, that "it is always the intention" of the state government "that persons whose hands are employed on any publick work belong to the state." Still, slave owners believed then that when they offered their slaves' services to the state, they would "receive a fair profit on their labor instead of the loss of them."[43]

White Carolinians expected to be compensated for their slaves who died while laboring on public works in part because this had long been the state's policy. For example, at the start of the Revolutionary War, South Carolinians desperately sought to complete defensive works along the coast. Daniel Cannon, a prominent Charleston contractor and carpenter, was charged with "erecting and completing the intended works upon Sullivan's Island." To allay any of the public's fears regarding the potential sacrifice of their slaves to such works, the Council of Safety promised, "the public will make good any loss that may be sustained . . . by negroes killed, maimed or lost in this service." During the Revolution, just as they had in the 1740s, South Carolinians relied upon the support of enslaved pioneers and laborers. But just as in the 1740s, South Carolinians perceived the sacrifices being made for the cause of the Revolution as those not of the enslaved but rather of their owners. For example, when preparing Fort Johnson for what South Carolinians feared was the initial British invasion of the rebellious state, the Council of Safety told the commanding officer, "Negroes may be found to assist your company at that battery to good purpose." To alleviate the concerns of slave owners who might be concerned about placing their slaves in the way of the British military, the council promised to "indemnify the owners for any loss which may happen by death or other injury to such negroes by the enemy."[44]

"To Be Made a Public Example"

Of course, black Carolinians were not simply the passive material means through which the early state produced its infrastructure and defensive works. They struggled and pressed against the demands of their owners and the government, staked their own claims to the spaces they were producing, and challenged the legitimacy of the government and the property claims of their masters, making them at times what de Brahm termed the "within enemy." Black Carolinians subsequently confronted a terrible situation: as the private property of dutiful citizens, their lives and labors were considered essential to the state and the formulation of the public good, but as potential and sometimes real enemies and rebels, their deaths were deemed equally important to the maintenance of the early state. Slave deaths, in this way, became as valuable to the formation of the early state and its territory as their lives and labors.

This is clearly evident in the compensation awarded to white Carolinians whose slaves were found guilty of a crime or deemed a threat to the public, and who were subsequently executed. As early as 1712, the colonial assembly established the precedent of compensation for executed slaves, arguing that in certain circumstances, the property lost through the public killing of enslaved men and women should "be borne by the public." Consequently, throughout the eighteenth century, the assembly read petitions for compensation, debated the merits of each case, assessed the value of each slave, and awarded financial recompense to individual slave owners for their loss. For instance, in early 1756, the assembly considered the case of Tony, "an old fugitive Negro man" who was killed for "resisting" when James White attempted to apprehend him. John Edwards, Tony's owner, was rewarded £50 by the colonial assembly. Compensation varied from case to case; thus, in the same year, Sarah Purry was awarded £200 each for two slaves, Jemmy and Robin, who had killed Charles Purry, her husband and their master. While the value of murdered slaves varied from owner to owner, their death's significance to the early state and the "publick" was marked less by monetary assessment than by the provincial government's willingness to bear this burden for individual owners.[45]

The brutal murder and policing of black Carolinians was of considerable importance to the production of South Carolina's early territory. Officials made this clear not only through the compensation they provided slave owners but also through the varied ways that they reshaped South Carolina's early state space to accommodate and emphasize this ruthless aspect of governance in a slave state. This is nowhere more obvious than when South Carolinians sought to alter and reshape their territorial boundaries in direct response to their rising concerns of possible slave revolts. Members of the colonial assembly made this clear in a letter to the Lords Commissioners for Trade & Plantations concerning "a Boundary Line between it & North Carolina." The report, written in the context of the Seven Years' War, argued that since "Georgia yet remains in a weak & infant state," South Carolina was in fact the southern "frontier of His Majesty's North-American Dominions." While they were willing to guard that southern frontier, they acknowledged that "the great disproportion there is between our white Men & Negros, renders us less formidable to a foreign enemy." As South Carolina's leaders argued, in the event of an invasion, their "whole Strength, from every Quarter," would be needed not only to repel the assault but also to keep their "Slaves from a Revolt." This reality demanded, at least as they argued, that the northwestern border between South and North Carolina be shaped so as to include all of "those inhabitants who are settled upon the upper parts of our several rivers." In other words, South Carolinians sought to reshape the border between South and North Carolina—no simple task—to ease the policing of the enslaved population.[46]

At the conclusion of the war, South Carolinians revisited this topic, seeking to include not just more white settlers but also the Catawba (a Native group that lived between the two colonies) within their borders, for the explicit purpose of aiding the colony in searching for and killing runaway slaves. During the winter of 1765, a large number of slaves had absconded into the swamps along the coast near the Ashepoo River, leading colonial leaders to worry "that some dangerous conspiracy and Insurrection was intended." The assembly gathered the militia, but the runaways' recesses proved "impervious to White people at that season of the year," and the governor requested the aid of the Catawba in their search for the rebellious slaves. The Catawba "immediately came down and partly by the terror of their name, their diligence, and singular sagacity," the report noted, they were able to disperse, capture, or kill most of the runaways, who did not want to "expose themselves to the attack of an Enemy so dreaded." Subsequently, the report suggested "it would be convenient and reasonable that the Catawba Indians should be comprehended in the proposed Boundary as a very useful body of men to keep our negroes in some awe."[47]

The inclusion of the Catawba within South Carolina's state space was not a slight adjustment, and when one considers the political and social upheaval that existed in the western portions of both North and South Carolina in the late eighteenth century, this concession takes on added significance. White Carolinians on both sides of the border were charging, at times violently, for equitable political and legal rights. Surveying and demarcating the border was an important part of the overall process that marked who (and what) was to be considered South Carolina—and subsequently, how legal and political rights and power would be administered. If one also considers the economic importance of access to trans-Appalachian territories—which the British received in the Treaty of Paris—the ramifications of where South Carolina's northwestern border would lie become profound. More importantly, as politicians and residents of South Carolina constructed boundaries and textually represented the polity through cartography, they gave form to their very idea of the early state. In South Carolina, this process was intimately connected to efforts by white Carolinians to maintain supremacy over the enslaved population.

South Carolina's leaders worked to reshape the borders and boundaries of their territory to accommodate their brutal control of black Carolinians. That such pitiless rule was a constitutive aspect of the early state's governing praxis was also made clear in the prominent public display of executed black bodies alongside the very roads, causeways, bridges, and canals that slaves were tasked with constructing. The ruthless subjugation of black Carolinians became a prominent feature of the constructed state landscape, as noticeable as the shade trees, distance markers, and public houses that were mandated by the provincial government. For example, in 1739, following the Stono Rebellion, a ranger serving under General James Oglethorpe noted that "about fifty" of the slaves who participated in the rebellion "attempted to go home" following their eventual defeat. As the ranger noted, however, the rebel slaves were "taken by the Planters" who subsequently "cutt [sic] off their heads and set them up at every Mile Post they came to."[48]

As the ranger made clear in the narratives of his travels, the landscape was already distinctly shaped by the early state: its man-made mile-markers signifying specific sociospatial practices that oriented travelers and allowed their calculated movement to and from the colony's economic and social center. Governing officials, many of whom traveled over South Carolina's hardscrabble roads as they went to and from the colony's seat of government, had mandated the appearance and comfort of provincial roads, ordering that shade trees remain preserved alongside the roads and establishing punishments for anyone who violated this provision. Thus, despite the fact that South Carolina's roads were, by English and European standards, rather primitive, to eighteenth-century travelers they were among North America's finest. After crossing one of South Carolina's early engineering feats, a "7 mile ... cawsway [sic] as straight as possible & as even as a bowling green," John Bartram remarked in his diary, "I believe no roads is finer to travail then ye Carolinas."[49]

Bartram came to this conclusion because the roads he traveled in South Carolina's Lowcountry were "level except over ye branches where we gradualy [sic] ascend or descend by slow degrees 6 or 8 foot" and "mostly shaded with lofty pines oaks [and] tupelo." Yet, even Bartram's gaze, curated though it was by his wealthy hosts, could not help but take in the brutality that accompanied what he described as South Carolina's picturesque progress. After visiting Jacksonboro, Bartram noted that it was "prettily scituated [sic] on ye river Pon Pon," that it contained "about 30 or 40 dwelling houses & several prety large & ye people very civill." He also immediately observed, however, that among the town's notable features were "two negroes Jibited alive for poisoning thair Master." Bartram's observation of the two men publicly displayed in Jacksonboro's gallows was almost casual, just one of the town's and the Lowcountry's many noteworthy features. Even his description of the men's suspected crime focused more on the science of their poison—after all, Bartram was a leading naturalist at the time—rather than the cause of their crime or the palpable fear it must have stirred up among the town's populace, white and black. Bartram did find the violent landmarks noteworthy, but the sight of tortured bodies in no way diminished his praise for the town and its white inhabitants. Bartram's seeming nonchalance about this government-sanctioned disciplinary display was the consequence of its normalization. Just as white Carolinians would grow accustomed to particular traveling procedures and governing techniques along South Carolina's manicured roads and carefully cut canals, so too, through the spectacle of disciplinary cruelty, they became habituated to the necessity of black repression for the maintenance of the early state. South Carolinians expected their slaves to be on the roads: as mobile laborers transporting goods and supplies between their plantations and the various economic nodes scattered across the territory; as infrastructural laborers, producing the network of thoroughfares, causeways, and canals that knit together the nascent state; and as bloodied sacrifices, signaling to South Carolinians, white and black, the means by which security was maintained throughout the provincial territory.[50]

CHAPTER TWO

The Strength of This Country
Securing and Rebuilding the State in the Revolutionary Era

In the years immediately following the American Revolution, South Carolina's elected officials engaged in a heated but often forgotten debate over the future of the Atlantic slave trade. The question of a slave embargo revolved around the state's post-Revolutionary economic malaise, compounded, many felt, by South Carolinians' enthusiasm for slave purchasing. As one member of the General Assembly argued, in the face of profligate spending on enslaved men, women, and children, the government was "bound in duty to restrain an exuberance in any that had a tendency towards injuring the public interest." That South Carolina, a state whose reputation would come to hinge on its commitment to free trade and the individual's right to own slaves, would decide that the inhumane traffic in human beings jeopardized the public interest is, of course, noteworthy. And yet, as the debate itself reveals, much more was at stake in this moment than simply a temporary policing of South Carolinians' spending habits.[1]

While many of South Carolina's political leaders confined their comments during the debates over importation to the issue of debt and the propriety of legislated commercial restraint, some focused their attention on the possible broader consequences of the trade's prohibition, reflecting specifically on the importance of slaves to South Carolina's existence. No voice was louder in this debate than that of Charles Cotesworth Pinckney, who argued for the continued unfettered importation of African men and women. Pinckney contended that enslaved black Carolinians were "the strength of this country" and "constituted its riches." Beyond stridently articulating that "this country was not capable of being cultivated by white men," Pinckney more importantly reminded his colleagues, who were safely gathered together in Charleston, that slaves were essential to the maintenance and security of the state and had only recently "saved this city, in the war." Few could argue the point, and most would have agreed that the initial defeat of British forces in 1776 was the consequence of "the number of bastions hastily thrown up" in defense of the city, "a service performed entirely by the negroe pioneers." Pinckney declared that slaves, beyond their role in constructing emergency public works, also allowed individuals to complete their civic duty, and knowingly asserted that it was a "moral impossibility for any planter to pay" a land tax "or any other tax" if he was deprived of slaves. Pinckney concluded by reminding his fellow legislators that the government itself was maintained by the "large duty paid to the state for negroes imported," an income the state would forgo if the trade was interrupted.[2]

Pinckney's argument ultimately failed to sway most of his legislative colleagues. Nevertheless, his state-centered, proslavery position illuminates the everyday, material role that slaves played in the production of the Revolutionary-era state. For Pinckney, the slave trade needed to endure not simply because it was the natural right for white Carolinians to own slaves and not only because the closure of the trade threatened to undermine South Carolina's economy but also because without slaves the state would falter. Importantly, Pinckney made his argument at a vital moment in South Carolina's history. In the months and years that followed the American Revolution, South Carolinians charted their initial path beyond British rule—carving out the contours of citizenship; erecting the infrastructures of trade, governance, and jurisprudence; and mapping and marking the physical dimensions of the state's territory. Pinckney crafted his argument about extending the international slave trade at the precise moment that the process of post-Revolutionary state-creation was initiated. Given the circumstances, white Carolinians (whatever their position on the slave trade) had to confront a glaring truth that few besides Pinckney were willing to openly acknowledge: slaves were, and had long been, the primary material means through which the newly established state was created, developed, and sustained.

As state leaders would make clear in the years during and following the war, enslaved Carolinians were the primary material technology at the heart of state practice. They provided the labor necessary for defensive and infrastructural development and construction, underwrote the state's finances through taxes on their bodies and the fruits of their labor, and provoked the creation of new administrative bodies and techniques of control. When the state sought to punish loyalist Carolinians, it took away their slaves; when it rewarded patriots, it provided them with slaves. When legislators conceptualized the roads and canals that would reinvigorate their economy and bind together the farthest reaches of the state, they imagined an army of enslaved people who could and would make real these developmental dreams. In almost every conceivable manner, enslaved black Carolinians stood at the center of the emergence of independent South Carolina.

This chapter examines the several ways that black Carolinians participated in the production of South Carolina as a modern independent state. Beginning in the Revolution and building upon colonial practices, South Carolinians immediately turned to slaves to build their fortifications, maintain their armies, recruit their soldiers, and provide for the material needs of their rebellious state. As a result of this labor, by the end of the war government leaders, state planners, and private citizens could hardly imagine South Carolina's material improvement and development without enslaved labor. In this way, slaves became embedded into the bedrock of South Carolina's postcolonial governing practices, which themselves were shifting in the face of postwar challenges and opportunities. Slaves' state labor remained essential even as South Carolina's government turned to private companies and independent contractors to implement their developmental agenda. In this way, slaves provided an important bridge between local infrastructural maintenance and state-led internal improvement. And yet, slaves did more than simply support the early state. Black Carolinians ran away from confiscation agents, built social networks with their fellow state laborers, and used the state's infrastructure for their own purposes. These acts were equally vital to South Carolina's development. Black Carolinians' rebellious and mundane actions alike directly shaped statecraft and challenged the state's claims to authority. In these ways, slaves produced the state, secured and shaped its territory, and gave meaning to the very ideas of freedom and sovereignty in post-Revolutionary South Carolina.

Securing the State

South Carolina's political leaders turned to the enslaved during the Revolution at a scale never before matched in previous generations. The enslaved labored on roads, bridges, and a variety of defensive structures. They worked in shipyards, in iron foundries, and as pioneers on the front lines of local militias, state troops, and the Continental army. From the initial moments of the British invasion until the very last British soldier was gone, South Carolina's government charged enslaved Africans and African Americans with the maintenance and security of the nascent state's fragile territorial integrity.[3]

The success of South Carolina's rebellion hinged on the Revolutionary government's ability to call upon and employ enslaved labor. For instance, in early January 1776 after the state successfully routed a growing body of runaway slaves occupying Sullivan's Island, the Council of Safety ordered the immediate construction of batteries and forts to guard the entrance to the harbor. The grounds had previously been a quarantine, a place where white doctors inspected recent African arrivals for disease before approving their bodies for sale in the Charleston slave markets. South Carolinians swiftly transformed the island, constructing the iconic palmetto-reinforced Fort Sullivan. Charleston contractor Daniel Cannon was given the lucrative contract to complete the construction of the fort, the price of which was a charge to "provide all the materials, workmen and labourers, that shall be necessary for erecting and completing the works." It was not a simple task: slaveholders were reluctant to supply the state with the requested slaves, whom they wanted for labor at home. Moreover, many slaves had taken advantage of the British presence, seeking their freedom behind enemy lines. The council promised that the "public will make good any loss that may be sustained in boats, or by negroes killed, maimed, or lost in this service, by means of the enemy." Such promises, alongside the looming threat of British invasion, convinced at least some slaveholders to offer their slaves for state labor. Subsequent reports on the status of South Carolina's defensive works verified their labor, if also highlighting the shortcomings of the state's reliance on coercion. As Major Bernard Elliott noted, "I saw a number of Negroes, perhaps 40: some tying the Palmetto Logs to a stake drove in the sand, others doing nothing, & but 4 Carpenters actually at work." Still, not everyone felt so dimly about the state's laborers. Struggling to complete the works in the face of a possible British attack, Continental General Charles Lee wrote to William Moultrie that notwithstanding his concerns regarding necessary materials, "I think the Negroes you have with you may be usefully employ'd—they may fill up the Merlons which are not yet full—they may palisade (for I believe you have palisades sufficient) the low, and most accessible parts of the Embrasures & angles."[4]

While Cannon, Moultrie, and the other men charged with building the harbor's defenses sought out men and materials, they competed with similar demands being made in the interior of the state. On December 11, 1775, the *South Carolina Gazette* ran two separate advertisements for laborers. The first requested "Any number of Able-bodied Negro Men, for the Public Works, on Charles-Town-Neck, near the Quarter House." The second, reflecting the fear that Charleston would soon be invaded by the British, demanded "Three to Five Hundred Stout Negro Men, to work on the Fortifications at Dorchester." Such advertisements, though effective, rarely drew the number of necessary laborers to public works; even the promise of payment and indemnity could not sway owners to part with their most valued property. Legislators subsequently passed an ordinance "to Direct the Manner of Procuring Negroes to be Employed in Public Service." Revealing the importance of slaves to South Carolina's security, the preamble to the ordinance stated that "a number of able male slaves are frequently wanted on very pressing occasions for the public service, which will not admit of delay." The General Assembly argued that "it would be very detrimental to the State if speedy and effectual means are not provided to supply the public, from time to time, with such a number of male slaves as the exigency of affairs may require to be employed on the public works, for the defence [sic] and security of this State." Even as political leaders were imagining their newly independent state into being, they were binding together its future with the enforced labor of black Carolinians.[5]

Following the example set forth by colonial commissioners of roads and fortifications, the ordinance established the practical means by which the state would procure this labor. First, the "President and Commander in Chief, by and with the advice of the Privy Council" was given the power to "issue orders to the several committees of the parishes and districts throughout this State" to demand "such number of able male slaves, fit for labor" that he "thought adequate to the exigency of the case, and the circumstances and abilities of the district." To facilitate the governor's request, the local committees were "required, immediately on receiving such orders," to "rate and fix the proportion that each owner of slaves within their respective parishes and districts shall be obliged to furnish towards completing the number of slaves demanded." As in colonial precedents, the administration of slave state labor hinged on the "information or knowledge they [commissioners] can obtain." In addition, the government promised that every owner who agrees to "send his slaves to work on the public account" would "receive for each negro, per day, the sum of ten shillings."[6]

While the promise of payment privileged the property claims of individual slave owners, the threat of invasion witnessed the further extension of state power and highlighted the fragile contingency of individual property rights. The legislature ordered the slaves of intransigent and unwilling property owners "to be immediately impressed, seized and conveyed to Charlestown, or other place of destination, there to be employed and kept in public service, for and during the space of three months." Because of their owners' lack of cooperation, those slaves would labor "without any pay, wages or allowance whatever to the owner or owners thereof." In other words, if the state demanded labor and slave owners did not immediately comply, then the government would simply take that labor and, at least temporarily, suspend individual property rights over the needs of the public good. What had been the duty and sacrifice of citizens as outlined by Henry Laurens in the late colonial era became a prerequisite for residence in Revolutionary South Carolina. An even more punitive stance was leveled against potential loyalists. Local public works procurement committees were granted the power "to cause a double proportion of slaves to be sent to work for the public benefit" from those individuals who "have not subscribed the general association of the inhabitants of this State, and taken the oath of fidelity to the present government of the same." If individuals refused to offer their allegiance to the newly created state—a difficult choice for many to make—then their property rights became forfeit. Even then, if they pledged their loyalty to South Carolina but did not comply with the demands made by the General Assembly, governor, and military, then their rights were abrogated. Importantly, this annulment of individual property claims did nothing for black Carolinians. Their condition as slaves remained intact in their transformation into public property.[7]

It is difficult to ascertain the degree to which local committees wielded the cudgel of this legislative ordinance. On the ground, their efforts likely resembled those of colonial commissioners of roads, who were already in possession of the requisite information regarding individual slave ownership that the law required. Over time, their work probably also became more difficult, as the number of runaways grew and the number of white Carolinians unwilling or unable to hire their slaves' labor increased. The evidence that exists would suggest that while the act initially provided the state with many laborers, by 1780—when the war seemed to be turning in favor of the British—procurement no longer met the state's needs. "It has been found impracticable to procure the number of Negroes which are wanted for completing the proper works for the defense of this town and harbor by virtue of the Act made for that purpose," noted John Rutledge in a message to the assembly at the start of 1780. The problem was not simply that the number of slaves fell short of what the state needed but also that the Act failed "to keep those who have been obtained by that law so long here as to perform much real service." By 1780, the exigencies of war, particularly the internal strife of what many considered a civil war in South Carolina, made it increasingly difficult for the state to acquire slaves for labor. This was particularly problematic given South Carolina's defensive needs following the British capture of Savannah. In the face of an invasion, South Carolina's government sought hastily to augment the state's defenses, a project it readily admitted would require considerably more slaves.[8]

Continental general Benjamin Lincoln, who led the failed defense of Charleston in 1780, argued to South Carolina's government, "No consideration can authorize one moment's delay in putting this State, especially this town, in the most ample posture of defense." Lincoln asked the governor "to order fifteen hundred Negroes to assemble in the vicinity of this town with the necessary tools for throwing up lines immediately." Rutledge presented Lincoln's request to the General Assembly. Charles Cotesworth Pinckney, chair of the legislative committee charged with considering Lincoln's request, reported, "It is also the opinion of this committee that Charles Town should be immediately put in the best posture of defense, and for that purpose, that 2,000 Negroes between the ages of 18 and 40 years be immediately ordered to town to throw up lines and necessary works of defense." It is unclear if Lincoln's request was ever completely fulfilled. Louis Antoine Jean Baptiste, Chevalier de Cambray, the Italian-born engineer who oversaw the construction of Charleston's fortifications beginning in 1779, reported in early 1780 that he was in possession of only 600 laborers. Even then, engineer Ferdinand de Brahm would report in his journal that as late as March 30, "the fortifications of Charlestown were, even at this time, very incomplete. All the negroes in town were impressed, who, together with the parties detailed from the garrison, were henceforth employed upon the works."[9]

Beyond the emergency defense of Charleston, between 1775 and 1783 the state consistently tasked black Carolinians with the maintenance of a variety of public works. On October 17, 1776, the commissioners of the Navy ordered Alexander Horn to "hire a sufficient number of Negroes to cleanse the entrance" to the state's shipyard, "in order to make it convenient to receive the boats belonging to the public." This was a more difficult task than they imagined. Less than a year later, the commissioners wrote Governor Rutledge arguing that with such high demand for slave labor across the state, "the public are at a considerable expence [sic] in hiring Negro Labourers." They thought time and money might be saved, and "the work more certainly & regularly conducted, if your excellency would be pleased to order twenty of the laboring negroes, employ'd in the public service to assist in the works of the naval department." In 1778, the commissioners of the Navy ordered Captain Hezekiah Anthony "with all possible dispatch" to prepare the "Brig Polly—of which you are Capt." for "a cruise." To facilitate the ship's preparation, the commissioners ordered Anthony to acquire slaves "to fill your water and cut your wood &c." Such seemingly mundane tasks are rarely the focus of Revolutionary annals. Yet without this labor, South Carolina's navy would have been severely hamstrung given their lack of white manpower and other material resources.[10]

The state's upstart iron makers, a group especially vital to the Revolutionary War effort, also depended on black Carolinians. In 1779, South Carolina's legislature provided Colonel William Hill with a capital loan to create an iron foundry near present-day York, South Carolina. Hill quickly partnered with Issac Hayne to run the mill, and advertised that the foundry, named the Æra Furnace, "being the first and only one ever erected in the State of South Carolina, is now in blast, and if no unforeseen accident happens will so continue." Given that the war shut South Carolinians off from both regional and Atlantic trade, the Æra Furnace offered vital metal goods for commercial sale: "Bar and Ploughshare Iron, Smiths and Forge Anvils and Hammers, Salt Pans, Pots of all sizes, Kettles both for kitchen and camp, Skillets, Dutch Ovens, Sad Irons, Spice Mortars, Waggon, Cart and Truck Boxes, [and] Stoves." Beyond these everyday consumer products, Hill and Hayne also promised to provide important munitions to the South Carolina military, such as "Swivel Guns and Cahorns, of any size, 2, 3, or 4 pounders, with balls to suit, with any sized Cannon Ball or any other casting in iron."[11]

Black Carolinians provided the bulk of the iron works' labor force. The initial agreement between the partners stipulated that Hayne would provide forty slaves for the foundry. This force, it seems, was insufficient to the foundry's needs, and in the same notice advertising the opening of the furnace and its commercial wares, the partners let it be known that "one hundred working NEGROES are wanted to hire, for whom good wages will be given." Given the furnace's labor demands, the partners requested that "the more men and fewer children in the gang the better." Obviously, competition for hired slave labor was intense in the midst of war, so Hill and Hayne suggested to slave owners that "no situation in the State is more healthty [sic] and secure from an enemy." Or so, at least, they claimed. As it happened, the British attacked the furnace shortly after their successful capture of Charleston, burning "the forge furnace, grist and saw mills together with all other buildings even to the negro huts." They also "bore away about 90 negroes." Such figures illuminate black Carolinians' early industrial labor, but more importantly highlight the range of jobs South Carolinians entrusted to the enslaved. The Æra Furnace's dependence on slave labor also reveals an early instance of shared private and public enterprise. Hill and Hayne, like the proprietors and partners who would take charge of postwar public works, ran a private enterprise but depended on government aid to provide material for the public good. As this example makes clear, beyond borrowing capital from the state, the owners of public-facing private enterprises borrowed the state's reliance on enslaved labor as well.[12]

Perhaps more importantly than their wartime labor, slaves also sustained the early state's security and survival during the war as the promised payment to military volunteers. Though their policy was only secured by legislation after the fact, South Carolina's military began confiscating loyalist property in the final stages of the war. Out of these confiscations, Thomas Sumter and other state officers provided volunteers with compensation for their service in the form of slaves. While some of the enslaved were captured aiding the British, many were simply taken from the plantations of presumed loyalists. For example, William Ancrum would complain following the war that "thirty one of his Negroes were taken from [his] Congeree & Wateree plantations... by General Sumpter, and disposed of in payment of the troops under his command." Similarly, Anne Lord, who inherited her accused loyalist husband's property, claimed, "74 Negroes was taken away by Order of General Sumpter [sic] and distributed among the State Troops" after "the reduction of the Fort at Congaree." In addition, she argued, the troops seized "22 head of horses, 100 head of cattle and upwards of 100 head of sheep besides other considerable property." As Lord made clear, all of the losses were the responsibility of the "State Troops commanded by General Sumpter [sic]." State leaders would ultimately reprimand Sumter—clearly, not all of his marks were loyalists—but the results of the scheme were a resounding success, strengthening the state's army at a turning point in the war.[13]

What South Carolina's military leadership had undertaken without official approval, the 1782 Jacksonboro legislature sanctioned into law. Individuals who volunteered for military service in 1782 for the duration of the war were, on a sliding scale based on their rank, to be awarded enslaved men, women, and children. This policy was vital to South Carolina's security and maintenance at the end of the war. Confiscation not only sustained the military but also consecrated the massive readjustment of property ownership that occurred in the shadows of the war. Various individuals, especially well-placed officers, accumulated considerable numbers of slaves at a time of terrible economic disruption. As importantly, this payment procedure married the individual right to slave ownership—and the power that such ownership assumed—to the cause of the Revolution. Just as the earlier 1776 procurement act invalidated the property rights of possible loyalists, the 1782 recruitment act promised patriot soldiers slaves that they could call their own. The bounty policy made clear that in South Carolina at least, the Revolutionary War was being fought in part for the right to own slaves.[14]

Officials' payment of military recruits worked, for very few men in South Carolina or elsewhere were willing to fight without the guarantee of payment. Given the massive debt that South Carolina found itself in at the end of the war and the terrible depreciation of their currency and total lack of specie, state leaders had little choice but to provide payment in one of the only stable commodities available to them. "We were obliged to turn our thoughts to recruiting with Negroes," noted Edward Rutledge in a letter to Arthur Middleton, because "we have not the ability to raise a tax." In one of its first actions as a gathered body, then, the House of Representatives directed Colonel Wade Hampton "to recruit a sufficient number of men" for three years' service, or the remainder of the war, and to that end insisted that "he be furnished with one hundred negroes." The ability of South Carolina's nascent government to simply take slaves, though often disputed by the policy's targets, not only reveals the importance of black Carolinians to the successful prosecution of the war but it also illuminates the substantial augmentation of state power, and how such growth, like earlier and later development, often hinged on enslaved men and women.[15]

Dreaming of Development

The slaves promised to the state's soldiers by the General Assembly were to be distributed from the property forfeited by South Carolina loyalists following the passage of the 1782 Confiscation Act. While there is much to be said about confiscation and its important role in shaping the early state, of particular interest here are the varied ways that simply the rumor of the state's acquisition of enslaved men and women shaped South Carolina's earliest postwar developmental policies. The combination of prewar and wartime slave state labor established the important precedent of slaves working for the production and maintenance of the state. Once reports began circulating that the state would be acquiring a substantial number of slaves through confiscation, the imaginations of improvement-minded South Carolinians across the state were unleashed. For example, the executors of Isaac Hayne's estate argued in a 1782 petition to South Carolina's General Assembly that the loss of the Æra iron works was "an object of Public and National Concern." The petitioners argued that local farmers "derived their whole supply of Instruments of Husbandry" from the works. While this may have been somewhat of an overstatement, South Carolina's citizenry did require agricultural implements to sustain their newly won independence. Moreover, the petitioners noted, "The great importance of this useful Metal to the purposes of war, is equally conspicuous, and it is well known that without the Iron works ... the brave Garrison of Charles Town could not have made that Gallant defence [sic], which will transmit their names with so much éclat to posterity." Given the foundry's importance, Hayne's executors requested slaves from the state to reconstruct the iron works. They noted that if rebuilt, the works could provide supplies directly to the state since "the Southern army is, at this instant in extreme want." The petitioners felt "particularly emboldened and encouraged to solicit the assistance of this Honorable House upon this occasion," as they had heard rumors that "a Bill will soon pass for the confiscation of a number of Estates in this Country." Given, they argued, that a number of slaves would remain "in the possession and at the command of the Public" until their distribution as payment to state troops, the "petitioners humbly conceive that the Negroes cannot be fixed in a more safe and healthy situation or be employed more beneficially to the Public than in rebuilding the above mentioned Iron Works." For South Carolinians, the faintest whispers of state-owned slaves led to dreams of rebuilding their lives and reconstructing the state.[16]

The House of Representatives voted down the proposed aid for the iron works, not because political leaders averred the idea of the enslaved laboring on public works—Hayne's partner, Colonel William Hill, would eventually rebuild the foundry with fifty of the state's confiscated slaves, alongside eleven slaves he had personally taken from loyalists during the war—but rather because there simply were not enough slaves to accommodate all of the assembly's proposed projects. The state's ambitions, as they were, far outstripped the enslaved men and women at their disposal. The postwar slave population had decreased substantially over the course of the hostilities. This was at least in part the consequence of the British evacuation of loyalist property at the Revolution's end, wartime deaths, and the rebellious actions of black Carolinians who took the opportunities war provided to reject their enslavement. But it was not simply the significant diminution of slaves that limited their distribution. It was also the consequence of South Carolina's overwhelming reliance on the enslaved during and in the immediate aftermath of the war: there simply weren't enough slaves for all of the state's needs. Beyond their role in the recruitment of state soldiers, the enslaved were also meant to augment the strength of the military, as upon confiscation 440 black Carolinians were immediately sent to aid General Nathanael Greene's forces, which were scattered across the Carolinas. Confiscated slaves, or rather their sale, were also meant to supplement the state government's meager income. For example, in 1783, Governor John Mathews was empowered to "order two hundred Negroes belonging to the confiscated estates to be sold directly to raise a sum of money as a contingent fund." The wide distribution of slaves was further complicated by the slow process of acquiring enslaved men and women. State leaders and private citizens could imagine numerous ways to use slaves, but they needed to first be acquired and processed by state administrators.[17]

Still, what's important here is not that the measures failed or succeeded but rather that when state leaders initially imagined the production of their new state, they did so through the acquisition, sale, and labor of the enslaved. This is nowhere clearer than when South Carolina's legislature turned its attention to the physical reconstruction of South Carolina's territory. South Carolinians had long sought to develop new, more commodious means of transportation, focusing primarily on clearing the state's rivers and creeks and constructing new canals to connect the distant and disparate parts of the state to Charleston. Crisscrossed with numerous rivers and creeks, many of which flowed from deep within the state's interior all the way to the coast, South Carolinians had long dreamed of ways to improve their navigability and accessibility. The Revolution interrupted many of these developmental plans, but they were quickly revitalized once the tide of war turned. At the 1782 meeting of the General Assembly, a committee for the improvement of inland navigation was established and tasked to craft a plan for South Carolina's infrastructural improvement.[18]

The leader of the five-person committee was wartime governor John Rutledge, a man who had grown quite comfortable seizing planters' slaves and distributing them throughout the state for the completion of public works. Joining Rutledge was William Hill, the operator of Æra Foundry. For both Rutledge and Hill, the previous seven years had been a nearly constant affirmation of the centrality of slaves to South Carolina's improvement and security. The committee was filled out by Joseph Kershaw, a prominent resident of the backcountry; Thomas Ferguson, who had previously run Parker's Ferry near Goose Creek; and George Robinson, an esteemed resident from the southern part of the state who had acted as both a tax collector and commissioner of the roads for the district near the Edisto River, the latter role giving him a unique understanding of the importance of slaves to infrastructural development. These men had all invested in the idea of slaves laboring for the state, whether it was on colonial roads, in an iron foundry, aiding state soldiers, or constructing military fortifications. The promise of publicly owned slaves acquired through confiscation only whetted their appetite for a significant increase in this type of slave-led development.[19]

The committee reported back to the assembly that the land between the Santee and Cooper Rivers—long a site that South Carolinians had sought to develop—should be immediately surveyed for a canal. The region south of the Santee River, which flowed deep into the central part of the state, was covered by dense swamps interlaced with some of the oldest and largest inland rice plantations in South Carolina. Once the survey was complete, they argued, the work of canal construction would be accomplished with the labor of "two thirds of the slaves which shall be taken for public use." If such a plan was found to be impractical, they thought the slaves should "be directed [instead] in clearing Catawba River, so as to render it navigable from the North Carolina line to Camden." The remainder of the slaves assigned to public service would "be employed in clearing Edisto River and the Forks of it." In other words, South Carolinians sought to task state-appropriated slaves with the difficult job of opening up social and economic commerce with the backcountry. The job at hand was of the utmost importance, as the infrastructural development that the committee suggested was no less than the means by which South Carolina's state space would be made materially manifest. The improvements to inland navigation promised to bind South Carolinians together, effectively uniting seemingly disparate regions. Moreover, this infrastructure promised to unleash the liberal promise of the new state, as canals and river improvements were meant to remove physical obstacles to mobility. Slave labor, in short, would unleash the unfettered movement of commercial traffic and unite South Carolina's newly reborn citizenry.[20]

The committee's proposal received support from both the House and the Senate, but little work was actually accomplished. Notwithstanding the committee's inability to actually see its ideas put into action, the plans and legislative debates themselves reveal a great deal about the important ways slaves influenced early statecraft following the war, including the unique manner in which developmental plans became tethered to enslaved labor. Slaves enabled improvement; it seems, in fact, that for early South Carolinians state development was imagined primarily through the labor of slaves.

Just as important as the physical labor that actually went into internal improvements, the committee meetings, petitions, and legislative debates were part of the broader everyday social practices that resulted in the production of the state. In the committee report on the improvement of inland navigation, for example, the marriage between coerced labor and free economic movement—a cornerstone of the liberal state—was cemented and woven into the very fabric of South Carolina's early existence. Moreover, the debates on how best to use the government's newly acquired slaves moved past the commonplace assumption that South Carolinians were simply committed to the institution of slavery, as if bound and fixed by the historical inertia of their slaveholding past and the overwhelming reality of an enslaved majority; and instead revealed the specific ways that slaves were tied to emergent ideas of citizenship and the public good, and thus were deemed essential to the development of the newly created state.

Still, one must not overlook the important ways that slaves were more than simply the imagined heart of the state's development or solely the subject of legislative debate. Regardless of the outcome of the government's grandiose plans for reconstruction and development, the government eventually confiscated hundreds of loyalist-owned slaves. The sale and distribution of those men, women, and children proved vital to the state's survival in the months and years following the war's end. In order for South Carolina to sustain itself financially and fulfill the promises they had made to their troops, state leaders necessarily had to establish a practical procedure through which the procurement and redistribution of slaves could be accomplished. To that end, the General Assembly, shortly after the passage of the Confiscation Act, appointed a five-person Committee of Forfeited Estates. Even as the General Assembly debated the merits of South Carolinians who petitioned to be removed from the lists of accused loyalists, the committee's work began in earnest. The committee sent troops in small groups, armed with the names of their neighbors, across the state to seize loyalist property. For example, on May 30, 1782, Robert Miscampbell, a lieutenant in the state army, arrived "with a wagon and a small guard" at John and Theodore Gaillard's St. Stephen's Parish plantation, "for the negroes." At plantations across the state, such arrivals occurred again and again in the days and weeks following the war's cessation. Such moments, however mundane they may seem, were actually hugely significant, both to the nascent state and to the individual men, women, and children who experienced this process firsthand.[21]

In the earliest stages of confiscation, black Carolinians were immediately distributed to the state's recruiting service, deployed to aid General Greene's army in securing the peace, and sold to provide much-needed funds for the everyday maintenance of the state. To facilitate such exchanges, administrative bodies and hierarchies were created, and relationships established between South Carolina's government and private merchants. For instance, near Georgetown, the state relied upon local merchants Robert Heriot and Daniel Tucker to facilitate the state's sale of confiscated slaves. To expedite the acquisition of those men and women, Governor John Matthews wrote to Colonel Peter Horry, "I have directed Heriot and Tucker to apply to you for a party of men to take charge of some negroes to be brought from Mr. Smith's plantation on Santee." The governor ordered Horry to provide the merchants with the soldiers required for this task, and to have the forfeited "negroes secured in Georgetown until the day of sale." Beyond considering the practices of the state army and the private merchants, both of which were significant in the development of early governing practices, one must also keep in mind the experience of the enslaved. Heriot, Tucker, and Horry's men traveled south from Georgetown to the "Smith plantation" on the Santee River. There they confiscated an unspecified number of enslaved black Carolinians and marched them back to Georgetown, where they were held until sold by Heriot and Tucker. The experience of the men, women, and children sold in Georgetown's slave mart are lost, but the trauma of the domestic slave trade is well documented, and must have been similar in this moment. Except in this instance it was South Carolina's government that seized and sold Smith's slaves. Moreover, the proceeds of their sale did not benefit individuals (in this case Heriot, Tucker, or Smith), but rather provided much-needed funds that sustained the struggling state government.[22]

Such transactions occurred numerous times in the months and years following the war's end. Lieutenant John Martin found himself in charge of receiving and distributing just some of the hundreds of slaves seized by state troops. In official ledgers, Martin reported the number of black Carolinians the state acquired, their names, to whom the slaves previously belonged, and the names of their new owners. The physical movement of enslaved people, their sale, and Martin's ledger work operated as types of knowledge production that stood at the very center of early state activities. These material social practices—the organization of government workers, the movement of enslaved people, and the sometimes meticulous record-keeping that took note of each of these actions—repeated again and again, bore the state into being. June 23, 1782, provides an illustrative example. That day Martin noted that he received from the commissioners of forfeited estates "the following negroes delivered by order of his excellency, the Governor: 20 [slaves], late the property of Mr. Charles Ogilvie; 29 late the property of Mr. John Rose." The list goes on. On June 6 of the same year, Martin reported receipt of "Pompey, Rachel, Will, Hector, Miriah, Hester, Jemey, Catey, Salley, Diannah, March, Betsey, Tilly, Nancy, Rinah, Ishmal, Sam, Elcey, [and] Malboro." Some of these men and women went to the army; others were sold to balance the state's accounts or pay the state's soldiers. Regardless of enslaved people's fate, their movement, alongside the flow of information to and from the committee of forfeited estates, sat at the center of South Carolina's earliest governing practices.[23]

The human element of these moments, however, must not be overlooked. To acquire confiscated slaves, South Carolina's government established a bureaucracy, shaped governing hierarchies, and established administrative techniques, but at the heart of all of their efforts were individual men, women, and children. Black Carolinians, presumably with little to no warning, were seized from their homes and delivered to the state's commissioners, to recruiting agents, or in some cases to the frontlines of the continuing conflict. For example, Robert Dillon—a colonel in the duc de Lauzun's French army—reported receipt of "two negro men named George & Robin, in part of the negroes appropriated to the use of Gen'l Greene's Army." These were not men whom Dillon personally confiscated or who willingly joined his army in the fight for liberty. They were men who were hand-delivered to the French forces stationed near Charlotte Courthouse by agents of the state. In addition to George and Robin, Dillon also received from the commissioners "two wenches and six children," perhaps the wives and offspring of George and Robin, as the General Assembly had ordered that all confiscated slaves be sold as families.[24]

George and Robin, alongside the children and women who accompanied them to the army's front lines, took up the work that so many of their enslaved peers had undertaken from the war's outset. Their efforts are remembered not because their feats were recorded in the annals of Revolutionary heroism, but rather because their movement and labors were an integral aspect of South Carolina's early statecraft, and as such were regularly noted in comptroller reports and committee journals. Chronicling their move to the front lines—creating the paper trail, so to speak—was as important to the initial substantiation of South Carolina's transition from province to state as were the men and women's labors for Dillon's regiment. In the administrative completion of property transfers recording the movement and labors of individual black Carolinians, slaves became the objects of informational and material transactions between individual white Carolinians and their government. This process, of course, had begun well before the Revolution, as parish residents regularly sent information regarding their enslaved property to road and tax commissioners. Such transactions not only created a relationship between individuals and their government but also solidified slaves' role as state laborers. The idea that slaves were the strength of the state was only augmented during the war itself, when South Carolinians—Whig and loyalist alike—called upon the labor of enslaved men (and some women) to sustain their armies and to construct the very infrastructure of war. As a result, by war's end, South Carolina's government and citizenry alike often intuitively imagined improvement synonymously with the labor of enslaved black Carolinians.

Producing South Carolina's Territory

This equation between state development and slave labor was fortified through everyday practice. For example, in early 1782, with peace not yet secured, South Carolinians and the Continental army feared an impending British attack on Georgetown. Governor John Matthews, upon hearing General Nathanael Greene's concerns about the city's defenses, sent state engineer Christian Senf to General Francis Marion, "to confer on the necessity and practicability of Fortifying the harbor of George Town." Marion suggested plans for a fort to Senf, and then ordered Colonel Peter Horry to "collect negroes for the above purpose." To that end, Marion provided Horry with strict instructions, which are worth noting at length, for they illuminate both the types of everyday actions that normalized the relationship between slavery and the state and the way that the acquisition of slave labor directly shaped statecraft.

> Whatever negroes may be wanted for public service, you will first make requisition of the inhabitants in proportion so that no unequal burden may come on any person; the negroes will be paid whatever has been usual. A certificate must be given for their term of service; if the number of negroes required is not furnished, we must be obliged (however disagreeable) to send parties to take them. The number of males each man has may be nearly ascertained, if it cannot, you must rate them by guess, and let the owners make it appear they have not the number; every district around George Town must furnish their quota, and if not sufficient to extend it to the North of Santee up to Lenud's Ferry.

Marion's orders were similar to those the state developed in 1776, which closely resembled the practices of colonial road and fortification commissioners. South Carolinians were to provide their slaves to the state when ordered, and if they refused, procurement officers, in this case Horry's military command, were allowed to take the said slaves from their owners. Just as in the colonial period, the state's process of slave procurement made the relationship between individual subjects and the state materially manifest.[25]

While the system of labor procurement may have seemed familiar, the scale and variety of work being undertaken during the war's final moments and into the postwar era were substantially different. Wartime neglect and strategic destruction ruined a substantial amount of South Carolina's existing infrastructure. Moreover, local road commissioners were in disarray following the war, such institutions did not yet exist in the farthest western portions of the state, and what had seemed like a citizen's duty in the prewar decades by the turn of the century was increasingly perceived by many as an onerous and unfair imposition. Repairs, reorganization, and reconstruction alone could have preoccupied the state's resources for years, but state leaders and improvement-minded individuals had more grandiose aspirations, some of which—like the improvement of inland navigation—were nurtured by their slave-fueled, postwar developmental dreams. John Rutledge, who had chaired the 1782 House Committee on Inland Navigation, was one of the central promoters of postwar inland navigation schemes. Unstymied by that committee's failure to secure supporting votes in the General Assembly, Rutledge along with forty of the most powerful and wealthy white Carolinians successfully petitioned the General Assembly four years later for a charter to construct and operate a canal between the Santee and Cooper Rivers.[26]

Among all of the postwar infrastructural projects, none reflected the larger ambitions of state planners more than the Santee-Cooper Canal. The canal, at least as it was envisioned by company stockholders, Charleston merchants, government leaders, and aspiring planters, promised the inland connection between the backcountry and Charleston that white planters had long sought. Surveyor and cartographer James Cook made the initial suggestion for the canal to the General Assembly in 1770. At the time, he argued that a canal would significantly increase communication between the coast and the provincial interior, predicting that the state's waterways would subsequently be "crowded with rafts and boats, loaded with articles of various kinds, producing necessaries for home consumption, and merchandizes for exportation, at an easy freight." A new canal would also decrease the high cost of transportation and travel to Charlestown, the seat of economic and political life in colonial South Carolina. That was no small thing: one of the backcountry residents' chief complaints during the Regulation movement that began in the 1760s was the high price and difficulty of travel. As Cook noted, "at present the settlers and proprietors on that river [the Santee] are deterred from improving, on account of their remote situation, and the length of a tedious land carriage." The twenty-two-mile, man-made inland waterway, South Carolinians believed, could tie together the interior and coastal regions through the free movement of goods, improved communications, and an ease of social access.[27]

That South Carolina's initial plans for the canal were suggested by Cook and further developed in the pre-Revolutionary era by his fellow surveyor and cartographer Henry Mouzon is revealing. Both Cook and Mouzon offered provincial leaders, and perhaps more importantly individual consumers (through the sale of pocket maps), a perspective of South Carolina that allowed them to imagine disparate parts of the state in ways they never had before. In fact, both Cook's and Mouzon's maps created an image and idea of South Carolina as a territorial whole, an idea Cook was uniquely positioned to assert, not simply as the creator of a map of the province but as a member of the South Carolina–North Carolina boundary commission. When suggesting the canal to the public, Cook maintained that as a surveyor and provincial cartographer, he had gained a unique perspective of South Carolina. In an open letter to the residents of Charlestown, lobbying for the benefit of the canal, Cook requested that his fellow Carolinians allow him "to convey to the public, my sentiments of an improvement, which the nature of my employment has made me perfectly acquainted with; a new opening to commerce, of the greatest utility to this province." As Cook made clear, the canal would be a boon not just to Charlestown merchants but "to the community in general." Mouzon similarly argued for a more holistic perspective of the state in an advertisement for his pocket map of South Carolina, which was meant to distinguish it from Cook's recently published maps, "as in every Map or Plan it is necessary for the Eye to command the Whole at one View, in order to form a just Idea of the Relation and Connection between the several Parts." Mouzon sought to make the geographic perspective he and Cook acquired through detailed surveys of the state accessible to everyone who purchased his map.[28]

The idea that maps provided viewers with a unique viewpoint of territory—bounded, whole, and knowable—was not new, but Cook and fellow surveyor Henry Mouzon created the first maps of South Carolina by South Carolinians, and they did so precisely at the moment when white Carolinians were increasingly contemplating the geographical expansion of early state rule. Their maps conveyed to Lowcountry residents something that had otherwise been represented only through newspaper reports, travelers' narratives, and gossip, permitting them to imagine the colony and state as a singular space.

Maps and surveys alone could not produce South Carolina's territory; governing practices that promised to bind together the disparate parts of the state, infrastructural projects, and the everyday activities of South Carolinians—both white and black—were necessary as well. As Cook argued, the Santee-Cooper Canal could provide South Carolinians with the necessary infrastructure that communication between the interior and backcountry demanded. Of course, provincial South Carolina's grandiose developmental agenda was interrupted by war. But the war—fought along the coast, in the Piedmont, and all the way to the mountainous backcountry—only solidified what Cook and Mouzon argued through their maps: that the early state's survival and success

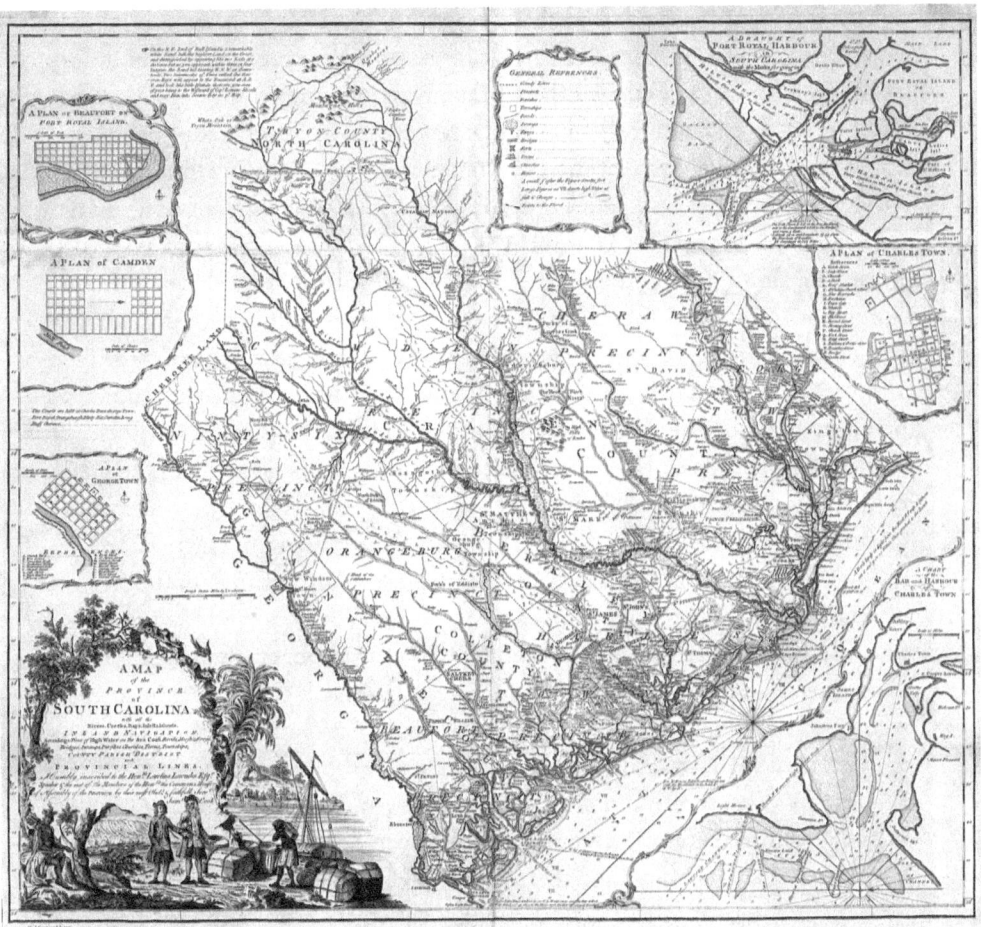

James Cook, *A Map of the Province of South Carolina*, 1773. David Rumsey Map Collection, www.davidrumsey.com.

required not only an infrastructure that bound Lowcountry plantations to Charlestown but one that tied together all of its disparate regions.

It was unsurprising, then, that when the Jacksonboro Assembly met at the end of the war its leadership turned to the promotion of inland navigation. The idea of infrastructural improvement never stopped fascinating the nascent state's leaders. As David Ramsey noted in a letter to Benjamin Rush, "This business [confiscation] got over our next business will be to improve our country cutting canals & building bridges." Moreover, he continued, "A plan for uniting Cooper & Santee rivers is the subject of much conversation. This would reduce the price of provisions in Charlestown one half."[29]

The war's end precluded immediate action, but in 1785 plans for inland navigation moved forward. That year, a group of powerful planters, merchants, and politicians created the Company for the Improvement of Inland Navigation. A year later they were granted a charter by South Carolina's General Assembly. Like many of the governments across the early United States, South Carolina turned to a private company, chartered by the state, to implement its plans for internal improvement. Much has been made about the private development of public works in the early nation, yet a close examination of entities such as the Santee Canal Company reveals a great deal about the relationship between the state and such private entities. Not only was the company composed of numerous members of South Carolina's government, including the wartime governor and longtime advocate of inland navigation, but as will be clear later, the Santee Canal Company was sustained and shaped by its relationship to the government, blurring any distinctions between public and private in the early state. The company hired an engineer who labored for both South Carolina and the Continental army during and after the Revolutionary War; was granted special access to African imported slaves in the midst of a multiyear ban on the trade; and most importantly directly borrowed the system of slave labor procurement and oversight that had evolved over several generations of development in South Carolina. Just as local commissioners of roads and fortifications relied upon the labor of slaves to complete their works, so too did private contractors and companies come to rely on enslaved men (and some women) to fulfill their contractual obligations to the state. In this way, slaves and their labor provided an important connection between private and public development in early national South Carolina.

After receiving its charter, the Santee Canal Company immediately began consultation with James Brindley, a nephew of the British engineer who designed the famed Bridgewater Canal in Britain, and charged Johann Christian Senf to supervise the canal's construction. It took several years of stock sales and planning for construction to begin, but work on the canal finally commenced in 1793. Senf offered an initial cost estimate of £55,620 (approximately $233,000) for three years of work. By the time the canal was completed, it had taken an additional four years of construction and the total costs were nearly three times Senf's original estimation.[30]

The bulk of the company's expenses was bound up with the cost of labor. The Santee Canal Company began advertising for laborers in 1792, specifically requesting "two hundred and fifty negro labourers, for one, two or three years, or until the work is compleat." The company noted that it would need "carpenters, bricklayers, and blacksmiths," and that it would hire enslaved women,

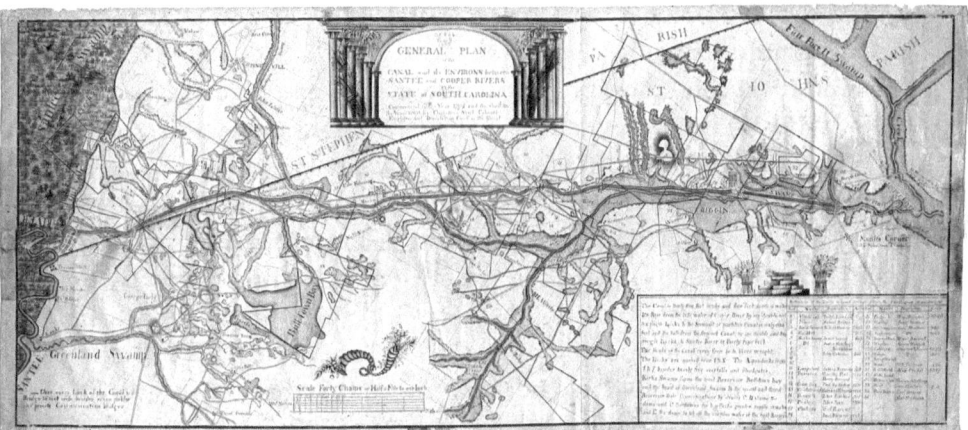

Johann Christian Senf, *General Plan of the Canal*, 1800. South Carolina Historical Society. General Plan of the Canal and Its Environs. From the South Carolina Historical Map/Plats Collection at the South Carolina Historical Society.

but in "a proportion not exceeding one third women to two thirds men." The company's openness to hiring women—which was not allowed for road construction—emerged in part, it seems, as an effort to keep down its labor costs. By the end of 1793, the first year of work on the canal, the number of workers employed by the company had exploded to nearly 1,000 slaves, straining the company's already tight budget. In the face of quickly spiraling labor costs, in 1794, the directors of the Santee Canal Company "resolved that the number of negroe labourers to be employed at the canal for 1795 must not exceed 700; and that the price to be allowed for their labour, for that year must not exceed 16 pounds per head." Planters, it seems, were eager to hire out their enslaved workforce in the early years of construction, as many had not yet recovered from the war or the loss of British bounties for their crops. The canal offered them an alternative to an idle labor force, and the company's liberal pay, £16 per year for each slave, was a boon to most slave owners who desperately needed liquid capital.[31]

Over the next seven years, the company's enslaved laborers built a canal twenty-two miles long, thirty-five feet wide, and five and a half feet deep, with draw-paths ten feet wide on either side of the canal. They built two double locks and eight single locks, catch basins for water reserves, eight aqueducts for the continual passage of streams beneath the bed of the canal, warehouses for the storage of goods, and housing for themselves, their overseers, and company management. In addition to this direct labor on the canal, slaves also cooked, butchered meat, cleaned, delivered supplies, assisted white tradesmen, and made bricks for the canal's locks.[32]

Beyond a sizable labor force, Senf also desired and requested stability among the workers "because such an undertaking much depends on regularity and system." According to Senf, "the work will not make that progress or be executed so well, until the Negroes and Overseers are acquainted with the Business; but should their Engagements be for short periods, the same disadvantage will always attend the executing of it." Such stability was difficult to secure. The constant removal of slaves by their owners at year's end regularly threatened to disrupt the project. Senf hoped that "several Planters" who were building complicated tidal rice irrigation systems might "not hire their Negroes for the Wages alone, but to have them instructed for such a time." Some did, like Henry Ravenel, who noted in his plantation diary, "My Negroes return'd home from the Santee Canal after working there three years." Peter Sinkler's slaves labored on the canal for six years. Nevertheless, as the state slowly recovered from the war, slaves' labor became ever more prized, and their prices soared. By the end of the eighteenth century the canal was paying £24 for the labor of men and £20 for the labor of women, an increase that reflected the growing market for slaves across the state, a consequence of both the expansion of cotton planting and the state's prohibition of the Atlantic slave trade.[33]

To avoid work disruptions in this context, the directors of the Santee Canal Company petitioned the General Assembly to relieve their slaves from additional public service, making clear that while the company was a private entity, their slaves' labors were for the public as a whole. The directors argued that "the slaves now working on the Santee Canal are engaged in a service extremely beneficial to their country," and thus should not "be called upon by the commissioners of the high roads in the parish where they are now employed to work on the roads." If they were, the company argued, it would "retard the accomplishment of that undertaking." In essence, there was competition between different state agencies—local road commissioners and a publicly chartered private company—for enslaved labor. Local road commissioners, however, simply could not ignore such a sizable work force, particularly when so many parish roads needed repair following the Revolution. For example, in 1795, 122 canal slaves were required to do road work in St. John's Parish. Only Daniel Ravenel had even close to that number of slaves, and only fifty-six of his slaves were responsible for road work. Similarly, in St. Stephen's parish, the number of company slaves ordered to work on the roads was 385, which more than doubled the total number of black Carolinians liable for parish road work. Throughout the 1790s, commissioners from both St. John's Parish and St. Stephen's Parish had no choice but to regularly demand that the company contribute its male slaves to annual road labor, effectively making the company's slaves responsible for the development of the most important elements of South Carolina's infrastructure. In doing so, the company, and more importantly its slaves, confounded the presumed distinctions between private and public development.[34]

And yet, as much as the state, local commissioners, and independent developers relied upon slaves, the labors of those slaves were often easily dismissed and forgotten. Which is not to say that South Carolinians did not notice the infrastructure of the state. Indeed, residents from both the state's interior and the coast heaped praise on the canal and Senf as it neared completion. In a letter to the *City Gazette*, one "gentleman now on a visit at Santee Canal" wrote that the "construction, the workmanship, both brick and wood, and the attention paid to secure it from any and every accident of water exterior or subterraneous, must result greatly to Col. Senf's honor and fame." Another correspondent noted the ease with which a boat "of many tons burthen" floated down the then-completed section of the canal. He argued that the alleviation of the high costs of transportation would create immense wealth for the "upper country." He added, "Nor will the advantages of the lower country be less; for they will be supplied in their turn, with every article with which the upper country abounds." In fact, he argued, the backcountry "will be so immediately connected with Charleston, by the means of this canal when finished . . . that the whole of those parts of the country, will from thenceforth, be considered as in the vicinity of this great seaport." Just as Cook envisioned, the canal seemed to promise a remarkable transformation of the state's territory. Missing from these assessments of the canal and Senf's leadership, of course, were the ceaseless, dangerous labors of the hundreds of black Carolinians who made the canal possible. To be sure, those planters who hired their slaves to the canal were well aware of their sacrifice. For example, Henry Laurens Jr., lost Samuel Massey, his recently deceased father's most valued and trusted slave, to the dangers of canal work. Laurens mourned Massey's death, while questioning its circumstances: "Whether it was merely an accident or whether it was in consequence of want of care I know not—Alas, poor fellow! What shall I do without you?"[35]

For many South Carolinians, the canal's completion signaled the fruition of their territorial ambitions and harkened the shift in orientation and meaning of the nascent state's infrastructure. Rather than the colonial emphasis on security, the Santee Canal seemed to unleash instead the liberal economic potential of all of its white, male residents, regardless of where they resided. One celebratory article told the brief story of "Mr. Warham Buford, an enterprising citizen, who lives on the banks of Broad River, near Pinckney Courthouse, which is more than ninety miles above Granby." Buford arrived in Charleston through the Santee Canal "with his own boat, built on his own land, and loaded with his own crop." Not only did Buford embody the ideal individual, independent citizen celebrated in the newly formed United States; but his trip, it was reported, was the first to occur from such a "distance from the sea-coast, and from its success, leads to the most pleasing anticipation of the immense advantages, which are likely soon to result from the easy intercourse that may now be carried on, between Charleston and the interior country by means of the Santee Canal." As the company directors themselves argued in a feat of self-adulation, "This great public work, unequaled by any thing of the kind in the United States . . . will, it is confidently believed, remove obstacles that, in times past have embarrassed the agriculture of our interior country." In other words, the canal promised all of Buford's equally industrious neighbors the same opportunity for individual economic advancement.[36]

Like earlier assessments of the canal's construction, these laudatory announcements emphasized company leadership rather than enslaved labor. As one writer noted, referring to the Canal Company directors and stockholders, "the gentlemen who persevered so successfully, and at such great expense, to complete the canal, will possess a property, which while it contributes to the welfare of the state, will yield them an income that will amply repay all that they have expended in an undertaking which is unequalled in the new world!" South Carolinians reported on the independence of Buford, the perseverance of the company stockholders, and the diligence of Senf, but completely overlooked the everyday labors of the enslaved, without which the canal would never have been completed. Still, company directors themselves could not so easily disregard the significance of slaves or their labor.[37]

This is nowhere more obvious than in a petition the president of the company, Adam Gilchrist, submitted to the General Assembly shortly after the completion of the canal. According to the petition, completion of the canal went well over budget, and the company went into significant debt in finishing the project. The company argued, "In order to insure, improve, and facilitate the benefits and advantages of the said inland navigation, it will be absolutely requisite to undertake and effect several other works." These projects included "the making of a ferry canal through Santee Swamp, and the opening [of] several new roads." These new works were in addition to the "continual strengthening and reparations of the said canal and its appendages." Beyond the high costs of materials, the company anticipated "increased difficulty of procuring workmen and other labourers," particularly since "the wages of workmen and other labourers being very much enhanced in price from a variety of concurrent causes within these few years." Moreover, the petition argued, "It is for the interest of every commercial and agricultural country like this state, to promote and encourage works of this kind." With all this in mind, the company requested that the legislature grant them "the licence [sic] of importing a competent number of negro slaves from Africa"—a privilege, the company noted, "the legislature was pleased to grant to the Company for opening the navigation of the Catawba and Wateree Rivers." As this petition reveals, no matter the company's pretentions to private initiative, it overwhelmingly relied on enslaved labor for its construction and maintenance, labor that could be procured, in the face of a prohibition on the African slave trade, through the direct intervention of the state.[38]

The General Assembly had in fact included this prerogative in the 1787 charter of the Catawba Company. This privilege was the consequence of the defining piece of legislation passed in the 1787 session of the General Assembly: the prohibition of the African slave trade, which would last until 1803. The ban on the slave trade itself reflects the extraordinary powers of the early state, just as its willingness to allow exemptions to the ban for public works companies reveals the innovative ways that the government retained control over developmental policy. The Catawba Company was given this dispensation at the precise moment that the trade was closed in South Carolina. By including the right to import African slaves in its charter, the General Assembly guaranteed the companies that they would have continual access to the requisite labor necessary for their projects. More importantly, such allowances reinforced the centrality of slave labor to infrastructural improvement.[39]

Still, it seems, such guarantees were not adequate to the company's needs. The Catawba Company continued to pursue its goals, pressed to do so in part by the General Government's decision to construct one of three national armories on the Catawba River at Rocky Mount. This project required that the Catawba Company construct a canal around the shoals near the proposed site of the armory, a project that was slowed by a number of factors. Not least of which, as the directors of the company argued in a petition to the General Assembly, was that "many of their members being also members of the Santee

Canal Company, the very great expences [sic] that have hitherto attended that work, have prevented them from contributing sufficient funds to give efficacy to their designs." Upon the Santee Canal's completion, the directors of the Catawba Company noted that they intended to "proceed without delay to the completion of their proposed object." To do so, however, they sought an amendment to their original charter, which allowed them "to import three hundred negroes to carry their works into effect." As they argued, "many among them [the imported slaves] may be unfit for immediate labor," and subsequently they sought an increase in the number of imported slaves so "that the company may be enabled to select that number of efficient labourers from the numbers imported."[40]

Ultimately, the Catawba Company was unsuccessful. Workers fell ill; Senf, who served as engineer for both projects, was removed from directing the canal construction; and the company failed to raise the necessary funds required to complete its project. What is of concern here is less the success or failure of these early projects than the implicit connection state leaders, independent contractors, private companies, and individual citizens made between South Carolina's development and enslaved labor. Such assumptions were quickly forgotten in the memorialization and celebration of developmental projects, but state planners, engineers, and company directors made clear that no project could move forward without the labor of the enslaved. The state government itself lacked the resources to directly provide enslaved laborers to most of these developmental projects, as it had initially planned during the height of confiscation. Instead, it counted on chartered corporations, independent contractors, and local road commissioners to both manage projects and procure the enslaved laborers necessary for their completion. Like road commissioners who called out laborers at appointed times throughout the year, independent contractors and private companies posted notices for hired slave labor at the start of their varied projects, and chartered corporations imported African slaves, even amid the prohibition of the trade. In almost every instance, be it public, private, or a combination of the two, black Carolinians remained the primary laborers for the state's developmental agenda.[41]

In 1788, for example, the state legislature appointed three commissioners to oversee the reopening of Wall's Cut between the New and Wright Rivers. Wall's Cut provided inhabitants from May River Neck and the islands of Hilton Head, Daufuskie, Bull's, and Savages important inland access to the city of Savannah and its markets. John Joyner, William Hort, and Daniel Stevens were named the commissioners, and they eventually hired a local contractor, Richard Proctor, to complete the work. From the outset of this project, the commissioners struggled to complete their charge. Stevens, in a letter to the General Assembly, explained that the government had provided only limited funds for the project, and to make matters worse, demanded that the cut follow its original route between the two rivers. This was problematic, the commissioners explained, because the marshy landscape surrounding the cut, as well as the tidal action of the two rivers, rendered permanent mud removal difficult if not impossible. Proctor, Steven's argued, was one of the only contractors willing to accept this challenge at the offered price.[42]

The contract secured, Proctor and his enslaved laborers immediately went to work on the cut, slowly removing mud by hand, wheelbarrow, and flat, a project they continued well into the 1790s. "Mr. Richard Proctor's Negroes" were hard "at work upon Walls Cut," Charles Pearl noted in testimony defending Proctor's work on the canal. Similarly, Robert Jones commented on Proctor's work after piloting a boat through the cut. He "found the navigation rendered easy through the cut there being a sufficient depth of water from the work already done by Mr. Proctor's Negroes who were then at work upon the same." The cut, for all of its troubles, allowed boatmen to access more easily the Savannah River, and it owed its existence to the ceaseless toil of Proctor's slaves.[43]

Richard Proctor's petition to the state reveals the important work black Carolinians did on a day-to-day basis to promote the free movement of goods and people along South Carolina's southern coast. So too, the petition of James Brown, a carpenter contracted to build South Carolina's state house, illuminates the vital part enslaved Carolinians played in the development of the state's newly created capital. In late 1789, with the state government's move to Columbia looming, the commissioners in charge of organizing and building the new city were disappointed to find that the most important of the new structures, the state house, was still not finished. Brown provided them with an explanation for the delay: the state had not yet supplied him with the necessary materials to finish construction. Despite an agreement that the supplies would be furnished and the work completed in two months' time, Brown complained that he had never received the necessary materials and so "was finally obliged to withdraw his hands & labourers." In the intervening years between that decision and his petition, Brown reported, "his creditors have seised [sic] his negroes & sold them under executions and put it out of his power to compleat [sic] the work." Brown's economic misfortune is fascinating. Still more fascinating is his revelation that it was slaves who provided the labor to build the state house. Without them, he simply could not do the work. Indeed, this was true for almost all of the state's developmental projects: the labor of slaves was vital to their construction. For Brown, the seizure of his enslaved workers completely compromised his ability to complete the contract.[44]

Just as Brown and Proctor acknowledged their dependence on their slaves to fulfill state contracts, local road commissioners also regularly signaled the continued significance of enslaved labor to government-led, postwar infrastructural work. At the beginning of the nineteenth century, South Carolina's economy grew significantly with the expansion of plantation production in the Piedmont and backcountry. As a result, the state's infrastructure was strained to the point of breaking, demanding continual maintenance and repair. A growing traffic of heavy wagons filled with tobacco, wheat, and most frequently cotton taxed the roads closest to Charleston in particular. The Santee Canal eased some of this traffic, but new planters and small farmers with limited river access more often used the state's roads to transport their crops to market. As one planter from the Upstate noted, however, "The difficulties, the hardship and fatigue that the planters and their beasts have to encounter with, in taking their crops to market along these roads . . . is truly a serious evil, and calls aloud for a speedy remedy."[45]

The same anonymous planter suggested that a turnpike system might remedy these issues. South Carolinians began demanding that turnpikes replace the local administration of road maintenance as early as the turn of the century. As one commentator noted in 1804, a turnpike system was necessary given "the almost impassable situation these roads have been in for some years past and which the labor required by law to be bestowed on them is by no means equal to keeping them in any tolerable repair." In response to that petition and others, in 1806 the General Assembly demanded that the commissioners of roads for each parish and district report on the quality of the existing system of road maintenance, the laborers at their disposal, the miles of roads under their jurisdiction, and whether or not the current system needed to be replaced.[46]

Reports from the commissioners of roads from Lowcountry counties and parishes not only revealed the unique nature of the difficulties confronting South Carolina's highway maintenance but also highlighted black Carolinians' singular importance to infrastructural upkeep. The commissioners from St. James Goose Creek most clearly illuminated the problem confronting Lowcountry commissioners, arguing, "We think the present mode of keeping the roads in order extremely oppressive to those districts which are nearest to the market." They then continued: "The most distant districts from the market [have] to prepare its roads only for itself. The next in the direction of the market prepares the road for itself and its neighbour [sic] behind it. The third has two neighbours [sic] to work for as well as itself. And that which is nearest to the market actually groans under the accumulated weight of all the wagons and travellers in the state who direct their journey to Charleston." Of course, enslaved Carolinians, not the district as a whole, bore most of this burden, forced to labor in the heat of the summer to maintain the state's most vital thoroughfares. Henry Middleton, representing the commissioners from the Lower District of St. George's Parish, echoed the complaint of their neighbors, noting that the "total number of miles worked upon by them in their district is sixty five, and that the number of hands liable to work on the same is two hundred and seventy six." Still, he complained, as a consequence of "a great portion of the produce of the upper and middle country passing over said road," including many overloaded wagons from North Carolina and Georgia, "the said roads are very much cut up during the winter season, particularly that part which is situated between Dorchester and Charleston." These last roads, it seems, were both the most important and the most difficult to maintain. "Owing to a great part of said roads passing through a low & swampy country," concluded Middleton, "it is utterly impossible to keep them in order."[47]

Maintenance of the roads that nearly every planter and farmer in the state used fell disproportionately on these Lowcountry districts. As Middleton argued, it was nearly impossible to maintain their highways "with the force of labourers which is now allotted to [us] notwithstanding that all the hands are always kept at work during the whole time allowed by law." Peter Galliard, writing for St. John's District, similarly noted that the district had "one thousand seven hundred & fifty persons," the vast majority of whom were slaves, "liable to work" on their roads. Even with such a large labor force at their disposal, Gaillard noted that of the roads in his district, "seventy miles are generally very bad & from the constant run of heavy waggons, can never be otherwise while the present mode of working is pursued." To be sure, not all Lowcountry districts experienced the same strain on their resources. In St. Luke's Parish, the commissioners reported that the present system of road maintenance was sufficient for the developmental demands of the state, noting that "the length of roads being ninety three miles & the number of male slaves liable to work said road being one thousand five hundred & fifty two." But the parish was far from Charleston, and commodious traffic in the southern portion of South Carolina was often diluted by the nearby presence of the Savannah River.[48]

The General Assembly heard the complaints of the coastal road commissioners and responded by chartering the Charleston Turnpike and Bridge Company, which was required to build a bridge over the Ashley River and a connecting turnpike to Rantowle's Bridge. The new bridge and road would provide an alternative route into Charleston, avoiding the heavily traveled road that approached the city via Charleston Neck. The company completed construction of the bridge in 1810, but ultimately failed to provide a long-lasting alternative route to Charleston, a consequence it seems of the bridge's destruction in a tropical storm just three years after its completion. For the most part, then, the General Assembly never fully responded to the Lowcountry's cries of relief from onerous road duty. As an 1811 petition noted, turnpikes had been rejected, as they were "deemed oppressive to that class of citizens who's [sic] circumstances cannot well afford any deductions from the fruits of their industry." In other words, because small planters and poor farmers could not afford the cost of travel on a private turnpike, the existing road system would have to suffice. Lowcountry petitioners, however, continued to press for some relief, as the "present mode of keeping the Roads in repair operates as a very unequal tax on them." While earlier generations of planters like Henry Laurens may have perceived road maintenance as their duty as citizens, heavy traffic on roads, which increased the cost and labor for upkeep, placed new stresses on their willingness to so easily sacrifice for the state. Lowcountry planters subsequently requested that the General Assembly consider an appropriation "for the express purpose of hiring labourers to be employed throughout the year in working on the roads . . . to Charleston, and to employ proper persons to superintend the work." In other words, the petitioners wanted the state to purchase or hire slaves to labor on the roads year-round. As they argued, this was not an "improper application of the public funds, since it is by these Roads the Produce of the whole upper Country, part of North Carolina & Georgia are conveyed to the City of Charleston, thereby contributing to the Commercial Interest of the State." The petitioners made clear that they felt the upkeep of South Carolina's infrastructure was of vital importance, but they argued that responsibility for such maintenance fell unevenly on their shoulders. Still, they made clear, if such work could not be accomplished by private turnpike companies or an outdated local road maintenance system, then it should be borne by the state itself, or at the very least by state-owned slaves.[49]

This petition, alongside the reports of the commissioners of roads, and the Santee Canal Company's records make clear that black Carolinians' everyday labors bound together the whole of South Carolina, uniting distant regions and neighboring states with both Columbia and Charleston. The cuts, roads, and canals that slaves built facilitated the very type of independent economic activity that lay at the heart of South Carolina's nascent liberal state. Farmers and planters alike were able to send their goods to market, travel to the administrative seats of power, and attend social, religious, and political events with relative ease. The enslaved enabled, at a heavy cost to themselves and to their owners, this type of movement. Black Carolinians also allowed the governing practices of the early state to remain flexible in the face of immense change and financial strain. Slaves provided the bridge between state-directed improvement and privately contracted development. Company directors, engineers, and contractors—most of whom had worked for the Revolutionary and early state government in some capacity—not only gained access to special privileges and funding through their previous and existing relationships to South Carolina's government, they also duplicated their reliance on slaves, the process of labor procurement, and the everyday management of the enslaved. Slaves were, in short, the material means through which developmental plans were both born and made reality, providing the most concrete connection between what state planners envisioned and what independent contractors, local commissioners, and private companies produced.

Challenging the State

Step by step, South Carolinians—government officials, army officers and soldiers, private merchants and slave buyers, engineers, contractors, company stockholders and the enslaved themselves—established the practices that produced and reproduced the early state. The routine of planning, slave acquisition, distribution, deployment, and the coerced labor black Carolinians regularly performed gradually established the state as everyday practice and produced its physical infrastructure. But of equal importance to such governing praxis were the various ways that slaves rejected, resisted, and exploited the plans and aspirations of government officials and individual South Carolinians.

For example, on July 26, 1782, Governor John Mathews directed General Francis Marion "to deliver to Mr. John Taylor of the State of North Carolina Six negroes from confiscated estates." Taylor purchased these men and women from the commissioners of forfeited estates, who had taken them "from the Estate of Elias Ball, Jr.," paying "cash in specie two hundred & forty guineas." This sale was likely part of the transactions authorized by Mathews in the summer of 1782 as an effort to acquire much-needed money for the government's contingency fund. Marion (or one of his men) completed the business between Taylor and the commissioners by presenting Taylor with a "certificate likewise for the same." Despite the seeming ease and success of this transaction, shortly after the slaves were delivered to Taylor, four of the six left, and "returned to Mr. Ball [Sr.]." As Governor William Moultrie reported in a message to the General Assembly, in early 1785, Taylor visited "this state with his credentials & applied for the delivery of the said negroes, which Mr. Elias Ball refuses, alleging they never were the property of his son." By repatriating themselves to Ball Sr.'s plantation, the slaves refused the state's desire for their fate, and, at least for a time, returned to the life they had previously known. Similarly, John Orde's confiscated slaves "made their escape" from their new owner "and returned to the plantation." The movement of the enslaved and the meaning of space, including the value of home, will be discussed in chapter 4, but here it is important to highlight the way that Orde's and Ball's slaves reveal the way that individual black Carolinians came to shape state policy—not simply in their everyday labors, but in their refusal to accede to state desires.[50]

In 1783, William Wayne published a runaway notice in the *South-Carolina Gazette*, notifying the public of his runaway slaves, "all of whom formerly belonged to the confiscated estate of Elias Ball." It is not clear if these men, women, and children returned to the estate of Ball's father, but the group was composed of "nine Negroes, viz. Sam, Saby, and Syfax, with their wives Nanny, Harriet, and Tenah, also three children, two males and one female, the eldest of the children Cain, the other Amos, the female child named Mary." Along with the three young children, Wayne also noted "Nanny is far advanced in pregnancy." Wayne's note not only highlights the pressures black Carolinians put on the state through their refusal of the confiscation policy, but also makes clear black Carolinians' efforts to maintain their families in the face of confiscation and distribution. Similarly, Charles H. Simmons notified the public that "Three Negro Wenches" had run away from his property in July 1785. The women, "Jenny elderly, short and pitted with the small pox; Dido, her daughter, middle stature; and Tissey, her grand daughter, with a female negro infant," were all confiscated from Gideon Dupont's property, and were presumed to have run back to the vicinity of his estates, where they were "well known, particularly at Ponpon, Bees-Creek and Wando."[51]

Merely the threat of confiscation led many slaves to run away from plantations. For instance, at the exact moment Francis Marion began ordering Peter Horry to gather up slaves for Heriot and Tucker to sell, and to labor on Senf's

Georgetown defensive works, a number of slaves began leaving nearby plantations. "A number of negroes I am told are going northwardly," Marion subsequently wrote to Horry. "You will stop all such negroes, and prevent as much as possible negroes travelling anywhere without a pass from me or some officer commanding any detachment in the Continental service." Among those runaways may have been seventeen of Henry Mill's fifty-two confiscated slaves, who absconded rather than face distribution by the commissioners of forfeited estates. Some confiscated slaves not only undid the state's plans but also undermined the government's claim to their labor and bodies by turning instead to the British troops who remained in South Carolina at war's end. Former lieutenant governor William Bull reported that South Carolinians took "160 of my best Negroes." After their capture, twenty of Bull's slaves escaped and joined the "King's army."[52]

The experience of Horry's troops, in particular, illuminates the various ways that the enslaved shaped early postwar statecraft through their everyday actions. At least some of the enlisted men who made up Horry's command at the Georgetown Garrison were likely enticed to join the army at this late stage of the war by the promise of payment in the form of slaves. While many joined expecting to fight the British in the waning moments of the war, instead their primary labors included procuring confiscated slaves and delivering them to slave merchants, ensuring the delivery of black Carolinians to the public works being erected near Georgetown, and policing the roads and waterways north of Charleston to capture runaway slaves.

Of course, just as South Carolina's public works and governing practices were shaped by the enslaved, so too were slaves shaped by their experiences laboring for the state. To be sure, their ceaseless work, as well as the diseases and dangers that lurked around every corner of the swamps, rivers, and forests in which they labored, defined most of their experiences. Nevertheless, working on canals, roads, cuts, fortifications, and public buildings also gave black Carolinians an opportunity to expand their communities and familiarize themselves with different parts of the state. New social ties and a more intimate knowledge of nearby people and places subsequently transformed black Carolinians' social worlds. For example, on October 20, 1779, thirty-five-year-old Chloe ran away from her owner, Thomas Butler, and took her four-year-old son, Barny, with her. As Butler noted in his runaway advertisement, Chloe had become close with "all the negroes who have worked for the public these last two years." Similarly, Robin and Wauney ran away from Samuel Dubose in January 1800. As Dubose noted, both men "have been for six or seven years past in the service of the Santee Canal Company," and he assumed that they could be found "lurking in the neighbourhood of the Santee Canal." Seven months after posting his first notice for the runaways, Dubose again advertised for the return of Robin, who was "either harboured in the neighbourhood of the Canal, or gone high up into the country." Robin's labor on the canal made both outcomes a possibility. The canal was bordered on both sides by some of South Carolina's oldest plantations. Over the course of seven years, it is likely that Robin had come to know the enslaved communities that resided on and around those plantations quite intimately.[53]

Dubose's other fear was that Robin had gone "high up into the country," and it reflected one of South Carolinians' greatest unspoken anxieties: that black Carolinians would use the same infrastructure meant to promote the free movement of white people and commodities for their own purposes. Such fears were not unfounded. Black Carolinians' mobility and the various meanings of their movement will be discussed in chapters 3 and 4. It is important to note here, however, the most striking postwar case of black Carolinians using South Carolina's (and Georgia's) infrastructure for their own ends: the Savannah River Maroons. According to government documents and newspaper reports, in the years following the Revolution a significant group of runaway slaves had taken up residence on a Savannah River island roughly twenty miles from the coast. The full duration of the community's existence remains unknown, but at least one historian has argued that the former slaves established their residence shortly after the 1779 siege of Savannah. The first official mention of the maroons, however, did not occur until late in 1786, when a Georgia grand jury filed a complaint "that large gangs of runaway Negroes" were "allowed to remain quietly within a short distance of this town."[54]

The community's size fluctuated greatly in the wake of the war, as runaways from both Georgia and South Carolina steadily arrived at the encampment. The increased numbers strained the group's meager resources, leading the maroons to begin raiding nearby plantations for supplies. Such raids were dangerous. They alerted residents of both Georgia and South Carolina to the slaves' presence, and a grand jury soon reported that about one hundred "runaway negroes" were sheltering "themselves on Belleisle Island, about 17 or 18 miles up Savannah River." The discovery led to two violent encounters between the maroons and the Georgia militia. By the time the militia returned for a third attack, the maroons had retreated upriver to the swamps near Purrysburg, South Carolina, where they had established a second encampment fortified by "an almost impenetrable swamp."[55]

What the Georgia militia found in the abandoned camp must have surprised all involved. On their island refuge, the maroons had accumulated provisions and built shelters, establishing a seemingly permanent community. Militia leaders reported finding "a number of their houses" and at least fourteen or fifteen boats. They also found small fields with crops growing, along with harvested rice waiting to be processed. While these provisions were limited for the presumed size of the community, they signaled the seeming durability and stability of the community. This was no hideaway for slaves seeking a brief reprieve from plantation labor; it was an attempt to construct a new home.[56]

Practical knowledge of the coastal plain gave the maroon band a distinct advantage over their would-be captors, as did their likely work on fortifications during the war, as Georgia's military leader James Jackson noted in a letter: "Their leaders are the very fellows that fought & maintained their ground against the brave lancers at the siege of Savannah, & they still call themselves the King of England's soldiers." After the abandonment of their initial encampment, the maroons took shelter in a swamp near Purrysburg, on the vast property of Joachim Hartstone. There, slaves who had spent the Revolution securing British, Georgia, and South Carolina positions built what must have seemed an imposing fortification. They filled the creek leading to the camp with felled trees and positioned sentries at outposts along the approach. Fortified breastworks surrounded the camp itself, and the runaways were armed with guns and had ample ammunition. Moreover, as many of the maroons had previously labored on nearby plantations, they each possessed at least some vital knowledge of the surrounding landscape and communities that would allow them to survive and evade capture. They knew, for example, that they could take "cattle at Abercorn" and "corn at Mr. Greenhow's." The maroons also knew that if they posted sentries at "Long Reach" on the Savannah River they could capture and ransack boats as they traveled downriver with supplies. Still, such raids—a necessity after the loss of their provisions at the first camp—led to increased attention from South Carolina's government.[57]

Officials in South Carolina and Georgia, then, at the very start of their self-governing experiment, confronted the very real prospect of a permanent maroon community in the contested borderlands of their respective states. In response, South Carolina officials not only pressed the local militia into service but also turned to the Catawba Indians, who had regularly aided the colonial government in the capture and killing of runaway slaves. In a letter to a militia colonel, South Carolina governor Thomas Pinckney argued that eliminating "the runaway Negroes who have late committed depredations in the southern parts of this State" necessitated engaging "some Indians to assist in effecting this purpose." Several skirmishes ensued. Though they guarded their community for as long as possible, eventually the maroons were overwhelmed by the combined forces of Georgia, South Carolina, and the Catawba. On May 7, the militias overtook the maroons' camp, killing six of the runaways and scattering countless men, women, and children into the surrounding swamps.[58]

The Savannah River maroons reveal a great deal, including the important ways that slaves' labors, both for the state and for individuals, shaped their resistance to the institution of slavery. But there was something much bigger at stake in the struggle between Georgia, South Carolina, and the enslaved men and women who settled on the Savannah River. At the precise moment that South Carolina's militia was gathering in Purrysburg, planning its assault on the maroons' encampment, just a few miles to the east in Beaufort commissioners from Georgia and South Carolina were meeting to negotiate a border dispute between the two states. The discussion between the two governments revolved around three primary issues: the western limits of the Savannah River, which had long formed the boundary between the two states; control over the islands in the river; and the contours and limits of future commercial travel on the Savannah.[59]

This meeting was not the first time South Carolina met with its southern neighbor to discuss their border, nor would it be the last. As early as 1784, South Carolina's government began receiving reports of Georgians and North Carolinians settling in the New Acquisition, western territory only recently ceded to South Carolina by the Cherokee. Likewise, the government had heard from individuals and local grand juries that ships traveling from Charleston up the Savannah River to South Carolina's backcountry were being stopped by Georgia officials who charged duties on their shipments. The commissioners who met in Beaufort negotiated these issues and quickly agreed on a settlement, signing the Treaty of Beaufort on April 7, 1787. To be sure, boundary disputes between South Carolina and Georgia (as well as between South Carolina and North Carolina) did not go away with the signing of this treaty. Throughout the early part of the nineteenth century and beyond, boundary commissioners and surveyors would meet several more times to more accurately define the borders between South Carolina and its immediate neighbors, but this meeting was the last time that such negotiations would occur beyond the oversight of the general government.[60]

Such negotiations were incredibly significant to the production of these modern states. Whether it was commissioners seated at negotiating tables or surveyors walking, measuring, and mapping the physical border, all participated in the manufacture of the state's territory, what one historian refers to as its geo-body. The maps made by James Cook and Henry Mouzon and later ones made by George Blackburn and Robert Mills provided government officials and private citizens with depictions of South Carolina as a unified, bounded entity, but it was boundary commissioners and surveyors who worked out the fine details of the state's borders, just as local road commissioners, private contractors, and slaves maintained the thoroughfares, cuts, bridges, and canals represented through the map.[61]

Nevertheless, discussing the contours of boundaries, establishing more precise measurements of state borders, and physically constructing the state's infrastructure were only some of the ways that South Carolina's bounded territory was produced in the post-Revolutionary era. Of equal importance were the activities of runaways like Chloe, Robin, and Wauney, as well as the Savannah River maroons and the armed militias who destroyed their communities. As scholars elsewhere have noted, both the state and its territory are consequences of particular social practices. The state, in other words, is an effect of these everyday activities. It is not difficult to imagine that the work of boundary commissioners, surveyors, state engineers, and government officials produced the state. It is, however, much more difficult to perceive the important ways that slaves' labor on infrastructure and fortifications and the slaves' role as the objects of informational and material transactions shaped the very meaning of the modern state. And it is nearly impossible to conceptualize runaway slaves as participating in that same project. Still, these practices were essential to the transformation of South Carolina into a modern state.[62]

When the maroons crossed back and forth from Georgia's side of the Savannah River to South Carolina's, for example, they directly defined the sovereign claims and jurisdictional responsibilities of each state at the border. Ownership of the islands on the lower end of the Savannah River was a prominent point of contention between the two states, and while Georgia planters and state officials proposed that the islands be considered part of their territory, responsibility for the actions of residents in and around those islands—enslaved Carolinians and Georgians—was an entirely different matter. At the end of 1786, General James Jackson wrote to Governor Thomas Pinckney arguing that while the maroon band was encamped on "an island in the Savannah River," which should have made it the sole responsibility of the Georgia militia, "they are now removed to or nigh Hartstones swamp in your state, from whence they frequently make irruptions unto Georgia." Highlighting the maroons' remove to South Carolina—a move that the militia could not definitively ascertain—transferred responsibility in the matter to South Carolina's government. Jackson strengthened this assertion by noting, "The majority of the runaways are Carolina property, but for the want of officers on your side, they seem to range at large."[63] Just as the border negotiators were discussing which islands fell under the sovereignty of each state and debating the western end of the Savannah River, South Carolina's apparent lack of governance at the border permitted the enslaved to commit raids on both sides of the Savannah.

The Savannah River maroons, then, represented much more of a threat than simply a loose band of men and women who had escaped their bonds; their lives and actions directly affected the meaning and shape of South Carolina's territory, as well as the governing practices on the border. Moreover, this small but growing community of men, women, and children was able to establish homes and pursue self-sustaining agricultural activities that still eluded many white Carolinians in the immediate aftermath of the war. In this way, this community's unchecked presence on the Savannah River not only pressed against Georgia and South Carolina's sovereign claims but also challenged the very idea of who could pursue freedom within these newly created states, and what that freedom would ultimately mean. By residing in the muddy waters of South Carolina and Georgia's borderlands beyond the watchful eyes of either government for more than five years, jealously guarding their position, the maroons made their own sovereign assertions to the space along the Savannah River. A correspondent for the *Columbian Herald* put it this way:

> To break up the camp, and destroy the confidence and strength of the run aways, cannot fail of producing the best effects, as they had got seated and strongly fortified in the midst of an almost impeneterable [sic] swamp, and opening a general asylum, which no doubt would have been embraced by many on the approach of hot weather: Indeed running away had become more prevalent than usual. When it is recollected how long a band of these people have rebelled, and opposed with success, the government of Jamaica, and look at the still more recent example to the southward of us, in the Dutch government of Suriname, where, from being contemptible fugitives at first, they at length fixed and fortified the recesses, and (what will always take place, where persons of any description are in the practice of independence and threatened with extreme danger) with the encrease of numbers, they exercised the principles of union, and

opposed and harrassed their masters until they were obliged to treat with them; and they are now an actual independent colony: the example of which is felt as the greatest inconvenience.[64]

In other words, the correspondent and other South Carolinians believed that the gravest threat the maroons posed was to the sovereign claims to the islands and swamps in and around which the Savannah River flowed. The runaways asserted and defended their own vision of self-governing independence on the very river that defined both Georgia and South Carolina's bounded territory, a river that facilitated the necessary movement at the heart of their economic and political projects. And they did so by using the skills and practices they had learned while laboring for the state. As the writer argued, "To have despised or neglected them, or permitted their robberies, might have led them on to equally ambitious and extensive views with those of Jamaica and Suriname, where the best stationary regiments could not subdue them."[65]

The maroons challenged the exclusivity of South Carolina and Georgia's claims to sovereignty along the Savannah River, and in so doing forced both governments to act. The maroons' actions, thus, gave shape and meaning to the state, arousing government leaders to articulate more clearly, in both statute and practice, the harsh limits around who could claim the very freedoms that were at the heart of their revolutionary project. For white Carolinians, and for that matter for most Americans, their new states were exclusively created for white men and their families. Expressing a sentiment shared by many across the new nation, the same correspondent to the *Columbian Herald* sighed, "It is, perhaps, the wish of interest, as well as philosophy, that they [slaves] were all in Africa." His frustration hinted at the predicament white Carolinians fostered in their effort to secure and bind the state together. They could not help but acknowledge that the slaves they feared were also the very people upon whom they relied to make the state real. Without them, without their labor, it could not exist at all.[66]

And therein lay the trouble. South Carolinians depended on their slaves for their economic wealth and their political development. They were unable to imagine either without the labor of tens of thousands of black Carolinians. This labor required slaves to remain mobile—traveling to work sites, providing seasonal labor across the coastal plain and into the backcountry, delivering commodities to market and supplies to plantations both distant and far. In this way, the enslaved became the circulating lifeblood of South Carolina's territorial infrastructure. Their movement not only maintained the state but also brought it to life, directly animating the economic and social ideas that state planners had envisioned. And yet, as the Savannah River maroons made clear, black movement did not always orient itself toward service. As will be made clear in chapters 3 and 4, slaves' travels and work on state roads, canals, and rivers provided them with opportunities to differently and defiantly define the landscape on their own terms.

CHAPTER THREE

Their Intentions Were to Ambuscade and Surround Me
The Necessity of Slave Mobility

At the beginning of his plantation diary for the year 1791, Charles Drayton meticulously documented his travels between his country seat along the Ashley River and his Wateree River plantation. As a member of the Road Commission in St. Paul's Parish, Drayton was especially attentive to the details of his everyday travels throughout the Lowcountry, particularly those that reflected the poor state of the region's infrastructure. On January 12, Drayton proceeded on a badly maintained road from Goose Creek Bridge to Monck's Corner. From Monck's Corner, Drayton traveled to the estate of General William Moultrie, making his total journey that day twenty-seven miles at the slow pace of "4 ½ miles" per hour. Drayton spent the evening with the Moultries and then proceeded west to Eutaw Springs, increasing his pace to six miles per hour. The next morning, Drayton traveled to "E. Rutledge's" house "on the Precipice on [the] Congaree" River, a journey of thirty miles that Drayton finished in five hours. After spending three days with Rutledge, Drayton left the Precipice and passed through the Congaree Swamp, a much more difficult five miles, after which he completed the remainder of his journey to his Wateree River property. Drayton took note of this information because of his role on the Road Commission and his own personal interest. But more importantly, documenting the distance and the condition of the roads between his country seat and Wateree Plantation provided him with important knowledge vital to the control of his enslaved labor force that was regularly on the move throughout the plantation complex. If Drayton knew how long the journey took, if he knew the landscape, he could more accurately dictate to his mobile slaves his expectations for their everyday journeys throughout the Lowcountry.[1]

The maintenance of Drayton's far-flung plantation empire necessitated the constant movement of information, goods, and labor—a mobility that was provided by enslaved black Carolinians. A prominent planter and a member of one of South Carolina's most powerful families, Drayton maintained several plantations across the coastal plain, and kept one of the most detailed existing diaries documenting his slaves' everyday travels. From the family manse on the Ashley River and his summer home on Sullivan's Island, Drayton controlled a plantation on the Wateree River, one on Jehossee Island, another along the Cossawhatchie River, and another near Rantowles's Creek. Itinerant field hands supplemented resident laborers when planting or harvesting dictated their necessity, and a team of trusted carpenters maintained the infrastructure on each of the plantations—one day building trunks at Jehossee, another fixing fences at Long Savannah, and another maintaining Drayton's schooner. Drayton's plantation drivers were also frequent travelers throughout the countryside, as they maintained a regular dialogue with Drayton concerning the everyday operations of his plantations. And the small team of boat hands that operated Drayton's fleet of canoes, flats, schooners, and sloops facilitated all of this travel. Day in and day out, Drayton tracked the nearly constant travel of his boats as they plied the waterways that crisscrossed the coastal plain, carrying commodities to Charleston, supplies and people to each of his plantations, and information to his country seat, Drayton Hall. But Drayton's logistical oversight occurred at a distance; he was not on the boats as his patroons traveled throughout the Lowcountry, nor did he accompany his itinerant labor force as they went from plantation to plantation. Thus, his control over enslaved mobility remained limited. While the enslaved labored according to his orders and by his authority, their actual activities took place far beyond Drayton's direct supervision.[2]

In the late colonial and early national eras, South Carolina planters and state planners relied absolutely on enslaved mobility. Slave movement was an integral aspect of plantation operations and state infrastructural development. This movement was necessitated by the rapid economic and social transformation of South Carolina at the end of the eighteenth and beginning of the nineteenth centuries. In this era, indigo ceased being a lucrative staple crop and inland swamp plantations reached their productive limits. This, however, did not mark the end of the plantation enterprise in South Carolina. Rather, planters turned to tidal rice production and cotton plantations as viable replacements for their capital allocation. This shift in production required that planters relocate their efforts, transferring labor and supplies to tidewater plantations and transforming backcountry cattle ranges and indigo plots into cotton fields. It also demanded an expansion of South Carolina's infrastructure, as discussed in chapter 2. This spatial shift hinged on the ability of the enslaved to move from one plantation to another, performing a variety of tasks in the construction and maintenance of the plantation enterprise.[3]

Enslaved movement not only was essential to the everyday maintenance and transformation of the plantation enterprise but also was a key component in the production of South Carolina's state space. Political leaders, local administrators, and slaves designed and built South Carolina's infrastructure in response to the increased transportation needs of a growing population, but constructing roads and clearing rivers were only one part of the development of state space. Everyday movement on the state's infrastructure, the circulation of goods, supplies, and people, cultivated and imposed territorial meaning on South Carolina's altered landscape. State planners imagined that roads and canals would facilitate the economic activities of South Carolina's citizenry, connecting Lowcountry plantations and backcountry farms to the coastal market. The ordered transportation of commodity crops, plantation supplies, and individuals on South Carolina's roads and rivers fulfilled the promises of internal improvement and on a daily basis materially brought the idealized state into being. But, at least in the Lowcountry, enslaved black Carolinians undertook most of this movement, just as they provided the bulk of labor for the physical construction of the state's infrastructure.

The exigencies of plantation agriculture and state development required slaves to regularly move, and subsequently, white Carolinians were confronted with a type of mobility that stood in stark contrast to the broad assumption that slaves' movement was limited and primarily centered on their owners' properties. To be sure, the state developed and honed a variety of tactics to control slave movement—slave passes, codes, patrols, and the state militia. While each of these efforts worked toward checking black Carolinians' travels, they all suffered from a variety of limitations. Overall, while the state and planters attempted to define and inhibit the mobility of the enslaved population, white Carolinians were regularly reminded that their world could not function without it. Like their peers throughout the early national South, South Carolinians' efforts at balancing their fears and their desires led them to often overlook the transgressions born out of black movement.[4]

Still, white Carolinians' fears of black mobility were not entirely unfounded. It was in and through this movement, understood as necessary labor by planters, rather than transgressive mobility or overt resistance, that black Carolinians crafted "rival geographies" of South Carolina. The regular, everyday practices of the enslaved not only produced the state but also made the space a region of possibility. As will be discussed in chapter 4, out of their laboring movement, slaves crafted social relations, forged illicit marketplaces, and maintained and created spiritual practices. Understanding South Carolina's state space through the prism of the sociospatial practices of the enslaved, as well as white responses to those practices, not only reframes our perceptions of power and territoriality in early national South Carolina but also illuminates how enslaved movement came to shape the state's earliest governing practices. Slave passes, patrols, and regulations must be understood as more than mere articulations of control over the enslaved population; they were also, and perhaps more importantly, part of the state's reactions and responses to the role that slaves played in producing and maintaining state space. In other words, slave passes and slave patrols were part of a governing strategy that sought to accommodate slave movement, rather than deny it. In this way, South Carolinians provided a model to their peers and to future Southern states, crafting a system that appeared to respond to white fears by limiting enslaved movement, while simultaneously ensuring that the mobility that lay at the heart of the plantation enterprise went unrestricted.[5]

Wealthy planters like Charles Drayton might wring their hands at the prospects of what happened on slaves' travels, but they could not seriously curtail it, no matter their fears. This irresolvable conflict—an unsettling reliance on a slave majority that was legally barred from public spaces but that remained necessarily mobile—became a defining characteristic of early national South Carolina. As we will explore in chapter 4, within this necessity slaves defined and valued South Carolina's landscape on their own terms. In particular, the coastal plain became a site of resistance, but it also became one of economic possibility, communal discourse, religious epiphany, and complex social relations—the very things the state had sought to provide its white inhabitants through infrastructural development. Planters perceived these realities only dimly, but the little they did understand was enough to drive them to distraction and violence.

When Tim, one of Drayton's boat-hands, was delayed at Rantowle's Bridge near the Stono Swamp, he did not idle in the schooner, but took the opportunity, as he had many times before, to travel among the black community that resided along the creek and to trade with other boatmen who were also held up at the crossing. Similarly, at harvest, when planters across the region sent their produce to market at Charleston, enslaved boatmen spent hours and sometimes days waiting to travel through New Cut—a short canal that connected the Stono River to Wappoo Creek and Charleston—to deliver their goods to the busy metropolitan port. Sitting on their schooners, flats, and sloops, boatmen forged relationships with other patroons, traded goods with their peers, and shared information with their neighbors. By focusing on this movement as a meaningful practice—highlighting where slaves went, how they got there, and how long they stayed—we can understand more clearly the various ways black Carolinians produced South Carolina's state space and its earliest governing practices.[6]

The Necessity of Mobility

After completing his travels through Britain's southeastern colonies in 1778, William Bartram left Charleston and headed north. He crossed Winyaw Bay and rode his horse across the sandy beaches along South Carolina's ocean shore. There he "observed a number of persons coming up ahead, whom I soon perceived to be a party of Negroes." Bartram noted that in such "a desolate place," the sight of so many slaves frightened him: "I was by this time several miles from any house or plantation, and had reason to apprehend this being a predatory band of Negroes." Bartram had heard, though from whom it is not clear, that people "were frequently attacked, robbed, and sometimes murdered by them at this place."[7]

Bartram was traveling on the King's Highway, in the northern edge of South Carolina's growing plantation enterprise. On the eve of the Revolution, groups of slaves, such as those that Bartram encountered—unobserved and alone, yet presumably coerced to labor through violence—were busy expanding South Carolina's plantation complex and securing the state's defenses. As he anxiously contemplated his gruesome demise at the hands of this "predatory band" of black Carolinians, Bartram was shocked to find that when he rode near them, "though armed with clubs, axes and hoes, they opened to right and left, and let me pass peaceably." One of the enslaved then addressed Bartram and informed him "whom they belonged to, and said they were going to man a new quarter at the West end of the bay." These men were not runaways; they were merely traveling through the Lowcountry to a new place of labor.[8]

Bartram did not write of checking their passes; instead, the slaves he encountered seemed to volunteer information regarding their owners and the purpose of their movement. But he did make clear his continued apprehension as he rode away from the group of black laborers, noting that he "kept a sharp eye about me, apprehending that this might possibly have been an advance division, and their intentions were to ambuscade and surround me." Bartram wrote of this group of black laborers as he had written of so many other aspects of the natural, southern landscape—something to be catalogued, an attempt to understand their presence within the landscape.[9]

Bartram's nervous assessment, however, revealed more than simply his naturalist preoccupations. Bartram took note of the unmonitored enslaved laborers and immediately made clear that regardless of their stated task, their movement evoked his strongest apprehensions. And yet, the presence of black Carolinians traveling throughout the countryside was a conspicuous aspect of South Carolina's late colonial and early national reality. Throughout the

1760s, South Carolinians imported more slaves than at any other time in the colony's history. Between 1750 and 1775, 64,000 African men, women, and children were imported into the province. These men and women joined the seasoned laborers who were already busy providing the muscle for the backbreaking project of expanding the plantation enterprise and constructing the provincial infrastructure. Slaves worked day and night constructing new rice plantations, clearing land for future development, and building the transportation infrastructure that a project of this magnitude required. Bartram wrote of the small band of slaves that he encountered along the King's Highway, but it is highly unlikely that these were the only itinerant laboring men that he confronted during his journey. For while Bartram busied himself ordering the Southeast through the spatial discourse of natural science, tens of thousands of enslaved Carolinians were physically constructing, maintaining, and securing South Carolina's territory.[10]

The latter half of the eighteenth century was not the first time that the coastal plain experienced this level of development. From the colony's founding, settlers and slaves labored to transform the space into a productive landscape. Beginning in the area surrounding Charleston, white Carolinians acquired the swamps and savannahs of the coastal plain and tasked their slaves with clearing the land for commodity production. As white Carolinians subdued their indigenous neighbors and the land, they spread their enterprise into the surrounding countryside, sending slaves into the inland swamps and marshes to pursue the production of rice.[11]

Not that rice was the only crop they grew. Rice was primarily marketed in Spain, France, and Portugal; subsequently, when England went to war with continental powers, planters were confronted with fallow markets and falling prices. Beholden to the fluctuating exigencies of the Atlantic economy, planters learned throughout the latter half of the eighteenth century to develop other crops in the productive soil of the Lowcountry. They subsequently experimented with a variety of commodious products, finding the most success with indigo for markets abroad, and cotton, corn, and lumber for those nearer home. The development of these secondary products, along with the continual increase of rice plantations, cattle ranges, and the timber industry, meant that enslaved Carolinians were regularly tasked with much more than simply planting and harvesting a single crop. Rather, black Carolinians regularly traversed the coastal plain, building up the productive capacity of the entire region.[12]

Establishing and maintaining rice plantations, indigo crops, and cotton fields and herding livestock required slaves to be available in more than one place throughout the year. Planters who owned expansive properties that had both swamp and highland could maintain their labor force within what they considered to be a bound space. But many planters, particularly those whose property did not have fields well suited to indigo, corn, or cotton production, purchased new lands and spread their property claims across the coastal plain. This was a wise business decision: diversifying their product base lessened planters' dependence on a single market. But such diversification required they increase and then disperse their labor force among their various plantations. It also meant that planters asserted less direct authority over the enslaved population. For example, from the end of the 1750s through the Revolution, Henry Laurens purchased plantations along the South Carolina and Georgia coast. From his Charlestown home, he directed slaves nearby at his Mepkin plantation, and as far away as the Altamaha River. The plantations closest to Charlestown focused less on staple crops and more on providing material for Laurens's properties along the southern coastal plain, as well as timber for the thriving lumber market. Laurens's boatman traveled up and down South Carolina's Lowcountry rivers and along the dangerous stretch of the southern Atlantic coast, delivering supplies, transporting workers, taking commodities to market, and conveying Laurens's orders to his drivers and overseers. Multiple plantations with varied production goals required specialized management. Individuals like Laurens closely monitored the activities on their plantations as much as they could from a considerable distance; nevertheless, they became more dependent on the knowledge of their drivers and skilled laborers and resigned themselves to the distant oversight of production, a management facilitated by enslaved movement.[13]

The Revolution interrupted the expansionary plans of planters like Laurens, but it did not stop the movement of their slaves. Black Carolinians continued to move throughout the countryside, delivering commodities to market for as long as that remained possible. Moreover, as discussed in chapter 2, slaves continued to serve their masters and the public through the construction of fortifications and the rebellious state's infrastructure. And once the British took control of South Carolina, those planters who were able moved entire labor forces to different locations throughout the southern Atlantic coast, or had them removed by the British. For example, the Colleton family estate manager reported that by war's end "62 Negroes [were] sent to Augustine (before the evacuation of this town by the British)." Additionally, "47 Negroes . . . were carry'd into No. Carolina & condemned as lawful Prize." According to the Watboo Estate manager, "55 Negroes remained" on the estate, but some had "been enticed away—or carry'd off, perhaps about 10 in number."[14]

In addition, during the war and in its final stages, slaves were regularly on the move outside of the control of their masters. They traveled to survive, to join the British cause, or to rejoin former plantation communities. In the earliest stages of the war, one of Henry Laurens's plantation managers wrote regularly of his slaves running away from his plantations, only to be found at some of his other properties. As John Lewis Gervais noted in a letter to Laurens, "Four others are gone from Santee viz. Doctor Coffee, Montezuma, Belfast & Shanut. Supposed to be gone to the southward. I wrote to Wright Savannah on the Subject & I hear by Mr. William Brisbane who is come to Town they are there." Other black Carolinians used the opportunity of war to quit the plantation enterprise altogether. For example, during the war, Esther, one of Samuel Mathis's slaves, left her owner's plantation and traveled to Camden. Mathis reported in his plantation diary for March 26, 1781, that "Esther having went to Camden yesterday without leave," he "threatened her and sent [her] to work." Two days later, Mathis reported, "Esther had run off in the Night & taken her Child & Cloaths." Apparently, Esther found shelter for herself and her child among the British troops garrisoned in Camden, for as Mathis reported after speaking to one of the British officers, it was "understood that she was hid in an Officer's room."[15]

When the war concluded, slave movement continued, as individual slave owners and state leaders labored to reinvigorate the plantation economy. Confiscated slaves, as noted in chapter 2, moved between slave dealers and their new owners. Planters who had not been ruined by the war gathered what slaves they retained and tasked them with rebuilding their disparate properties, and political leaders regularly called on slaves to reconstruct the state's roads and bridges. Among the wealthiest planters, rebuilding meant expanding and diversifying. Charles Drayton exemplified this process of diversification in the post-Revolutionary era. On each of his plantations, Drayton's enslaved labor force performed numerous tasks and grew a variety of commodity crops. For example, on Drayton's Wateree River plantation, the farthest inland of his properties, he focused his efforts on corn production, a project that ultimately failed. But he also maintained a shad fishery, grew subsistence crops, and rented out property to a number of tenant farmers. This region, along the Congaree and Wateree Rivers, was, like much of the backcountry in this period, rapidly orienting toward large-scale plantation agriculture. Drayton, like his wealthiest peers, hoped to participate in this development. But enlarging one's property holdings and transforming the land into a productive plantation were two very different tasks. As the plantation enterprise slowly expanded again following the war, wealthy planters purchased slaves, when they were able, to supplement their labor force, which was made more difficult during the ban on the African slave trade that lasted until 1803. More often, planters moved slaves from older properties to new plantations, sharing their expanding labor force as need and demand required. This was particularly the case for the skilled labor needed to fabricate the plantation's infrastructure, manage holdings, and keep planters abreast of daily activities. Planters with multiple properties usually relied on a team of skilled and trusted slaves to perform these tasks. Mostly men, these enslaved Carolinians moved continually throughout the coastal plain, rarely residing on a single plantation longer than it took to complete their appointed jobs.[16]

Wealthy planters and skilled slaves found this to be a mutually advantageous system, but when planters extended their enterprise across great distances, as Drayton did with his Wateree property, they stretched their limited resources thin, and occasionally found it difficult to address the everyday managerial needs of disparate properties. Throughout the 1790s, Drayton believed that his Wateree plantation was either mismanaged or incapable of offsetting production costs. After another bad year on the plantation, which his overseer blamed on a variety of ills, Drayton noted that on a "contiguous swamp," his neighbor "makes near 1/3 more corn than I do on 80 acres, 3 ploughs, & 11 negroes in the field. The badness of the crop must then arise from negligence, purely." There was little Drayton could do to rectify this situation, as the Wateree was quite distant from his country seat on the Ashley River. Nevertheless, Drayton sent his most trusted enslaved drivers to "survey the crop" and supplemented Wateree's labor force with field hands from his other properties. Drayton noted that the "Negroes set off from Bob Savannah for the Wateree." Still, the problems at Wateree continued. At least part of the problem, it seemed, was managerial malfeasance. Paris, one of Drayton's drivers, reported that the overseer "never lays on the plantation and comes over only every other day." The overseer's failures and oversights pushed Drayton to cease production on the Wateree, lease the land, and remove his slaves "nearer home." Drayton's experience with his Wateree plantation exemplified the difficulties planters confronted in the everyday management of a large plantation complex. More importantly it illuminated the necessity of enslaved mobility in the everyday maintenance of a diversified, dispersed enterprise.[17]

This was especially true in the development of tidal rice cultivation, which dominated the efforts of wealthy Lowcountry planters and thousands of slaves in the latter half of the eighteenth and beginning of the nineteenth centuries. In the early eighteenth century, most South Carolina rice planters raised their crops on coastal marshes or inland swamps. Inland rice planters burdened their slaves with the dangerous tasks of draining swamps, constructing massive earthen dams to prevent reinundation, and building reservoirs for irrigation. But while this system provided planters with significant early returns, it also presented them with a litany of associated problems. To begin, inland rice cultivation required a substantial amount of dangerous and difficult labor. Weeds thrived alongside the rice and kept slaves mired in thick mud during the hottest months of the year—months when they struggled to prevent a plantation from falling "in the grass." In addition, because most of the plantations lay in naturally flooded swamps and marshes that had been artificially drained, planters continually feared, and were forced to deal with, seasonal flooding. In the construction of inland plantations, slaves were tasked with the construction of massive embankments to prevent unwanted water from overwhelming the rice crops. But when floods, known as freshes or freshets, struck the Lowcountry, there was little that a man-made embankment could do to stop the rushing waters from affecting the rice fields.[18]

Freshets were devastating to rice production and the Lowcountry economy. Floodwaters regularly forced planters out of business or obliged them to abandon their productive fields for safer environs. For instance, in the 1790s, St. Stephen's Parish planters—some of the wealthiest in colonial South Carolina—were forced to desert their fertile Santee River swamp plantations, removing their slaves to new properties, after experiencing numerous devastating floods over a twelve-year period. As David Ramsay recollected, "Many of the planters discouraged by a rapid succession of freshets, abandoned the plantations subject to their baneful influence." Ramsay noted that old fields across the region lay bare "both on the high-lands along the edge of the swamp and in the swamp, which thirty years ago were in the highest state of cultivation, and produced luxuriant crops of corn, indigo, and rice."[19]

The worst of the floods, the 1796 Yazoo Freshet, affected all of South Carolina. This massive deluge slowed construction on the Santee Canal, and destroyed many of the infrastructural improvements South Carolinians had made in the aftermath of the war. As John Drayton remembered, newly built bridges were unable to "withstand the fury of its torrent, rendered more impetuous by the weight of large trees and houses" that the waters dangerously hurried toward the coast. The Congaree River was "upwards of forty feet high above the common level of the river." In Granby, across the river from Columbia, "the tobacco warehouse was destroyed; together with one hundred and fifty hogsheads of tobacco." A tobacco warehouse on the Wateree River met the same fate. Drayton noted, "Dwelling houses, corn houses, cattle, horse, and hogs were carried down by the violence of the current; and vast beds of sand, were strewn over fertile tracts of swamp land, to their irreparable injury." In the Lowcountry, slave quarters were "carried by the torrent entirely out to sea." Even tidal rice plantations, with their high embankments and sophisticated water-control technology, were unable to escape the raging waters, and "were overflowed for near a week." Charles Drayton noted that he lost over 200 bushels of corn on his Wateree plantation because of the floodwaters. Such natural disasters magnified slaves' labors, forcing skilled and unskilled slaves alike to rebuild plantation infrastructures across the coastal plain.[20]

The combination of these devastating floods and the high costs of inland cultivation pushed planters toward new crops and alternative methods of cultivation. Throughout the latter half of the eighteenth century, an increasing number of rice planters turned to tidal estuaries to provide irrigation for their rice fields. The power of ocean tides, sometimes reaching as far as thirty miles inland, pushed rivers above their banks. This daily occurrence, if controlled properly, allowed planters to flood their fields, sustaining their plants and preventing the growth of weeds. Tidal cultivation required less labor for the everyday maintenance of plantations—eliminating the incessant task of weeding—but the initial capital and labor costs were astronomical. Nevertheless, after the economic disruptions of the Revolution, more planters turned to tidal rice cultivation as a safer and more lucrative means of producing rice in the Lowcountry.[21]

Despite the high capital outlays, by the end of the century planters were rushing to the coast to claim river swampland that they had heretofore considered useless—and for good reason. Prior to the Revolution, inland swamps had produced between 600 and 1,000 pounds of rice per cultivated acre. By the last decade of the century tidal cultivators were able to nearly double that output. This production increase was reflected in the assessed value of plantations. Inland swamp plantations were typically valued anywhere between twenty and fifty dollars an acre, whereas postcolonial tidal lands were valued at seventy to ninety dollars an acre. The increased value of land and the promise of increased crop yields spurred wealthy planters toward the coastal rivers, where they subsequently sent thousands of slaves to labor.[22]

The slaves whom William Bartram encountered near Winyaw Bay were laboring in one of the primary sites of this expanded tidal rice production. Even as Bartram traveled, the Black, Pee Dee, and Waccamaw Rivers were quickly being transformed into plantation spaces, as planters purchased new slaves to settle their properties, or transferred entire labor forces from one plantation to another. This resulted in a significant migration of black Carolinians into parts of the Lowcountry that had been only sparsely settled through most of the colonial era. Because of the high costs involved, these new tidewater plantations were developed by wealthy planters, most of whom, like Charles Drayton, oversaw a range of developments from the safety of their Charleston homes, country seats, and summer residences.[23]

These new plantations were far from idyllic. Late colonial and early national tidal rice plantations were almost solely devoted to the production of rice and devoid of the plantation infrastructure that contemporary observers have come to associate with coastal plantations. No big house was constructed, only an overseer's home and slave quarters. Aspects of the plantation enterprise that would normally make each a self-sufficient island unto itself occurred off-site. Subsistence food production, the maintenance of plantation infrastructure, and even labor management frequently took place at other locations. For example, Henry Laurens supplied his Georgia plantations, which were solely dedicated to commodity production, from his Cooper River plantation Mepkin and the gardens of his newly built Ansonborough estate. This separation of functions was, in part, the result of the aggrandizement of plantation spaces by the wealthiest Lowcountry planters.[24]

Many of the planters who developed the coastal plain in the later eighteenth century were already well situated near Charleston. They were not concerned with constructing an outward display of their wealth at their rice-producing properties—that was the role of their country estates and Charleston townhomes. The tidal rice plantations, situated on the peripheries of settlement along the coastal plain, were constructed solely as labor camps for the generation of wealth. Eventually the lands became more settled and self-sufficient, as planters dispersed their holdings through sale and inheritance. But throughout the late colonial and much of the early national eras, coastal rice plantations remained wholly devoted to commodity production.[25]

At the heart of the coastal plain's dispersed plantation complex—its new plantations and intricate infrastructure—was a peripatetic enslaved labor force. Lacking the means to support themselves, these large-scale operations relied on the constant delivery of supplies, goods, and labor to function. Black Carolinians thus constantly traversed the Lowcountry to supplement labor forces, provide specialized labor, and transport goods. For example, when Henry Laurens set about constructing his new home in the Ansonborough suburb of Charleston, he borrowed "Caesar, Taff, George, Jack, Tom, Bennett, Billy, Tanner, July, Charles, and Adam" from his nearby Mepkin plantation. When Charles Drayton's lucrative Jehossee Island plantation neared the annual harvest, he ordered the overseer at Bob Savannah to send "Pompey, Nella, Lacey, Monday, January, Charles & if possible Sarah & Paris" to "assist in the harvest." Field hands—men and women—regularly traveled to neighboring and distant properties to address seasonal needs, but skilled laborers were constantly on the move. Woodworkers—coopers, sawyers, and carpenters—were especially integral to the upkeep of plantation operations. Overseer John J. Hales wrote to Isaac Ball of the theft of his Pee Dee River plantation's "grinding stone." Ball's resident coopers, Hale wrote, took the tool, as they worked "9 or 10 miles from home," and did not return it—a regular occurrence it seemed.[26]

Charles Drayton's carpenters never seemed to reside in any single space. Mobility was a defining characteristic of their labors, whether building "negro houses" at Savannah, repairing Drayton's frequently damaged sloop as it lay idle in a distant stream, constructing fences at Jehossee or Bob Savannah, or delivering timber to Drayton Hall. And as the plantation enterprise expanded in the late eighteenth century, the need for skilled labor directly increased. When building the vital embankments that lined tidal rice plantations, planters needed vast amounts of labor. But they also required the services of slaves who had experience constructing massive earthworks—laborers who were skilled as sawyers, trunk-minders, coopers, and carpenters. Reflecting this need, the number of specialized laborers increased dramatically following the Revolution. Prior to the war, skilled laborers represented 15 to 20 percent of South Carolina's labor force. After the Revolution, slaves with specialized skills represented over one quarter of all laborers.[27]

As important as mobile labor was for the Lowcountry's dispersed plantation complex, information was more valuable. Planters and plantation managers relied on regular updates from their overseers and drivers to maintain oversight on plantation business. Overseers sent plantation owners updates on crops and labor, and requisitions for needed supplies. And in return, owners regularly sent their overseers labor directives, requests for particular goods, and suggestions for the management of their slaves. To facilitate this exchange of information, planters relied on their most trusted slaves, who were subsequently regularly on the move, traveling between plantations, country seats, and summer retreats to deliver letters and information. Though often subtle, this movement was plain to see in the regular correspondence between plantation owner and overseer. Less obvious were the ways that slaves took advantage of such travels. For example, new overseer John J. Hales wrote plantation manager Isaac Ball, "I received your letter by Quacoo." It seems Quacoo used the opportunity of mail delivery to pursue his own business, as Hales added that he "was very much surprised at his not coming to you

Saturday by the middle of the day as I directed him to go." What Quacoo did in the extra time he took remains a mystery, but as will be discussed in chapter 4, there were numerous similar opportunities that mobile slaves took advantage of in their daily travels.[28]

Once plantations were settled and production began to peak, more demands were placed on plantation infrastructure. Higher yields meant a need for more efficient milling techniques. For most of the colonial era, slaves removed the grain from its husk by using a mortar and pestle. Planters interested in increased efficiency experimented with a variety of milling techniques, both human- and animal-powered. However, it was not until the introduction of water-powered mills that significant advances were made in this aspect of rice production. Slaves on tidal rice plantations were frequently able to use the same water that they harnessed for irrigation to power new mills. But not every plantation had the necessary equipment, skilled laborers, or power sources to construct this important time- and labor-saving technology. This was a boon to those planters who owned overly salinized riverfront property. These coastal landowners must have been frustrated by their proximity to seemingly lucrative tidal flows. But by developing water-powered mills, they could take advantage of their location by charging for their high-demand processing services. The development of off-site rice milling increased the need for mobile slaves in the coastal plain. Whereas before, enslaved boatmen simply transported the finished product to Charleston's harbors, this new development required teams of slaves to travel away from their respective plantations first to mill their rice, and then again for delivery to Charleston. Similarly, with the development of cotton as a lucrative commodity crop, planters sometimes sent their crops to plantations that maintained cotton gins.[29]

Critical to this mobile labor force were enslaved boatmen. Wealthy planters maintained small fleets of canoes, flats, schooners, and sloops for the transportation of material across the coastal plain. The patroons that traveled up and down the region's waterways, like skilled workers, were in perpetual motion. Henry Laurens's boats regularly traveled between his plantations, transporting information and supplies and delivering "Boat Loads of Ruff [sic] Rice to town." Charles Drayton's boatmen only lay idle for inclement weather, boat malfunctions, or heavy river traffic. And even then, they rarely lingered upon any one plantation. Instead, they ceaselessly traveled through the Lowcountry, transporting supplies to Drayton's far-flung properties, delivering produce to Charleston markets, and relaying important information to Drayton at his country seat.[30]

Of course, as the numerous runaway notices in Charleston attest, the freedom of movement afforded to black boatman provided them with numerous opportunities to transgress their owner's orders, something that will be discussed in more detail in chapter 4. White Carolinians recognized the inherent risks of unmonitored boatmen plying the region's waterways, but planters' absolute dependence on this method of transportation limited the state's ability to effectively check slave mobility. In 1818, residents of Georgetown District petitioned the General Assembly to address the "traffic carried out by negroes in boats upon our rivers." Little was done to address their concerns, and five years later Georgetown residents again petitioned the state government to address the "practice of negroes navigating the rivers and creeks in flats and boats, for cutting wood and other purposes." As the petitioners stated, "It is well known that many negroes have the free use and control of flats and boats and some also in companies and are generally supplied with firearms. In this way, the vigilance of the patrols is defeated and incalculable mischief results to the planters and others." In fact, the state required that all ships have at least one white boatman, but wealthy planters saw these regulations as a nuisance or simply were unable to comply and frequently disregarded them. For example, on March 19, 1796, Charles Drayton noted that the "Port Collector of Charleston seized my sloop & many other vessels for not having a white mariner to navigate." Such seizures may have given planters and merchants pause, but as they often made clear, black patroons were sometimes the only reliable boatmen available for their needs. John Lewis Gervais noted in a letter to Henry Laurens, "I am at a loss for a patron [sic], white men are not to be hired—In this situation Mr. Loveday advised me to take Turamoush, I will try him if he behaves well." Laurens, Drayton, and others were unable to comply, or just as often simply refused to adhere to the state law, for any number of reasons. Both continued to staff their boats with mostly or wholly black crews, a practice that most of their peers clearly emulated.[31]

To a certain extent, South Carolina's planters had no choice but to violate the state's navigation laws. They relied on their slaves' mobility to maintain distant properties, and their operations hinged on the unimpeded ability of enslaved boatmen to transport supplies, information, laborers, and produce between and among plantations and Charleston. As with drivers and skilled slaves, planters relinquished control and ceded substantial responsibilities to enslaved boatmen. In return, patroons, skilled slaves, and trusted servants were able to freely move about the Lowcountry. In the midst of such movement, black Carolinians took advantage of their owners' distant oversight, and used their relative freedom of movement to develop their own sociospatial practices, the results of which had profound implications for the meaning of South Carolina's territory and its earliest governing practices.

The Limits of Control

Though white Carolinians depended on mobile slaves to maintain the plantation complex, black Carolinians regularly reminded them that labor was not the sole reason for their movement. In 1816, a band of fugitive slaves led by two men named Mowby and Dunmore encamped themselves amid the swamps, rivers, and creeks that flowed throughout the jagged coast, just south of Charleston in the Pon Pon district. In this region—long familiar to South Carolina's enslaved population—the two men and their band frequented surrounding plantations and farms, taking food, supplies, and eventually weapons. The maroons' forays into surrounding plantations and within the intercoastal trade network quickly disrupted the perception of calm control white Carolinians tenuously maintained. After local inhabitants failed to do so, Governor David Williams sent General William Youngblood and a contingent of troops from the South Carolina militia into the area to disperse, capture, and kill the runaways.[32]

Mowby and Dunmore's white pursuers noted the difficulty of uncovering and capturing the runaways, complaining that "attempts were then made to disperse them, which either from insufficiency of numbers, or bad arrangement, served by their failure only to encourage a wanton destruction of property." Besides the arrangements and the apparent lack of sufficient support, the militiamen were unable to conquer the physical reality of the coastal plain. Governor Williams explained that "the peculiar situation of the whole of that portion of our coast, rendered access to them difficult." Mowby and Dunmore's gang of runaways used the dense coastal landscape to evade the pursuit of those who claimed legal title to the region.[33]

Mowby and Dunmore were not simply fortuitous in their choice of maroon camp; the area near the Pon Pon River had long been the destination of runaway slaves in South Carolina, as it lay at the center of the plantation complex south of Charleston. The Stono Rebellion had occurred in this part of the Lowcountry, and a short time later, in 1765, colonial officials feared that the slave population was planning another insurrection, aware that a number of runaway slaves were already hiding there, within the "great swamps near Horse's Shoe, and near Spoons Savanna." Like their predecessors, Mowby and Dunmore's group were readily familiar with the contours of this swampy landscape, and knew that they were surrounded by potential allies, traveling on the rivers and laboring on nearby plantations.[34]

Mowby and Dunmore's band maintained an everyday knowledge of the landscape and waterscape that frustrated the militia's search for them. These difficulties were exacerbated by the presence of thousands of black Carolinians in the region, the vast majority of whom were not runaways. White Carolinians, particularly wealthy planters, were of course well aware of this complex social order. In their instructions to the 1765 militia leaders who, with a band of Catawba, were searching the same Pon Pon region for a band of fugitive slaves, colonial officials requested "10 to 15 brisk young men to join the Indians, that they may do no harm by mistaking negroes who are not run away."[35]

Such an order may have calmed nervous planters who knew their capital was heavily invested in enslaved persons, but it did nothing to keep slave patrols and the state militia from mistakenly killing the wrong individuals. Numerous petitions to the state legislature spoke to the inability of slave patrols to discern the imperceptible differences between slaves that were *runaways* and slaves that were simply *not on the plantation*. Slaves frequently ran away to the same swamps and forests in which they worked. They had, in fact, gained their familiarity and intimacy with the space through their everyday labors. Runaways—who were, after all, slaves first—knew where they could retrieve supplies, where boatmen lingered, and the places least likely to come under the watchful eyes of planters and patrols. Such spatial practices complicated the distinction between slaves laboring in the countryside and slaves absconding from labor.[36]

This, then, was the dilemma that confronted planters and politicians, patrolmen and merchants. They were unable to reconcile planters' and the state's absolute dependence on enslaved mobility with the control necessitated by white Carolinians' fear of slave insurrection and black transgression. Officials had the difficult task of protecting planters' property rights over the bodies of the enslaved and encouraging economic expansion, and at the same time were responsible for maintaining a sense of communal calm, particularly given the overwhelming number of slaves who resided and labored in the coastal plain. Their task was made more difficult by the spatial practices and knowledge of white and black Carolinians. Property boundaries were vague and often unmarked; slaves carried passes easily forged and purposefully unclear in their prescribed limitations; and the patrolmen, militia, overseers, and planters, whose duty was to limit enslaved movement and monitor public spaces, often lacked familiarity with the region, knowledge that the enslaved had accumulated through generations of labor. Colonial and state officials thus struggled to develop sufficient laws that would simultaneously control enslaved mobility and permit the freedom of movement demanded by the exigencies of the plantation enterprise.

In the summer of 1819, David L. Rodgers and his slave Pompey, a resident of Williamsburg District, experienced this costly complexity firsthand. During the summer, according to reports, a large band of runaways "to the number of [seventy] Negroes had associated and imbodied themselves together, committing depredations of many kinds on the property of the inhabitants." Residents of the district unsuccessfully attempted to locate and disperse the runaways. Militia colonel William Salters strongly suggested to those concerned that "the people should turn out with fire arms and quell the negroes in their nefarious acts." Residents in the district initially resisted Salters's call to arms. Planters knew that many of their slaves labored in the backcountry forests and swamps, and were aware of their boatmen plying the region's waterways. They also knew that the swamps and forests of the region were dense and mysterious, making any efforts to uncover the runaways more difficult.[37]

Nevertheless, residents eventually agreed to Salters's suggestion, and "this last and only probable way, of subduing the negroes was agreed upon and pursued for some time." The band of runaways was eventually found "imbodied and measurable in a state of rebellion, against the peace and welfare of the neighborhood." The men who found the group noted that they "manifested in their conduct no pacifick disposition to surrender," and "when ordered to give up" they "endured as far as possible to effect their escape." What this actually looked like, on the ground, remains a mystery. While it is possible that Salters, local residents, and the militia uncovered a sizable maroon community, it is more likely that a small band of runaways and itinerant laboring slaves met at what was most likely a popular gathering space for black Carolinians, perhaps inflating the purported number of rebellious slaves. What is certain is that when the armed and angry white search party discovered the group, the resulting confrontation quickly descended into chaos as slaves scattered, immediately blurring the distinction between those with permission to be in the countryside and those who were there illegally. It is possible, as the militia report suggests but David Rodgers disputed, that this large group of black Carolinians was made up entirely of runaway slaves who had joined together "to commit depredations" upon the community. Of course, this claim may have simply been intended to cast the militia's subsequent actions in a better light.[38]

Whatever the case, the militia treated the entire group of black Carolinians as hostile and fired haphazardly into the mass of people as they attempted to escape. In the shadows of the swamps, amidst the chaos, Pompey, "a prime negro fellow" belonging to Rodgers, "was shot dead." In his mid-forties, Pompey was a valuable enough slave to warrant a petition for financial redress. Rodgers described him as "a very prime field hand; a good sawyer, and was quite handy in the use of mechanical tools of different kinds." Rodgers believed and argued that it was unlikely Pompey was participating in any type of rebellious activity at the time of his death, for he "had sustained previous to being killed, uniformly, a good character, with the exception of running away once or twice at the most." Ebenezar Gibson, a neighbor, corroborated Rodgers's petition, noting that he "has had the said negro Pompey frequently in the Boat as a hand," and that he subsequently considered him "a valuable boat hand, and also valuable in many other respects."[39]

As a boatman, sawyer, and skilled slave, Pompey needed to travel frequently throughout the swamps, forests, and waterways of Williamsburg District. Rodgers depended on Pompey's mobility, both for the maintenance of his own property and for the supplemental income he accrued by hiring him out to his neighbors—men like Ebenezer Gibson. As mentioned above, skilled slaves were essential to the Lowcountry complex and highly valued. It is no surprise, then, that Rodgers requested financial recompense for what he considered the wrongful murder of a slave who was worth at least "nine hundred or one thousand dollars." Pompey's presence in the swamps was, according to his master, a regrettable but necessary consequence of his labors. Rodgers had likely heard of the runaways in the nearby swamps, but he could not restrain Pompey from traveling through the region. To bar his movement would have hamstrung the maintenance of Rodgers's plantation operations and limited the income he received from hiring Pompey out to neighboring planters.[40]

Yet, when Colonel Salters, Captain Isaac Nelson, and the armed citizenry approached the gathered slaves, all of the black Carolinians instantly became runaways—regardless of their status or circumstances. Deposed, both Salters and Nelson reported: "Pompey had been in the woods for some time with other negroes who had imbodied themselves together against the peace and property of the citizens of the district." In the rush of that moment and its aftermath, it did not matter if the group of slaves was a conglomerate of runaways and itinerant laborers. All black Carolinians gathered together beyond the gaze of planter and patrol, viewed through the complicated prism of civic order in the midst of racial slavery, were ultimately deemed a threat to the safety of the district and the property rights of individuals. Salters and Nelson's actions reflected the cumulative frustration and fear that white Carolinians experienced in the Lowcountry. They did not have the same familiarity with the landscape that slaves possessed, nor did they recognize most of its inhabitants. How could they? Even in this relatively small district, slaves outnumbered whites almost four to one. Yet white Carolinians were expected to respect the property rights of their neighbors—particularly the wealthy planters—while all around them, at the behest of masters, the enslaved regularly transgressed proprietary boundaries. And in doing so, mobile black Carolinians instantly revealed the tensions intrinsic to a world maintained by the very group that white Carolinians feared most.[41]

Throughout the first decades of the nineteenth century and despite their reliance on black mobility, white Carolinians, particularly nonplanters, increasingly conflated the everyday movement of the enslaved with illegal, rebellious, and insurrectionary motives. In 1810, residents of Georgetown petitioned the General Assembly for a stronger law to prevent slaves from trading with shopkeepers. The petitioners recognized the centrality of slaves in the production of rice within the district. But, they stated, a "considerable portion of the crops raised in the vicinity of the said town is sold by Negroes, without tickets." This seems a strange point of contention given that Georgetown slaves outnumbered white residents by an astonishing ten-to-one ratio. Any resident privy to the surrounding rivers or harbor would have instantly recognized that enslaved boatmen, besides being a ubiquitous laboring presence at the harbor, delivered virtually all of the crops from the countryside to Georgetown. But the petitioners believed that these ticketless slaves were responsible for selling substantial quantities of rice to "petty shopkeepers, who raised no rice and who could hardly, in any other way, have obtained such large quantities of produce." Residents believed that this practice induced "persons of bad character to make establishments in their town." Once there, these "evil disposed persons" reportedly raised the illegal ante. Being "not satisfied with the gains arising from illicit traffick," they "attempted to set fire to the town." Black Carolinians may or may not have had arsonist designs for Georgetown; regardless, when slaves reoriented South Carolina's infrastructure for their own survival and economic gains, they threatened to destroy the very meaning of the city and the state for its white inhabitants. In the face of this, residents of Georgetown acted upon their fears and formed themselves "into a guard for the protection of their lives and property."[42]

They were not alone. In the wake of the Denmark Vesey conspiracy, police associations, beginning with the South Carolina Association, were founded across the state. In 1823, residents near the Black River swamp created the Blackswamp Association "for the purpose of enforcing the laws of this state," and specifically "for the better governing and managing [of] Negroes and other persons of colour." At a meeting of the Pineville Police Association, also founded in the 1820s, members gathered to "devise a plan for apprehending or dispersing a gang of desperate Runaways" who were "encamped in the vicinity" of the Santee-Cooper Canal. Members of each of these police associations pooled their resources, devised night watches, and searched for runaway slaves. But police associations had only limited success in capturing runaways and enforcing South Carolina's slave laws. More importantly, the formation of local police associations reflected local residents' frustration with their white neighbors and state leaders, who they felt too often disregarded state laws directed at the oversight and control of the enslaved population.[43]

Such frustrations and fears grew in direct relationship with the growth of the slave population. Throughout the early national era, the number of slaves throughout South Carolina continued to rise, while the number of white residents, particularly in the Lowcountry, either decreased or experienced only small gains. The discrepancies in the two populations in the coastal plain were astounding. In 1820, Georgetown District had 15,000 slaves compared with just 1,800 whites. In Colleton District, there were 21,000 slaves and only 4,000 whites. Even in Charleston District, which had the Lowcountry's largest white population, slaves outnumbered whites three to one, with 57,000 slaves compared with just 19,000 whites. Given these profound population differences, white Carolinians throughout the early national era, particularly those who did not directly benefit from slaves' labor, often experienced enslaved mobility with a real sense of dread. Like William Bartram decades earlier, residents of the Lowcountry (and increasingly across the state) were continually confronted with what seemed to many a profound dilemma: with tens of thousands of slaves forcibly laboring and moving throughout South Carolina, how could one know the difference between an itinerant laboring slave and a potentially insurrectionary black Carolinian? For most white Carolinians, black Carolinians were always already both: their race presupposing their simultaneous status as slave and rebel, criminal and loyal servant. The emergence of paternalism as a discourse of mastery provided some ideological comfort to South Carolinians, but such control seemed to dissipate on the roads and rivers that black Carolinians frequented across the coastal plain.[44]

Provincial leadership and state legislators were aware of the fear and dangers that accompanied a large enslaved labor force, and thus maintained strict laws regarding the oversight of black Carolinians. In 1740, in 1743, and again in 1751, the provincial assembly strengthened the slave code, crafted harsher punishments for violators, and built in more inducements for planters and merchants to obey laws considered essential for the colony's safety. Planters who did not live on their plantations "six months in every year" were required to "keep upon the same, some white man, capable of performing patrol duty." The acts drew clear lines around a slave's ability to move freely through the coastal plain, stating that a slave could not be "out of the house or plantation, where such slave resides, or without some white person in company." If a slave was caught beyond the boundaries of his plantation and refused to submit to an examination by any white person, it became "lawful for such white person to pursue, apprehend, and moderately correct such slave." If the slave were to "assault and strike such white person, *such slave may be lawfully killed.*"[45]

White Carolinians not only were given the right to control the enslaved population but were expected and even ordered to participate in the governance of slaves. The new laws clarified that "masters, overseers, or other persons, have the power to apprehend and take up any slave found out of his or her master's or owner's plantation at any time." The 1740 statute further delineated the worrying circumstances it sought to address, requiring white Carolinians to apprehend slaves "especially on Saturday nights or Sundays, or other holidays, not being on lawful business, or not with a ticket from the master, or not having some white person in company." Because the 1740 law was written in the shadow of the Stono Rebellion, it ordered white Carolinians to apprehend slaves with or without tickets if they found them "armed with wooden swords or other mischievous and dangerous weapons, and to disarm such slaves."[46]

Upholding the slave code was the responsibility of all Carolinians; and in this way the spatial governance of black Carolinians tethered together citizen and state. Patrols were typically made up of five local men, and after 1740, those men were to be drawn from local militia companies. Their duties were to visit each of the plantations in their neighborhood at least once a month, and to "correct" any slave they found outside of their homes without a pass. They were also tasked with searching slave quarters for firearms, or any goods they suspected were stolen. Taverns, homes, and boats could all be searched for suspected runaway slaves. The patrol's duty was, thus, to control and define acceptable spaces for black congregation. The slave code and patrolmen did this, theoretically, by forcibly keeping slaves on plantations and out of particular places such as taverns or markets. In such ways, slave patrols and state regulations turned all slaves—in their homes and in their daily travels—into suspected criminals. Nevertheless, despite the brutal stories frequently associated with the slave patrol, and their wide-ranging powers, the state's police power over the enslaved was never absolute, as regulations and patrols were administered only haphazardly. White control over the enslaved population and the coastal plain was easier to assert than to actualize.[47]

Slave patrols, in fact, only sporadically traversed South Carolina's countryside, and the actions of individual patrollers, planters' prerogatives, the state's lax enforcement of the slave code, and judicial interpretation of slave law all worked to check their power. The 1740 act required patrols to meet "at least once every fortnight" to search for slaves, thus from the beginning making them a periodic rather than regular undertaking. Patrols also limited their searches to constructed roads and well-known paths. While this growing transportation network provided important connections between and among plantations, they provided patrols access to only a small fraction of the coastal plain. The subsequent difficulties that patrols faced were exacerbated by the continual growth of the plantation complex. The patrol's responsibilities were further complicated by the dispersed and enlarged slave population that was necessarily crossing perceived plantation boundaries—which themselves were not well known or fixed in this era of growth. In addition, patrolmen traveled along roads looking for runaway slaves, but it was the enslaved who had constructed the roads and subsequently knew the paths in a different and more intimate way.[48]

Perhaps because of the overwhelming odds against them or the difficult terrain they were required to cross each night, throughout the eighteenth and early nineteenth centuries the patrol duty remained poorly administered. In the Patrol Act of 1740, the provincial assembly noted that many "irregularities have been committed by former patrols arising chiefly from their drinking too much liquor before or during their time of their riding on duty." Despite colonial leaders' attempts to enforce patrol duty more closely, by 1766 residents in Charlestown presented as a grievance "the want of patrol duty being duly done." Patrols were hard to organize and more difficult to keep orderly, particularly in times of seeming quiet and peacefulness. In coastal parishes, wealthy planters, who were considered most responsible for the situation, frequently shirked their duties or paid others to patrol in their stead. Governor John Drayton argued that "in the lower parts of the state, where regulations of this kind are particularly needed those who are most interested in the preservation of peace and order, have, from a mistaken notion of things thrown the whole of this burden on others less fortunately circumstanced." In 1820, Governor John Geddes noted that the patrol duty "is still so greatly neglected in several of our parishes and districts, that serious inconveniences have been felt and cannot fail to continue."[49]

The patrols' dereliction of duty stemmed partly from the severe limitations to their power that planters sought and achieved. Throughout the colonial and early national period, the state and individual planters acted to limit and check the power of the patrol. For the most part, these limits were meant as precautions against the likelihood that patrols might trespass against the property rights of the slaveholder. For example, while patrols were able to punish suspected runaway slaves, they were "restrained" to a maximum of twenty lashes and could not execute their suspects. More importantly, patrols were limited by the slave pass system, which while perceived as a check on slave mobility is better understood as an extension of slave owners' property claims.[50]

Many scholars have asserted that the slave pass was one of the many ways that planters maintained their control over the slave population, limiting their movement beyond the boundaries of the plantation. And in many ways the pass did act as a check on the freedom of the enslaved population, forever premising their movements on planters' needs and permissiveness. But the pass served multiple purposes in South Carolina during the late colonial and early national eras. Given the frequency and necessity of everyday slave movement in the coastal plain, passes importantly extended planter authority and claims of ownership over mobile enslaved bodies, and provided an important differentiation between slaves who had run away from plantations and those simply, and obligingly, beyond the plantation's walls. Slave passes were, in effect, written extensions of planter power. They acknowledged a planter's liability for an enslaved person's actions while outside of the plantation boundaries, and simultaneously maintained the planter's abstract claims of property ownership over enslaved persons' bodies. Tickets, then, transformed slaves into abstracted, embodied extensions of their owners' desires—granting them the legal rights to move to and fro and into places that might otherwise have been deemed dangerous. With a ticket, a slave could travel up and down South Carolina's numerous waterways, visit neighboring plantations, and even enter stores and markets to conduct trades for their owners and, some feared, for themselves.[51]

Moreover, given the variety of slaves' activities, both on and off the plantation, passes were necessarily and intentionally vague. It would have been virtually impossible for slave owners to articulate detailed sketches of their slaves' numerous activities beyond the physical limits of the plantation space. For example, on a single day in October 1796, Charles Drayton recorded that he sent his boat hands to his Long Savannah plantation to repair his sloop. After making those repairs, they were to load the boat with lumber and other provisions for the maintenance of Drayton's Jehossee plantation. At Jehossee Island, Drayton's boatmen were to load the sloop with calves and travel along the Stono River up the coast to Charleston. Any or all of these activities could take longer than Drayton accounted for in a ticket, might require additional travel or labor, and could take the enslaved boatmen through any number of available routes.[52]

Drayton frequently wrote of his sloop's delayed arrivals. On April 12, 1798, he noted that the "sloop from Jehossee unloaded [rice] yesterday morning & yet laying in the dock idling—she passed by Prasilla [April] 8. [Jack] said he arrived [April] 10 at evening being detained by Campbell's raft in Wappo Cut." Given the number of plantations in the Colleton and Beaufort districts, planters expected travel through Wappo Cut to be slowed by high traffic, and accepted these delays. These types of contingencies, which reflected everyday labor and mobility in the Lowcountry, required that passes maintain planters' property claims on enslaved bodies while simultaneously excusing and permitting slaves' unmonitored movement. A plantation complex that relied on the constant movement of goods and supplies necessitated that slave tickets do more than provide checks on slave mobility; they also had to provide slaves and their owners a sufficient degree of flexibility to maintain their agricultural enterprises.[53]

South Carolina's Constitutional Court recognized this, acknowledging the inability of planters to provide detailed descriptions for their slaves' frequent absences from the plantation. In an 1819 decision, they interpreted the state's slave-pass legislation accordingly. In a suit brought by Lewis Hogg against a "Mr. A. Keller," Hogg argued that Keller and the slave patrol that he managed had wrongfully whipped Hogg's unnamed slave. Keller and the patrol came across the enslaved man traveling through the countryside. Though Keller admitted that the victim of his violence produced a ticket from Hogg verifying his absence, Keller and the patrol acted on the belief that the slave was a runaway with an illegal pass. Again, many white Carolinians like Keller operated under the presumption that black Carolinians were always already potential criminals, and acted accordingly. Keller and his band argued that their actions were reasonable and legitimated by the state, as "the pass was not according to law; because it did not state to what place the negro was going."

The Constitutional Court, however, disagreed. It clarified the law in judging against Keller, stating, "The law does not require a master to state in every pass, to what place the negro shall be permitted to go. It is sufficient if it express a leave of absence."[54]

The state's acceptance of this "general pass" system lingered well into the antebellum era, as did the discomfiture that it caused among whites. An 1848 article in the *Daily Telegraph* noted that a general pass "to enable a slave to go at large, when and where he pleases, is an outrage on the community, illegal in itself and will no longer be recognized. With a proper and specific pass a slave is always safe." The editor's threats and guarantees were not directed at the enslaved community, members of which probably did not read the *Daily Telegraph*. His audience was rather the planters who did.[55]

The Constitutional Court's decision acknowledged a tacit approval of slave movement throughout early national South Carolina and reinforced wealthy planters' power throughout the state. The *Hogg* decision followed a familiar legal pattern of giving first priority to planter prerogatives and the requirements of the plantation enterprise. Despite regular complaints from citizens across the state regarding patrol impotency and the ability of slaves to move freely across the Lowcountry, there was clearly a limit on how many restrictions could be placed on the mobility of black Carolinians. This pattern would persist throughout the nineteenth century. Even in the face of their worst fears—slave insurrection—political leaders would not or could not restrain the economic engine of South Carolina: the enslaved labor force whose deployment and movement created virtually all wealth. Thus, while the state passed laws, pressured patrols, and acknowledged local police associations, empowering citizens to guard against rebellion and the feared depredations of runaways, it also had to place some limits on those powers, or risk injuring the plantation enterprise. The role of the slave patrol in South Carolina was not to stop slave mobility between and among plantations—such an action would have seriously hampered South Carolina's plantation enterprise. Rather, the role of the slave patrol was to monitor and limit the activities of the enslaved, an altogether different and perhaps more difficult goal. When a patrol ventured into a tavern, shop, or swamp, it was attempting to define the spatial limits of black South Carolina. But white claims on this space were also narrowed in this era because of the restrained power of the slave patrol, individual slaves' knowledge of the countryside, and white Carolinians' unwillingness to participate in the constant project of slave observation. The state's slave code and the actions of the patrol did serve to transform the enslaved into a class of always suspect subjects, but the plantation enterprises' need for mobile laborers prevented the state from altogether prohibiting enslaved movement.

Out of slave mobility, the Lowcountry became, then, a space of possibility. Each time enslaved boatmen traveled through the rivers and streams of the coastal plain, every time skilled laborers ventured to neighboring plantations to work, and whenever field hands sought reprieve from harsh labor by absconding into nearby swamps and marshes, they marked and gave new meaning to the landscape. Black Carolinians infused the coastal plain with religious significance, marked out economic entrepôts, and created heterogeneous neighborhoods and communities throughout the region. White Carolinians consistently encountered these places and bore witness to slaves' everyday spatial practices, which black Carolinians painstakingly maintained throughout this era. As planters and politicians sought to assert their economic and social ideas onto the space, they were continually frustrated by the black landscapes that made up the South Carolina Lowcountry.

CHAPTER FOUR

This Negro Thoroughfare
The Meaning of Black Movement

In February 1825, sixteen slaves left their new owner, George W. Morris. Morris reported that the men, women, and children were "living together in the woods near Col. Cattle's place" from "whence they were purchased and removed last February." Like countless other slaves in the early national era, the group returned to what they had previously known, the material world surrounding the plantation where they had for so long labored. Morris noted that the group was supported "by the negroes of the adjoining Plantations" and that the runaways had developed an entrepreneurial livelihood in the countryside. For the better part of the year, the group was known to "pick black moss, make baskets and take them to the city in boats through Wappoo Cut," where they subsequently sold their wares at "Mr. Bennett's Mill," a site that was a central hub in the illegal trade network of mobile slaves on the Ashley River side of Charleston. At Bennett's Mill, the group would have been able to exchange their handmade baskets for the supplies and food that enslaved boatmen delivered to the city in the course of their labors, as well as the licit and illicit goods that Charleston slaves offered for exchange. Morris's slaves took advantage of the very infrastructure designed by the state to liberate white Carolinians' economic activities to support their own independence. In doing so, they, alongside countless others, articulated a spatial politics that disrupted the presumed racial exclusivity of state space. While planters, state planners, and political leaders may have imagined that black Carolinians' movement was limited to the whims and desires of their masters, African and African American slaves consistently undermined this narrow presumption, and in so doing challenged and reshaped state space.[1]

When Morris's slaves traveled back to the edge of their former plantation, they were not simply avoiding harsh labor or merely resisting the power of their new master. Rather, they were participating in, creating, and maintaining the dense socioeconomic world that black Carolinians painstakingly created in the coastal plain over generations of habitation. On a daily basis, in the everyday performance of their duties as mobile enslaved laborers, black Carolinians traveled to the city from surrounding plantations, ferrying boats and carts filled with commodities bound for the city's harbors. They floated lumber, rice, and cotton down the region's rivers through busy canals and cuts to mills in Charleston and Georgetown. And, of course, they continued all the while to labor on plantations throughout the expansive Lowcountry complex. But while in town, during their travels, and amid their daily toils on their owners' plantations, black Carolinians inscribed their own meanings onto the landscape. South Carolina's slaves subsequently undermined and redefined the state's infrastructure and territory. At the same time, black Carolinians became rooted to the landscape, staking their own differential claims to South Carolina's landscape and waterways—the specific places where they buried their loved ones; where they practiced their religion in the region's swamps and marshes; where they crafted trade networks along the banks of rivers, at busy intersections, and by the edges of plantations.[2]

This chapter examines the sociospatial practices of enslaved Carolinians in early national South Carolina—in particular the Lowcountry, where the majority of black Carolinians resided—and uncovers the varied landscapes, communities, and politics that their practices produced. As discussed in chapter 3, the everyday experiences of the enslaved in the late colonial and early national eras revolved, in part, around their mobility and subsequent everyday presence in South Carolina's public spaces. No group embodied this mobility more than enslaved boatmen, who daily transported goods and supplies between plantation and market. At well-known and hidden spaces, black boatmen marketed wares that they acquired during their travels—pilfering from the goods they transported and trading with the slaves, free blacks, and poor whites they encountered in their journeys throughout the coastal plain. These daily travels made coastal waterways central to black Carolinians' experience of the Lowcountry, and black boatmen essential to the development and maintenance of black Carolinians' sociospatial practices.[3]

But enslaved patroons were not alone in the construction of the early national black Lowcountry. At the plantations that boatmen visited, as well as in the swamps and marshes that honeycombed the Lowcountry, slaves developed a variety of ideas concerning the landscape. Like Morris's slaves, many treated these spaces as vital to their economic practices: they raised their own crops, foraged for herbs and supplements to their diets, and hunted for subsistence and market alike. But their needs and desires were not limited to nourishment and purse alone. Black Carolinians also sought out spiritual and emotional sustenance and transformed the landscape through their efforts, imbuing swamp, marsh, and plantation with nature spirits, ancestral graves, secret initiation societies, and social networks. These sites provided sustenance to enslaved Carolinians and rooted them to the coastal plain as they developed a familiarity and intimacy with the landscape through their everyday practices. When new slaves arrived in the region throughout the first decades of the early national era, they found solace from the brutalities of slavery in the places that black Carolinians had carved into the Lowcountry. On Charleston Neck, at the edges of plantations, and within their quarters, newly arrived slaves saw familiar symbols, heard of spirits connecting them to their ancestors, and recognized the familiar cadence of West and West-Central African languages.[4]

The spatial familiarity that the enslaved established on plantations, alongside rivers and creeks, and in the alleys and wharves of Charleston and Georgetown continually drew the enslaved back to these spaces. Such places became marked, as it were, on black Carolinians' own map of South Carolina. Following the Revolution, slaves were regularly sold to backcountry plantations and transferred from one Lowcountry property to another as planters responded to postcolonial exigencies by redeveloping the plantation enterprise—transferring their capital from inland swamps to tidal rice and inland cotton plantations. In response to their ensuing displacement, many slaves ran away, but they did not run haphazardly into the countryside. Instead, many ran back to the plantations and regions from "whence they were sold," Charleston Neck, the wharves of Georgetown, or well-known maroon encampments. They ran, that is, to what they knew—be it the worlds they constructed or the embrace of distant spirits, languages, and cultural practice.[5]

Black Carolinians, then, made their own claims to South Carolina's territory. In transforming riversides into economic entrepôts, Charleston and the Neck into social centers, and plantation spaces into spiritual havens, black Carolinians challenged the very notion of an exclusively white state space. The dilemma for white Carolinians, of course, was that they relied upon slaves to construct, maintain, and secure the state; subsequently, black Carolinians were afforded numerous opportunities to inscribe the landscape with a variety of new meanings. This was not simply an inconvenience to planters and state planners. When the enslaved traded at river landings and gathered together on plantations and on the streets and alleys of Charleston, they transgressed the strict restrictions that were meant to bar access and give limited meaning to South Carolina's state space. State planners imagined roads, canals, bridges, and river landings as nodes in a complex economic infrastructure, specifically designed to promote the industrious, individual, slaveholding independence of its white citizenry. When the enslaved used South Carolina's infrastructure for similar purposes—economic gain, survival, spirituality, social conviviality—the exclusivity and presumed ascendancy of state space were disrupted.[6]

The complexity of meaning and frequency of black movement directly shaped the production of South Carolina's territory as well as the state's earliest governing practices. Slave owners, planters, and state leaders may have imagined that enslaved movement bent toward their own needs, but they also made clear in their diaries, their petitions, and their actions that the everyday mobility of their slaves undermined their power and claims to control. When Charles Drayton's boatmen pilfered his stock or were delayed in their journey, he labeled their activities "roguery"; when they absconded from plantations, they were "runaways"; and when they established encampments in the swamps and forests of the coastal plain, they became "banditti." Confronted with the results of black Carolinians' independent will amid their necessary laboring mobility, whites saw only resistance. Planters believed that when slaves ran away, when they participated in an illicit economy, or when they practiced their own forms of spirituality, they were doing nothing more nor less than defying their owners. That such activities were born out of the demands slave owners imposed on their slaves and took place in the very sites designed to promote white independence not only frightened white Carolinians but also came, by the end of the early national era, to dictate South Carolina's improvement agenda.[7]

The Possibility of Space

When smallpox struck Davison McDowell's plantation in 1826, "Toney took himself with the Red Boat the day we cut rice." Fleeing disease or the everyday brutalities of slavery, Toney reclaimed his body, taking himself from the plantation and floating up the Pee Dee River to Georgetown. There he knew he would encounter his peers, as well as a variety of shopkeepers, grogshop owners, and free blacks who would supply and perhaps even entertain him during his brief foray away from McDowell's plantation. The coastal city was the center of the plantation complex north of Charleston, and thus the social and economic hub of the region, and not just for white Carolinians. Residents of Georgetown regularly complained of "the illegal trade with negroes after night in and about the town & wharves of Georgetown."[8]

Toney knew what to find in Georgetown because the exigencies of plantation labor mandated that he routinely visit the coastal town to complete his everyday duties. Likewise, countless black Carolinians gained a familiarity with the coastal plain beyond the plantation as they labored on roads, bridges, and neighboring plantations; herded cattle; constructed and maintained causeways, canals, and cuts; hunted for fowl and deer; and foraged in nearby swamps and forests. They learned the region's urban landscapes, too, as they delivered goods, went to market, and processed rice and cotton at coastal mills. For generations, these activities provided black Carolinians with an intimate knowledge of the coastal plain, and that knowledge in turn grew deeper as it took daily shape in the toils of cattlemen, sawyers, boatmen, field hands, and hunters who ventured ever more deeply into the forests and savannahs of the Lowcountry, and who returned again and again to the places they knew so well. In 1817, Isaac Ball's cattleman left his Pee Dee River plantation after being "whiped for lettin' the oxen get in the oats field and ordered in the [rice] field to work." The cattleman absconded to the "Black River" region west of the plantation, an area to which his labors had frequently taken him, and about which he had accumulated a knowledge that would aid him in his time away from the plantation.[9]

Perhaps no other group among enslaved black Carolinians acquired more knowledge of the South Carolina countryside than boatmen. Vital to the maintenance of the plantation enterprise, enslaved patroons knew nearly every inch of the rivers, creeks, canals, cuts, and streams that crisscrossed the coastal plain. The constant movement of goods and supplies along the Lowcountry waterways provided bondsmen with a virtual smorgasbord from which they could illegally supply themselves. White Carolinians were well aware that their slaves used the waterways for illicit trade, but despite their repeated efforts they were unable to do much about it. When a 1771 law obliged owners of coastal vessels to maintain at least one white person on board each boat, many planters simply ignored the requirement. Planters and merchants relied on enslaved patroons, and maintained their dependence even when confronted with irrefutable evidence that their slaves were stealing goods. Henry Laurens considered selling Abraham, his enslaved patroon, when he learned the extent of his illicit activities. However, the importance of knowledgeable boatmen in the Lowcountry stayed Laurens's hand, and he eventually gave Abraham control of his own boat in the plantation's small fleet.[10]

Entrusted to transport commodities from plantation to market, enslaved boatmen used these lengthy, unmonitored trips to supplement their meager diets and acquire goods for trade. Henry Laurens ordered one of his overseers, when loading his boat for a return journey to Charleston, to "take care to prevent an intercourse between [the] boat & plantation Negroes & let me know how Abram the Patroon of the Boat behaves." Charles Drayton habitually noted the deficiencies of his ship's cargo upon arrival, and though he devised a variety of tactics to restrain his bondsmen, the thefts continued. Enslaved boatmen took pecks and bushels of rice from barrels destined for Charleston; stole rum, wine, and food meant for planter tables; and quietly redirected other supplies bound for plantations. Davison McDowell noted that his enslaved boatmen, John and George, each took three "bushels of corn while watching the flat." In 1796, the great Yazoo flood injured much of the coastal plain's corn crop, destroying 200 bushels of Charles Drayton's corn. This loss must have greatly affected his bondsmen's barely adequate food supply. Jack, Drayton's patroon, took matters into his own hands, stealing ten of the 104 bushels of corn that Drayton subsequently purchased in Charleston.[11]

Enslaved boatmen slipped more than food away from their owners. In August 1813, when his schooner arrived at Charleston with a supply of lumber, Drayton complained that it contained only "half a cord of wood. Rogues!" Coastal boats transported lumber, bricks, lime, seashells, turpentine, cotton, ammunition, guns, clothing, and tools throughout the Lowcountry. Henry Laurens noted a shortfall in the lumber his boatman transported. As he woefully explained to his overseer, "Abraham made out only 22 cords of wood which he was pleased to sell without orders & therefore I have the greatest reason to suspect him of knavery. You will be very watchful over all his steps & remember what I said to you about the wood put on board his schooner." On October 30, 1798, Will, one of Drayton's bondsmen at Drayton Hall, went to Charleston to retrieve "two barrels of lime and 500 bricks." In July 1808, he sent Sampson back to his Jehossee Island plantation with a "gun, keg of gunpowder, etc." Although Drayton did not suspect either Sampson or Will of plundering their loads, the transportation of these goods highlighted the possibilities that river carriage provided.[12]

In the completion of their daily tasks, enslaved boatmen supplemented their diets and acquired possession of important supplies and desired goods to trade in the Lowcountry's vibrant illegal marketplace located on the region's rivers, canals, cuts, landings, and plantation edges. Laurens complained to Abraham Schad, one of his overseers, about the actions of Amos, who Laurens believed "has a great inclination to turn Rum Merchant." Laurens believed that Amos "has or may send up some by my flat Boat to Mayrant's Landing," presumably to trade among his enslaved peers. In creating and participating in these markets, the enslaved altered the meaning of the state's economic infrastructure in ways that diverged from the meanings that white Carolinians had assigned the space. Provincial and state leadership, planters, and yeomen imagined river landings, roads, causeways, bridges, canals, and cuts as a way to connect distant properties to the metropole, and as routes for the safe delivery of goods and supplies in the expansive plantation complex. But white Carolinians entrusted slaves with the construction and maintenance of these thoroughfares, and tasked their boatmen and carters with the transportation of materials throughout the region. And, more often than not, these activities occurred outside of white Carolinians' watchful gaze. This granted slaves, particularly but not exclusively male slaves, an opportunity to reinscribe the landscape in their own varied ways.[13]

In part, black Carolinians were able to impose their own meanings onto the landscape because of the inadequacies of the outdated transportation system that crisscrossed the coastal plain. By the early national era, the coastal plain had outgrown much of its infrastructure, and the byways and thoroughfares, landings, and cuts designed for the transportation of goods were choked with boats, lumber rafts, wagons, and carts. The sheer volume of waterborne traffic between Charleston and the Lowcountry's commodity-producing plantations caused countless delays in boatmen's travels. Josiah Smith wrote of a monthlong interruption in the return voyage of George Austin's schooner, which was only traveling between Charleston and his property on the Pee Dee River. Meanwhile, in 1801 Charles Drayton's schooner arrived at his Jehossee Island plantation after four days of travel. Drayton noted in his diary that his boatmen were "detained in New-cut by rafts laying across it." New Cut, carved into the coastal plain by order of the colonial government in 1712 to create a direct link between the Wadmalaw and Stono Rivers, provided the numerous plantations within St. Paul's Parish, St. John's Parish, and St. Bartholomew's Parish in Colleton District access to Charleston's mills, harbor, and market. Boatmen from wealthy estates on Wadmalaw Island, Edisto Island, and the plantations that skirted the edge of the Edisto River all traveled through New Cut to transport commodities and supplies between the plantation complex and Charleston. It is no wonder that Drayton noted the delays caused by heavy traffic; the cut was originally designed to be but "ten feet wide and six feet deep," not nearly large enough for the volume of traffic that passed through it during the early national era.[14]

Spurring this traffic was the ever-growing plantation enterprise, and the motor behind that enterprise was, of course, black Carolinians. Although Colleton District witnessed an overall drop in population during the early national era, the number of enslaved residents remained well over 20,000 throughout the first decades of the nineteenth century, representing a staggering 82 percent of the overall population in the district. These men and women labored on plantations of immense size. In 1783, over 60 percent of the plantations in the Stono–St. Paul Parish area were over 500 acres in size, and more than a third were between 1,000 and 3,000 acres in size. The brutal labor of the bondsmen and bondswomen on these massive plantations was manifested in the steady production of commodities, which were regularly transported to Charleston through coastal waterways via New Cut. Correspondingly, the maintenance of this overwhelming labor force required the nearly constant arrival of supplies and materials transported through the same waterways. This incessant traffic resulted in an uninterrupted stream of canoes, flat-bottomed schooners, and sloops, and their enslaved crews through New Cut on the Stono River, Watts Cut on the Edisto, and Wappoo Creek near Charleston. These ships competed for space on waterways with the massive rafts of lumber as new planters in the state's interior shipped acres of freshly cut timber to Charleston. Similarly busy water-bound crossings were located throughout South Carolina, as planters throughout the state depended on boatmen to transport commodities and supplies between their plantations and Charleston.[15]

At these busy intersections, which were vital to the maintenance of South Carolina's plantation enterprise, enslaved Carolinians inevitably gathered to trade and socialize. At the end of each year, when the season's harvest was ready for market, the rivers and cuts that flowed to Charleston's harbors were inundated with boatmen. If during this busy time a schooner or sloop went to ground in a cut, or went sideways in the narrow channel, traffic would grind to a halt. While waiting for their turn to pass through the cut, or for enslaved carpenters to make repairs on damaged ships, boatmen sat idle and were afforded an opportunity to converse and trade among themselves. Boatmen also took these opportunities to disembark from their ships to interact with slaves on nearby plantations or runaways who resided in the swamps and marshes that surrounded the thoroughfares. Black peddlers paddled their canoes among the flats, schooners, and sloops that lay idle, offering a variety of goods. At Prasilla, a site somewhere in the vicinity of Wappoo Creek and the Stono River, enslaved boatmen frequently interacted with Joe, "the negro pedlar." In 1801, Charles Drayton's schooner lost both her masts because "Jack [was] loitering with the schooner at Prasilla or it might have been avoided." In March 1805, Jack took Quash, one of Drayton's carpenters, from Jehossee plantation, and three days later they were reportedly "at Prasilla rogueing." Their visit to Prasilla almost certainly involved illegal trading, for two weeks later Drayton noted that there was an "investigation of Jack patroon at Prasilla concerning his friend Joe the negro pedlar." These activities obviously concerned white Carolinians, particularly planters, who increasingly sought to limit their slaves' interactions with the outside world, even when doing so directly threatened to impede the free movement of goods along the state's infrastructure.[16]

For example, planters and private property owners were, in the face of black Carolinians' illicit trade, increasingly loath to share their riverside landings with their neighbors. Planters who created such impediments did so specifically in the hopes of isolating their slaves, limiting their interactions and movement. Nathaniel Heyward, John Gibbes, Ann Gibbes, and Daniel Blake responded to a request made by Colleton District residents for more riverside landings—which would have been built on the Heyward, Gibbes, or Blake properties—by pleading with the assembly to deny the request, arguing that "the establishment of a public landing at either of their plantations would be attended with very great inconvenience." Specifically they believed that "public landings" would be "productive of much evil," as they would provide "free access to their plantation to the bold and the vagrant who resort to places of that sort." They argued that there were "many pedling boats which frequent the river, who want only a public landing as a station to enable them to remain in the vicinity of the large and productive rice plantations." Peddlers were not the planter's primary concern. Instead, it was their potential customers: enslaved men and women. The petitioners believed that itinerant traders sought a landing "for the purpose of trading with the negroe slaves to the very great loss of the owners and corruption of such slaves." As these wealthy planters knew only too well, black Carolinians used the state's economic infrastructure for their own purposes. And white Carolinians were willing to alter the infrastructure of the state to bar the enslaved from such opportunities, even at the cost of limiting their neighbors' mobility and economic access.[17]

Black boatmen and peddlers, however, did not limit their activities to riverside meeting places. As the plantation system developed, slaves carved canals and cuts from creeks and rivers to the plantations where they labored, providing the properties with access to a ready supply of water for rice cultivation and to South Carolina's arterial transportation system. But these canals and cuts simultaneously offered boatmen, peddlers, and runaways access to plantations as well. In January 1803, Simpson, a black peddler, visited Jehossee Island to retrieve "his pedling canoe, rum cask, empty bags, liquor measures, tobacco & crops for trade." Drayton's Jehossee Island overseer captured Simpson as he traveled through the canal that connected the plantation to the river.[18]

The regularity of waterborne travel meant that these types of interactions occurred with surprising frequency, and through their repetition these cuts, canals, landings, and bridges, despite the concerted efforts of individual white Carolinians and state leaders, became central to black Carolinians' social and economic lives. As sloops, schooners, and canoes cut through the still waters of the man-made canals, black boatmen transgressed the boundaries of what many presumed to be exclusively white territory, and simultaneously remarked the sites as black spaces in the coastal plain; subsequently other slaves used the surrounding environs to trade, socialize, and survive. When Morris, the planter mentioned earlier, sought out his runaway slaves, he noted that they could be found at "Wappoo Cut and its landing." Patrols frequently found runaway slaves in the cut and its nearby marshes. White petitioners noted that Elliott's Cut, between the Ashepoo and Pon Pon Rivers, was "seldom if ever used but by runaways and Negroes unlawfully trading from River to River." By 1813, Elliott's Cut had become so central to black socioeconomic activity that white residents referred to it as a "Negro thoroughfare."[19]

Time and again, when slaves fled their owners' plantations, they immediately made for these busy intersections. They would steal canoes and rafts from their owners to make for the riparian hubs, where they knew they would meet their peers. In 1798, an advertisement in a Charleston newspaper reported that "a canoe, about 28 feet long and 4 ½ wide," was "taken from some runaway negroes." Runaways stole the yawl from Charles Drayton's schooner in the summer of 1800. When militia and patrolmen overtook maroon encampments, they typically found the groups outfitted with canoes and rafts, a veritable maroon flotilla. For instance, when the Georgia and South Carolina militia overtook the Savannah River maroon encampment, they found "14 or 15 boats or canoes." Residents of Colleton District petitioned the General Assembly for relief concerning the runaways encamped there. They noted that the "navigation of the rivers and creeks" was "excessively dangerous," because the runaways were furnished "with boats."[20]

Whether they had water carriage or not, runaway slaves continually made for the Lowcountry's waterways. There they knew that they would encounter friendly slaves and boatmen who would trade with them, furnish them with supplies, or at least entertain them on their brief forays. Terry, one of Davison McDowell's slaves, was "taken in Waccamaw," a coastal river near Georgetown. In 1793 the overseer at Elias Ball's plantation wrote of "Mr. Moultrie's Negro Man" who had "been skulking on Waccamaw Neck" with the overseer's "two wenches." In 1800, Arthur Hughes highlighted similar practices south of Charleston in his newspaper notice regarding his runaway slaves, Hercules and Tom, "who had been for three years past, and are now between Wappoo-cut and Ashley River."[21]

In addition to these heavily trafficked intersections, boatmen also visited and stayed on neighboring plantations as they traveled up and down South Carolina's rivers. In 1785, residents of St. James Santee Parish, near Georgetown, petitioned the General Assembly, presenting as a grievance "that patroons of Schooners and other small craft are allowed (as they pass and repass up and down our rivers) to trade, traffick, barter, and sell to and with Negroes." Planters and politicians long complained of this practice, and aspired to limit these types of visits. But throughout the early national era, the travels and activities of enslaved patroons remained unmonitored in any systematic way. It was only by chance that Charles Drayton found his schooner docked at Rantowles Bridge. When he questioned the toll-man at the bridge, he discovered that the ship had lain at anchor for over a day, as "Jack patroon left her last night to make some visits and is yet absent." Through these visits black Carolinians, and particularly boatmen, expanded the limits of their socioeconomic networks, maintaining intimate connections and economic contacts with their distant plantation neighbors. Toward the end of the eighteenth century, a planter on the Savannah River commented that it was "common practice for trading boats and others to land their people, and remain whole nights and days on the plantation." While white Carolinians may have imagined plantation boundaries as inviolable, slaves regularly demonstrated their porous qualities.[22]

Boatmen and peddlers knew they would meet other enslaved people in their daily travels, for the rivers and creeks that bordered plantations were also central to the everyday activities of resident slaves who were not on the move as a matter of employment. Enslaved men and women fished and oystered along the coast and in the rivers and creeks that surrounded their plantations. As one historian has recently argued, slaves also used the rivers and creeks for pleasure—swimming to cool off from their day's activities or to participate in competitive races. Black sportsmen dove into the coastal waters and rivers of the Lowcountry, wrestling sharks, alligators, and devil-rays. On some Lowcountry rivers, the enslaved even went so far as to alter the nautical landscape to facilitate their fishing exploits. Along the Ogeechee River, slaves "in the neighborhood were in the habit of getting fish and oysters." Below a certain point on the river, shellfish were known to be "available in abundance." To enable their acquisition at half-tide, the enslaved "cut rocks and removed other obstruction[s] from this creek to enable them to pass." The enslaved, it seems, sometimes made their own improvements to the coastal plain's infrastructure.[23]

To be sure, however, while the enslaved reshaped the Lowcountry landscape to address their varied needs, their encounters with the space always began with the brutal labor demands placed on them by both their owners and South Carolina's government. Building bridges and roads, digging canals and cuts, and constructing plantation spaces may have afforded slaves an opportunity to intimately engage the coastal plain, but these interactions came at a high price. Disease-bearing mosquitoes infested swamps and rivers where they labored, and the stagnant waters of constructed rice fields and canals allowed the deadly pests to thrive. If disease did not kill the region's slaves, the labor itself often did. Construction work was often the most toilsome and dangerous labor for slaves in the whole of the Lowcountry. Because the difficult labor was considered menial, planters frequently assigned the tasks to their newest slaves, who were often the most vulnerable.[24]

For those men and women who arrived in South Carolina from distant African ports, the initial experience of plantation labor was incredibly shocking. Unlike those who had long resided in South Carolina, new arrivals did not yet know the landscape as a space where survival was possible. When they arrived, particularly in the post-Revolutionary era, they most likely were placed in quarantine. There they sat, with their dead and dying peers—relieved to be off ship, but most likely exhausted, sick, and despondent from the months-long journey they had just completed. There they remained until it was time to be taken into the market for sale. For most of the roughly 30,000 men and women imported into Charleston in the early nineteenth century, coastal South Carolina was but a staging ground for the remainder of their journey. From Charleston, they were sent overland to the western territories, or by sea to Mobile and New Orleans for future sale to sugar and cotton planters. Still, many thousands of the recent African arrivals remained in South Carolina, taking up residence on tidal rice and Sea Island cotton plantations or transported to the backcountry to aid in the rapid development of western South Carolina.[25]

Wherever they went, newly arrived enslaved Africans had to adjust quickly. If planters purchased them for field labor, they were immediately put to work doing the most difficult tasks on the plantation. This most likely meant that they cleared swamps, marshes, and forests for the development of rice and cotton fields, or drained swampland and aided in the construction of massive earthen embankments. Lowcountry planters like Samuel Porcher, for instance, purchased many recent arrivals to aid in massive improvement projects like those he devised at Mexico, his Santee River plantation. Mexico rested directly beneath the southern bank of the Santee-Cooper Canal. After the massive flooding that destroyed so many plantations in the 1790s, Porcher purchased his neighbor's lands, adding to his already sizable holdings, and sought to protect his property from the still-dangerous floodwaters. Porcher sent his slaves into the dangerous Santee River swamp to build the massive earthwork. When completed, the embankment was four miles long, thirty feet wide at the base, nine feet in height, and wide enough at the top for two men to "ride abreast." To restrain the Pee Dee River's floodwaters, David R. Williams similarly built a five-mile embankment to protect his valuable tidal rice property. As newly arrived slaves labored on these projects, their first interactions with the landscape were the most dangerous and deadly. Such earthen dams became monuments to the early experiences of the recently enslaved, serving as physical reminders to black Carolinians that the landscape was defined, in part, by brutal and taxing labor.[26]

Still, for many of the slaves imported from West Africa and West-Central Africa in the late colonial and early national era, the Lowcountry was never simply a site of labor. Nor was it, for that matter, a wholly unrecognizable world. The size and brutality of the plantation system was certainly new and terrible, but to hear the rice stalks billowing in the ocean breeze or the sounds of mortar and pestle beating out the fine grain strangely echoed many of their seemingly distant lives. The overwhelming number of enslaved laborers resident in the coastal plain also meant that the men and women who arrived from West and West-Central Africa heard recognizable tongues, saw familiar symbols, and recognized their laboring peers' country marks. In the course of their labors, they possibly heard about the spirits that resided in the nearby springs and were introduced to the resident midwife or conjurer, spiritual leaders within the quarters.[27]

Nevertheless, it was an indescribably traumatic experience. And the countryside was filled with West Africans for whom enslavement was too much. Recently arrived Africans wandered the countryside as runaways and were routinely taken up by patrols and planters. For most, running away unquestionably reflected a refusal to oblige to the demands of driver and overseer. But many also left their new homes in search of the recognizable in the dense countryside. In April 1804, Charles Drayton noted, "An African lad strayed in" who could not speak English. Similarly, James Fraser noted that in 1805 "a young Negro fellow, cloathed in blue, his teeth filed, [who] cannot speak a word of English" arrived at his place on Charleston Neck. In 1786, a slave named June, "a new Negro fellow . . . of the Guinea country," was taken up by a patrol at Wappoo Cut. June either feigned ignorance to avoid harsh punishment or, just as likely, was unable to answer the patrol's questions because of a language barrier and the newness of his situation. Either way, when questioned he was only able to note that his owner's name was Spoone, but he did not know where he lived.[28]

Of course, these men and women did not simply wander aimlessly through the countryside. Dazed by the brutality of their enslavement, they also took note of the spaces and people they encountered as they worked. In the barracoons of the Central African coast, in slave ship and market, and traveling to plantations, the enslaved—even the newest arrivals—were never alone in their experiences. The conditions they experienced united disparate peoples, but more importantly, through each phase of the enslavement process, men and women found themselves beside their cultural brethren. This is not to deny that slaves crafted new cultural and social networks with those beside whom they lived and labored. It is merely to say that in the coastal plain, where mobility was a central feature of the plantation complex, black Carolinians had numerous opportunities to engage with one another while developing and maintaining the Lowcountry plantation landscape, through the course of which they often encountered men and women to whom they were connected culturally, spiritually, and linguistically.[29]

This was especially true in and around Charleston, where numerous slaves lived and labored and to which an untold number regularly traveled. A significant proportion of Charleston traffic passed through Charleston Neck—the strip of land that stretched westward from the city's edge between the Ashley and Cooper Rivers. White Carolinians came to consider it a "refuge for runaway negroes," both from the city and from the surrounding countryside. And while white residents in the city believed that slaves used the Neck as a convenient rendezvous for "robberies both in and out of the city," black Carolinians used the area for a variety of purposes. On the Neck, particularly on Sundays, slaves fished and hunted. And they gathered there to trade wares among themselves. As one witness to black Carolinians' activities on the Neck during a random weekend noted:

> Whoever may please to walk or ride, from this town, only so far as where the road divides near the Quarter-House, from about 3 hours before sun-setting on Saturday afternoon, 'till 11 o'clock at night, and from about two hours before sun-rising 'till an hour before it sets on Sundays, will not long be at a loss to answer the question; For tho' he will find the numbers passing and repassing between these periods, never to be less than four hundred; but often exceeding seven, yet he will rarely meet with more

than 40 or 50 tickets or letters in the hands of the Country Negroes, and never more than 4 or 5 such licenses amongst those that belong to the town, who generally make four-fifths of these strollers. . . . At such times likewise, those Negroes are, for the most part, provided with heavy hickory sticks or clubs, hanging to which they carry baskets, bags, or jugs, with provision, liquor, and perhaps plunder.[30]

Charleston Neck, as described above, was a social hub in the black Lowcountry, and for new slaves it served as a potential refuge and reprieve. Pierre Louis, "an African about 20 years of age," was sent to work on the Neck and never returned to his master. Likewise Jim, whose owner resided in the Mazyckborough neighborhood of Charleston, left his master and was "harbored by his countryman" on the "neck near the Race Ground." The racetrack was only a few miles across the isthmus created by the Ashley and Cooper Rivers from Mazyckborough, but for both master and slave it seemed a world away.[31]

Pierre Louis and Jim were not exceptions. Many enslaved Carolinians, including newly arrived West Africans who could more easily locate ethnic countrymen in an urban environment, escaped to Charleston after working in and learning about the city's spaces. Runaway notices accordingly noted the unique experiential knowledge that the enslaved acquired regarding the cityscape, as well as the ways they reconfigured the space. For example, Henry Doggett's slave tended his master's store in the Charleston market, and frequently visited the vendue district unmonitored by his master. Laboring every day in the economic center of Charleston gave Doggett's slave an understanding of the space, one he must have shared with numerous others. Meanwhile, when Plenty left the Goose Creek plantation where he labored, his master, Laval, advised constables to note that he "commonly strolls about the wharves and in the shops about Union Street at night." Laval also noted that Plenty was "well known in Charleston," and we can safely assume that he likewise knew the city quite well. In the execution of their duties, Plenty, Doggett's slave, and numerous others learned the location of merchants who would sell them wares, grog shops where they could wash away the despondency of their condition, the homes of their friends and family, and the places in the city where it was safe for them to gather. Such spatial knowledge also necessarily included the location of their countrymen—and this was especially the case for the newly arrived. In a landscape filled with new sights, sounds, and brutality, the welcoming lilt of familiar languages would be forever woven into slaves' sense of South Carolina's territory.[32]

It was this familiarity with the landscape—not simply an aversion to labor or a desire to escape from the horrors of bondage—that continually drew slaves back to Charleston, the Neck, and countless other locales scattered throughout the coastal plain. To be sure, gaining this familiarity was a process—one that included more than merely learning important landmarks. Ultimately, making the space their own meant that they had to remake the landscape in their own way. For example, one runaway slave recollected that after escaping construction labor on the Charleston-Hamburg Railroad, he made his way to the coastal city. Once there he visited the sites of economic exchange that he had come to know in the course of his everyday labors, going first "to the tavern where I used to stop when I carried eggs and peaches and other things to market." Despite being legally barred from many places within the city, black Carolinians were welcomed as customers and neighbors by many. Such sites were not created out of conspiracy, but as the unnamed runaway noted, were produced as a consequence of mundane laboring activities. Out of these daily practices, the enslaved remade spaces within and outside Charleston into sites of possibility.[33]

For many, the familiarity and possibility born out of daily activity was more difficult to acquire. The experiences in the countryside of Maddy, a recent arrival from West Africa, reflected those of many of his peers. In the early spring of 1805, Maddy reportedly wandered onto Elias Horry's South Santee River plantation. Horry noted that Maddy was a "Mandingo Negro Man" who could not speak English. Through one of his slaves, Horry was able to ascertain that Maddy did not know "his master's name, nor the way back to his plantation" from which he fled over a week prior. Horry was also able to gather that Maddy "was directed by a driver named Prince, who abused and imposed on him" while his absentee master was away; he knew this because the runaway "spoke the Guinea language to one of my Negroes." None of these details were exceptional. Drivers routinely abused recent arrivals as part of the seasoning process, and planters were mostly absent from their Lowcountry plantations. And it was not strange that a resident slave was able to communicate with Maddy, as at any point between 1750 through the beginning of the nineteenth century, tens of thousands of slaves born in West Africa labored in the Lowcountry.[34]

Horry's advertisement for Maddy presented his arrival as accidental and the presence of someone able to speak his language as fortuitous. But this was Horry's perspective. It seems possible (given the number of plantations in the region and the thousands of slaves whom he could have approached) that Maddy went to or was directed to the South Santee plantation to specifically rendezvous with Horry's slave. Certainly, some black Carolinians simply wandered onto Lowcountry plantations, shocked from the brutal conditions they experienced but struggled to understand. When a nine-year-old girl arrived at a store on Charleston's Gadsden's Wharf in the winter of 1808, it was probably safe to deem her a "strayed African." But Maddy was thirty-five: old enough to remember his home, his language, and his culture. While Maddy may not have known his way around the coastal plain, his cultural awareness could guide his experience; his language and spirituality remained the lenses through which he understood, traversed, and experienced the South Carolina Lowcountry. So while he may have been despondent at his situation and thus took flight, he also was attuned to that which he found recognizable in the countryside: he heard its whispers as he labored in the fields, glimpsed its symbols in forest and cabin niche, and recognized its purveyors among his distant peers.[35]

That Maddy ended up on a plantation alongside someone with whom he was able to speak in his native tongue may have seemed surprising to Elias Horry and other white Carolinians. But Horry and his planter peers conceived of the Lowcountry landscape as beginning and ending with their authority. They could only imagine a slave in the countryside as laboring, rebelling, or wandering helplessly and aimlessly. Through such presumed vulnerability, white Carolinians were able to imagine their own power. It was almost impossible for planters to imagine slaves traveling in the countryside with purpose beyond their demands. And even when they did, those acts were interpreted exclusively as resistance. But on plantations, in the countryside, on rivers and creeks throughout the coastal plain, and in the alleyways of Charleston, slaves crafted their own notions of space. And throughout the early national era, black Carolinians actively maintained these spaces, and in so doing defined and shaped the coastal plain.

Of course, South Carolina was not West Africa or West-Central Africa; newly arrived slaves encountered flora and fauna unlike anything they had ever known. But the intersecting streams, the proximity of the coast, and the dense swamps and marshes where they labored were not wholly different, either. Maddy and other recent African arrivals brought to South Carolina their own ideas of landscape. These ideas had been nurtured for generations in West Africa and West-Central Africa, had shifted over time as a consequence of a number of exigencies (including the slave trade), and necessarily affected how the enslaved experienced and subsequently defined the Lowcountry. Enslaved men and women not only saw and experienced South Carolina through such cultural lenses but also re-created important aspects of their spiritual lives within the Lowcountry landscape.[36]

For example, numerous limestone springs and sinks, with their constantly flowing and bubbling waters, proliferated throughout the coastal plain. Enslaved men and women recognized spirits, which they called *simbi*, within these flowing waters. Simbi spirits were an everyday aspect of Kongo spiritual lives, and were likewise significant in the experiences of black Carolinians in the Lowcountry, who incorporated these deities into their sociospatial understanding of the coastal plain. In their West-Central African context, simbi and other nature spirits were specifically associated with local communities, and especially to particular places. Importantly, when one clan or group rose to prominence within a community, these spirits, rooted in the landscape and not tied to any particular group, provided a nonlineal means by which land and natural resources could be administered. In other words, the spirits, rather than ancestral connections or kinship, became arbiters of political and social cohesion. The spirits gave outsiders with no familial connection to a particular domain a broader claim to the landscape, creating relationships and a sense of belonging where kinship ties did not exist.[37]

South Carolina's simbi spirits, many of which were located in some of the oldest settled regions of the Lowcountry, allowed newly arrived slaves, as one historian has recently argued, to "root themselves in a land that lacked adequate burial grounds, at least in the earliest times, and to form strong spiritual bonds with unrelated people." This would have likely been particularly important to the significant number of West-Central African men and women who were imported into the Lowcountry between 1800 and 1810. According to the Trans-Atlantic Slave Trade Database, of the 66,000 Africans imported into Georgia and South Carolina at the beginning of the nineteenth century, more than 26,000, or 40 percent, were from West-Central Africa. Their predominance in the Lowcountry had lasted for generations. West-Central Africans constituted over 30 percent of the Africans forcibly imported into South Carolina between 1730 and the Revolution. Moreover, according to one historian, West-Central Africans accounted for over 30 percent of all runaways in the same period. It is of course impossible to know, but it is possible that at least part of the reason why West-Central Africans ran away in such high numbers was precisely to locate such spirits.[38]

Simbi spirits were located throughout the Lowcountry. They were common and important enough among enslaved people to attract the attention of even the most modern, scientific planters. When traveling through the coastal plain, Edmund Ruffin heard of the "cymbee" at Woodboo Plantation. This particular spirit, according to the driver at the plantation, was "only seen when the sunshine is 'right up and down.'" Upon inquiring, Ruffin was told of other simbi that resided across the region. According to the black Carolinians he asked, the simbi typically came out at night, were "usually seen in a sitting position, on any low bridge or plank, crossing the water, or on the margin of a steep side." He also heard of simbi at Henry Ravenel's plantation, Pooshee Swamp, on the Santee-Cooper Canal, and at Eutaw Springs. The slaves who labored on these plantations and public works closely guarded the spirits, and Ruffin was told "it is bad luck to any one who may see a cymbee to tell of the occurrence, or refer to it." When Ravenel attempted to enclose "his fountain with masonry & confined & raised its water," an older black Carolinian "of the neighborhood" approached Ravenel and "remonstrated with him, upon the ground that the cymbee might be made angry & leave her haunt."[39]

The enslaved, particularly those from the Kongo-Angola region of West-Central Africa, were drawn to the springs, pools of water, and ponds where the simbi resided because they connected black Carolinians to the landscape and gave them spiritual strength in the face of slavery's brutality; furthermore, the water provided them with a connection to the land of the dead, and consequently their ancestors and former homes. In the mid-eighteenth century—when many West-Central Africans were forcibly transported to South Carolina—the Kongolese used the "reflecting surfaces of water as an avenue to communicate with the dead." When European traders introduced glass mirrors into the Kongo, they "transposed their notions of watery reflection onto the mirrors." Similarly, shiny and reflective objects were frequently placed atop the graves of slaves throughout the Lowcountry, allowing the living to continue communicating with their dead ancestors by connecting themselves to places where those ancestors lay buried. For individuals like Maddy who were recently transported to South Carolina—for those slaves who lacked ancestral gravesites in the Lowcounty—springs and streams where the simbi resided may have provided them with a portal to converse with their ancestors, and, despite the brutality they experienced as slaves, joined them to both the landscape and peers who resided there.[40]

The spirits that recent African arrivals found in the coastal plain were also central to the secret initiation societies to which many West and West-Central Africans belonged. The West African *Poro* and *Sande* initiation societies were the foundation for slave "seeking" in antebellum Lowcountry Christian conversion experiences. And West-Central African *kimpasi* societies were also progenitors of this process. In West African *Poro* and *Sande* societies, which were for men and women, respectively, individuals were socialized into their groups and prepared for an active role in their communities. Initiates in the groups withdrew from organized society for a period of time around puberty to participate in a spiritual journey "into the bush." They were then taken to a sacred site, "where they symbolically took leave of the earth and journeyed down into the spirit world, the world of the dead." This journey was meant to represent the "death of individualistic tendencies inimical to group survival." In other words, these experiences worked toward creating community, and because they were tied to spirits that were located in specific places, enslaved communities became united and attached to specific places through their shared experiences.[41]

The kimpasi, meanwhile, were initiation societies that rose up in Kongo society in times of social or physical misfortune. In times of famine, drought, warfare, or dire stress, kimpasi allowed people from a variety of groups to come together to reform themselves for the communal good. Initiation in the societies took place in isolated enclosures that contained sacred objects. Typically, these sites were located near a river, stream, or forest, which lay between the land of the living and the dead, and thus were considered the homes of spirits, like the simbi. Once initiated, members of the kimpasi primarily addressed communal suffering and strife. The violence and struggles that kimpasi sought to address in the Kongo "were the same forces that ensnared many West-Central Africans in the Atlantic trade in captives." Given the notable presence of West-Central Africans "amongst the first generations of enslaved people" in the Lowcountry, we can assume that some of the captives "included initiated people, or at least many familiar with the necessity of kimpasi."[42]

Given the secretive nature of these initiation societies, it is unlikely we could ever know the extent of their role in black Carolinians' experience of the coastal plain. However, because we know that black Carolinians believed simbi resided in springs, streams, and ponds in the coastal plain, and because we know that the cultural practices of the initiation societies were incorporated into subsequent Christian practices, it seems probable that these societies played important roles in the lives of at least some enslaved black Carolinians. At the very least, they were part of the cultural lens through which many African-born black Carolinians perceived and experienced the Lowcountry landscape during the late colonial and early national eras. Regardless, it is important to note that the enslaved men and women who sought out spirits and re-created distant societies were actively participating in a calculated political effort to undermine white claims to their bodies and lives. That such efforts revolved around community and place—two things that slave owners sought to deny them—was profound.[43]

To recognize the importance of these societies and spirits to the enslaved complicates our understanding of their everyday lives, and confounds our expectations of why slaves ran away, where they went, and how they survived in the countryside. In 1796, Ocra, a slave "of the Congo country with his country marks on his right shoulder and belly," was taken up by the patrol and brought to the Charleston workhouse after nearly four years' absence from his master's plantation. What did he do in all that time? Where did he go? How did he survive? That same year, a slave named Dinah was also captured and placed in the workhouse. A young woman, Dinah absconded from her master's plantation to give birth to her child, presumably with plans to never return. Why? For what reason did Dinah choose to depart her master—who was a doctor— at the time of birth? How did she and her infant survive in the unforgiving Lowcountry environment? To white Carolinians, Ocra's long survival alone in the backcountry and Dinah's choice to leave at the moment of her child's birth must have seemed astonishing. But to the enslaved, this movement was not out of the ordinary. Slavery, bondage, and brutality were extraordinary; the conditions slaves confronted as planters altered production methods, transferred them to new locations, and placed them under new management were bewildering; their decision to leave must have seemed, in many ways, normal. Movement away from and around the plantation, after all, was woven into the mobility that was already an integral aspect of their everyday labors.[44]

When slaves ventured into the countryside, they were never alone for long. Ocra, like his runaway peers, most likely developed a social network consisting of friendly slaves on Lowcountry plantations, his countrymen, boatmen who plied their trade up and down the rivers and creeks that crisscrossed the coastal plain, poor whites, or fellow runaways who resided in itinerant camps across the region. For example, in 1817, overseer John J. Hale wrote to Isaac Ball about one of his slaves named Lannon who "tuck himself of[f] the plantation without any provocation whatever." Hale believed that it would be "a long time before he is saw as he has a good many friends about hear [sic]." Lannon developed this network throughout the year, as according to Hale he had been "harbouring runaway negers about him all the summer." Like Lannon, Ocra likely was able to survive and even thrive in the coastal plain because similarly minded black Carolinians were always potentially at hand. Allies could be found throughout the Lowcountry. In 1765, Henry Laurens noted that Sampson, a recently purchased slave, ran away from his Mepkin plantation. As Laurens noted, "He went to Santee & fell in with a poor worthless fellow who entertained him near 8 months." There, it seems, Sampson learned "to make Indigo or at least to work at it & to speak tolerable good English." Despite eventually being returned to Laurens, Sampson "soon quitted it & returned to his former range which proves that he had not been unkindly treated there." In 1793, Charles Drayton complained of the late arrival of his sloop. The enslaved boatman told Drayton that he "was wind bound at the mouth of the Stono branch." But, as Drayton noted, the boatmen "had on board a run away wench." Drayton speculated that "roguery," not wind, "idled the voyage." And while this may have been true, for slaves like Ocra the conspicuous presence of boatmen on Lowcountry rivers—their sloops, schooners, and canoes overloaded with rice, corn, and other supplies—must have been a boon in their efforts to survive in the coastal plain, and were thus charted into their spatial conception of the region.[45]

Meanwhile, Dinah probably left her master's plantation to have her child delivered by an enslaved midwife. In 1829, John Peyre Thomas noted in his plantation diary that Old Peggy, a midwife, "left us this morning of her own accord & against our wishes." Although Peggy seemed to serve the wives of planters, traveling throughout the region for her various appointments she necessarily would have encountered enslaved women—both on and off plantations—who also required her services. Dinah and other pregnant slaves across the coastal plain knew of the existence of midwives like Peggy, and might have been able, if they deemed it a risk worth taking, to travel abroad to have their children delivered.[46]

Black Carolinians turned to more than the forests and swamps that surrounded their plantations for spiritual and bodily nourishment; they found those things at home too, on the very plantations where they spent the vast majority of their lives. And, just as they did in the countryside, on these plantations the enslaved crafted their own ideas of what this built environment meant. As noted above, several of the known simbi were located on plantations, including Pooshee and Wadboo. Also, when slaves buried their dead near where they labored, they transformed the landscape into a space to which they were connected, drawn in by the presence of their ancestors. In addition, archaeologists have uncovered evidence of some of the varied ways the enslaved transformed plantation spaces into sites specific to their spiritual needs. For example, Frogmore Manor on St. Helena Island contained a "conjurers house" among the enslaved quarters. Centered on the four walls of the midwife's cabin, researchers have uncovered the remains of four deposits consisting of fully articulated animals—a chicken and the remains of a cow—and in the other two, deposits of ash, burned shell, and metal. Taken together, the material remains represent a *Bakongo Cosmogram*, the presence of which would have transformed the cabin into a sacred site where slaves went to be healed or protected. Such a space provided Frogmore's enslaved inhabitants, as well as those who visited, with access to spirits, allowing them to participate in the "manipulation and maintenance of the supernatural world."[47]

The creation of such sacred spaces meant that specific places on specific plantations became central to the everyday lives of the enslaved. Plantations then, through the sociospatial practices of the enslaved, became the locus of extended kinship networks. There black Carolinians constructed their spiritual worlds, their access to the supernatural, and their ability to communicate with their ancestors. But these were more than simply sacred sites; the infusion of these cultural practices onto the plantation space ordered black Carolinians' everyday lives as well as their labor. Hugh McCauley, an overseer placed in charge of Isaac Ball's Pee Dee River plantation, noted the complicated practices that a particular community of slaves crafted on one plantation. McCauley was hired in 1814 to improve the output of the plantation by altering some of the enslaved community's everyday practices. To do that, his first order of business was to remove Jacob, one of the plantation drivers, from his post. According to McCauley, Jacob was "a great [sic] rascul." He was, reportedly, a dishonest man, though "also a Methodis[t] parson." McCauley wrote to Ball that Jacob did not "attend to orders," which Jacob argued was simply because he forgot. But McCauley believed that Jacob carried no authority with the plantation slaves, ordering them to do "only what pleases" them. This was in part, it seems, the result of Jacob's kinship to the majority of slaves on the plantation. McCauley noted that two-thirds of the slaves on the plantation were Jacob's "relations & he indulges them & then he can't do anything with the rest."[48]

Upon removing Jacob from his post, McCauley was confronted with a dissatisfied workforce that refused to participate in his prescribed labor arrangements. Slaves began running away from the plantation, tools went missing, and complaints steadily mounted. McCauley responded by making radical changes to plantation practices. He vaguely noted in a letter to Ball that he put a stop "to this pretended religion" that the slaves practiced at night, which he thought would put an end to "all those strifs [sic] and consternations." He also denied them access to additional provisions to which they had grown accustomed, in particular beef and salt-fish. But while McCauley intended to bring managerial order to the plantation by removing Jacob, monitoring nighttime religious practices, and curtailing access to provisions, he actually disrupted the social and spiritual world that the enslaved had carved into the space.[49]

In response to these changes, the Pee Dee River plantation slaves took matters into their own hands. When McCauley placed his own slaves in the role of driver, he erroneously believed he had resolved the issues of discipline and labor on the plantation. But when McCauley departed for Charleston, the plantation slaves resumed their previous practices. They did only as much work as they should have "dun in 3 days," and the new drivers were unable to keep the "negrows from stealing." The enslaved, meanwhile, also killed two "cattle [that] was on the Island" and hid a "morter and pisell" to grind their own private stock of rice away from the watchful eyes of both driver and overseer. As a result of their inactivity and theft, the crop fell short of expectations—so short, in fact, that McCauley, previously a sought-after overseer, noted that he was "positively ashamed for anyone to know [sic] the turnout of the present crop." Another overseer subsequently replaced him, just two years after beginning his service at the plantation.[50]

So connected were the enslaved to particular plantation spaces and the specific lives they constructed on them that they sometimes turned to violence to protect those lives. The murder of Thomas Merchant was one result. Charles Drayton hired Merchant to oversee his Jehossee Island plantation after it fell to disorder. According to Drayton, when he arrived at the plantation on January 8, 1800, to inspect the enterprise, "everything seemed backward." Crops were short, fields were overgrown with grass, and no cotton had been ginned. Drayton blamed this all on the overseer, fired him, and almost immediately hired Thomas Merchant. But as Merchant soon learned, the issues on the plantation transcended poor management. The enslaved at Jehossee had in fact created a dearly held social and economic world on Drayton's island plantation, one that they were loath to concede, no matter the expectations or demands of their new overseer. Because Jehossee was isolated along the coast but adjacent to heavily populated Edisto Island, it was well situated to act as a hub for illicit traffic. Moreover, as on many of the isolated plantations that dotted the coastal plain, the enslaved had grown accustomed to a certain level of labor demands.[51]

Merchant intended to alter all of this by transforming the site into a productive part of Drayton's plantation complex. He must have used a heavy hand, for only a month after his arrival, slaves from Jehossee began to arrive at Drayton Hall with complaints about Merchant's managerial methods and abuses. On March 7, Drayton noted, "Nella came from Jehossee complaining of the overseers licentiousness & threatenings." Later that month, Phillip, a driver on the plantation, complained directly to Merchant—apparently on Drayton's recommendation—and for his trouble was "whipped and dismissed from office." After that, Drayton noted "there appears a combination to endeavour [sic] to get the overseer turned off. He being more intelligent & industrious than suits their disposition." Just two weeks later, Drayton noted that six slaves left Jehossee, led by Phillip, the former driver. They did not go far, however, staying on nearby Edisto Island.[52]

Merchant's oversight severely disrupted the world that Drayton's slaves had created for themselves. But the momentary relief of running away or complaining to their distant master did not content them. The men and women on Jehossee Island had created a political community, one that they were unwilling to have disrupted by their new overseer. After a long summer under Merchant's direction, the Jehossee Island slaves took matters into their own hands. On October 23, less than a year after taking charge of the plantation, Drayton received a letter "announcing the death of my overseer at Jehossee." Two months later, he received word that "sundry negroes were carried from Jehossee to Edistow by warrant on suspicion" for the murder of Thomas Merchant.[53]

Undoubtedly angry, Drayton also recognized the real threat these labor disruptions posed to his prosperity. In the face of a violent challenge for control of what he surely understood as his own plantation space, Drayton sought an overseer who would maintain the island's productivity while avoiding the disruptions caused by Merchant's managerial methods. He ultimately chose Solomon Freer, a man he soon deemed "worthless & impossible," but one he continued to employ—"for he is acquainted with the disposition of the negroes." This "disposition" apparently included the maintenance of a thriving illegal trade network on the island. Drayton was notified by his neighbor "Mr. Seabrooks" of an "illicit trade to a very great extent at Jehossee." Even Paris, the driver at Jehossee, complained of the workforce's extracurricular exchange. After receiving one of his messages, Drayton noted "Roguery—pedlars, visitors, rum." Jehossee Island, which was only partially cultivated by Drayton's workforce, provided ample acreage for this hidden exchange network to thrive. Simpson, a local peddler, was apprehended in one of the plantation canals. Another time, two visitors "hunting about the fields at Jehossee" came upon Exeter, "a fellow belonging to Mr. Deas," whom they promptly shot in the back. It is not clear if Exeter was a runaway or was simply visiting the plantation for trade.[54]

While Exeter's motives are unknown, it is clear that black Carolinians' sociospatial practices made plantation spaces—along with swamps, canals, forests, landings, bridges, cuts, and city wharves—into spaces of possibility, spaces that Exeter and numerous others regularly took advantage of for their own political and economic purposes. To be sure, such spaces did not ameliorate the harshness of their labors, nor did they diminish the brutalities that the enslaved faced every day. But neither did those realities stop Lowcountry slaves from crafting their own ideas of the landscape, nor did it stop them from reifying those ideas through their everyday practices. Each shaped the other, and incrementally altered how the space was perceived by white and black alike. Exeter, Simpson, Nella, Maddy, Morris's slaves, and tens of thousands more lived in the coastal plain and throughout the state, and in their living, they experienced and remade South Carolina in a variety of ways. These experiences marked, and even at times dramatically altered, the landscape.

The Value of Space

As noted at the end of chapter 3, throughout the early national era, planters, yeoman, and state leaders were confounded by their absolute dependence on slave mobility to maintain the plantation enterprise. They recognized that the enslaved majority represented a very real threat residing in their midst. For the most part, the interests of planters remained the primary focus of South Carolina's slave law, as patrols and the pass system were crafted in such a way that consistently acknowledged the primacy of planters' property claims. However, over time, it became increasingly difficult to justify this approach to policing slaves. Many white Carolinians felt a sense of anxiety and dread as they found themselves surrounded and supported by those whom they feared most. How could planters prioritize their property claims in the face of what many believed to be maroonage, murder, and insurrection? As planters and state leaders alike regularly acknowledged, enslaved men and women's everyday acts—from the rebellious to the mundane—regularly transgressed white Carolinians' desires and expectations.

For many white Carolinians, slaves seemed to be everywhere, doing just about everything. Most troubling, they seemed to do so with little to no direct supervision, and at times in direct violation of both their masters' wishes and the law. Lowcountry residents petitioned the state government for tighter restraints on the enslaved population, requested that the existing patrol and pass laws be better observed, and even pushed for the more humane treatment of slaves. But still slaves continued to move throughout South Carolina, exacerbating white fears with each step. Surprisingly, though, given the volume of residents' fears, very little white blood was spilled in this era. The three major insurrectionary scares—Camden in 1816, Denmark Vesey in 1822, and Georgetown in 1829—were more rumor than action. And when slaves did kill white Carolinians, it was often the result of violence initiated by the victims.[55]

So why did white Carolinians increasingly fear their slaves? Historians have previously argued that the large black majority in the Lowcountry, the memory of the Haitian Revolution, and Gabriel Prosser's Virginia slave rebellion, as well as the increased calls for abolition both abroad and at home created an atmosphere of intense anxiety for white Carolinians. Planters worried that slaves, upon hearing rumors of freedom or of other revolts, would rise up against them. Undoubtedly these were all factors. But just as significant, though often overlooked, were the spatial dynamics that played out daily between black and white Carolinians throughout South Carolina, and the ways that such practices reconstructed and challenged South Carolina's nascent state space.[56]

White Carolinians did not, and perhaps could not, understand the varied ways slaves defined and experienced the Lowcountry. Throughout this era, white Carolinians remained fearful of the disease-ridden swamps, dependent on the labor of the enslaved, and sure of their abstract dominion over the landscape. They thus remained distant from many of the spaces slaves frequented, unaware of the values materially constructed along riversides, deep within swamps, and along the edges of plantations. Those whites who did encounter black sociospatial practices often maligned and misrepresented them: Hugh McCauley dismissed the "pretend religion" that slaves on Ball's plantation practiced, though in hindsight it seemed to be the glue that held that plantation together; Charles Drayton and Henry Laurens railed against the "roguery," or theft, that their boatmen regularly committed in their everyday travels, though it was often the means by which slaves provided for their own subsistence as well as the maintenance of the plantation enterprise; and Edmund Ruffin scoffed at the slaves who claimed that "cymbee" resided in the bubbling waters of St. Stephen's Parish, though those same spirits were the means by which enslaved Lowcountry Carolinians organized their lives in bondage.[57]

In the decades following the Revolution, such narrow perspectives had profound consequences. As planters sought to alter the plantation complex— selling or moving slaves to backcountry cotton plantations and shifting from inland rice to tidal rice production—they became privy to the extent of slaves' attachment to particular parts of the coastal plain. When forcibly sold to backcountry estates, many slaves attempted to return to their former homes.

They did not run haphazardly into the wilderness and away from labor, but rather back from where they came, to the spaces where they were rooted spiritually, communally, and economically—former plantations, inland swamps, the Neck, and the wharves of Georgetown and Charleston. Because slaves valued these places, they often went to extraordinary lengths to return to them. For white Carolinians, though, it did not matter where slaves ran, or why; white Carolinians experienced enslaved movement only as a threat to their authority.[58]

For many, the draw of the Lowcountry was not so much a particular plantation, but rather the people who resided there and their knowledge of local spaces. On one plantation near Savannah, the entire labor force ran away during the Revolutionary War with their driver, Andrew, but ventured only as far as the surrounding swamps. The owner of the slaves was able to retrieve them only after negotiating for their return with Andrew. More than a decade later, that same driver led seventy slaves away from Ca Ira plantation. Similarly, the slaves who built the maroon enclave on Belleisle Island near Savannah left their plantations but did not leave the Lowcountry, though they had supplies and weapons and were well organized. Instead, they remained in the coastal plain, where they had acquired a practical knowledge of the space and a connection to the landscape and the people who resided there.[59]

Despite their connections to the landscape and its inhabitants, following the Revolution black Carolinians' attachments to the coastal plain were increasingly challenged by the exigencies of a plantation complex in flux. In the economically turbulent decade immediately following the Revolutionary War, many white Carolinians returned home and were immediately confronted by slumping markets and properties ravaged by neglect and weather. Some simply abandoned the plantation enterprise altogether, selling their lands and their slaves. The wealthiest among them abandoned their inland swamp plantations and turned toward tidal rice cultivation. Others looked to the production of new commodities, chiefly cotton, and set their sights on the fertile soil of coastal islands, South Carolina's Piedmont, western Georgia, and the Mississippi Territory. Eventually, planters' efforts were rewarded as demand for their commodities increased and worldwide markets stabilized, finally ending, for many at least, the postwar economic malaise.[60]

But while these economic developments were a boon for planters and merchants, for black Carolinians the shifting plantation landscape precipitated a severe disruption to their everyday lives. When slaves moved from inland swamp plantations to the coast, the backcountry, or even out of the state, they were being removed from landscapes that many had labored on—and lived in—for decades. The plantations in St. Paul's Parish, St. Stephen's, or St. James Santee that planters abandoned in the 1790s were located in some of the oldest settled areas in the coastal plain and contained the trading sites, simbi spirits, and burial plots dear to black Carolinians. Many planters now deemed these spaces wasted and unproductive, and took their enslaved property elsewhere.[61]

Forcibly moved, black Carolinians often struggled to return to the spaces they had always known. Loved ones and friends, torn apart by sale or their planters' distant labor needs, sought to maintain their hard-won social ties, no matter the cost. For example, as already noted, six slaves confiscated from the estate of Elias Ball Jr., at the end of the Revolution were sold to North Carolinian John Taylor. Shortly after their sale and transport to North Carolina, four of them "quitted Mr. Taylor and returned to Mr. Ball" at his Lowcountry plantation. In 1820, Abram, a slave originally from the Lowcountry, was sold to Benjamin Courson in Columbia. After less than twelve months, Abram left his new owner, who believed that he would "first make for St. Stephen's Parish, and try to stay about Governor Alston's plantation or go to Georgetown, or come to Charleston." Courson believed this because Abram "has acquaintances in all the above named places." Abram, Ball's slaves, and countless others went back to the Lowcountry because of their communal ties to the region but also because life on a plantation along the coastal plain was dramatically different from life in the backcountry.[62]

Slaves sold upstate encountered a laboring experience that was unlike anything they had previously known. On Lowcountry plantations, slaves typically lived within a significantly sized community, as the majority of plantations averaged fifty slaves or more. When they moved to the backcountry, they frequently found themselves on plantations with ten or fewer slaves. In the Piedmont, only the wealthiest planters owned more than twenty slaves, and in the Upstate, the average planter only owned five. And while families or groups might be sold or transported together from one plantation to another, it was much more likely that they would be separated and their social worlds severely disrupted. Because they labored in much smaller groups, it was also less likely that they would be able to re-create the social networks and practices they had been able to develop along the coast.[63]

Besides the dramatic difference in the size of Lowcountry and Upstate slave communities, the interactive dynamics between master and slave were also different. On large rice plantations, interactions with masters and overseers were severely limited, and at times even nonexistent. Most planters chose to reside in Charleston, their summer retreats, country seats, or one of the small towns scattered about the coastal plain. Slaves on Lowcountry plantations might never see a white person during summer months, when even overseers abandoned their posts for fear of disease. On backcountry plantations, by contrast, slaves frequently worked shoulder to shoulder with their masters, for at the turn of the century the South Carolina backcountry was still only a nascent plantation society, with most white Carolinians busily working alongside their slaves, transforming their small farms into cotton plantations. In addition, because the region's climate was considerably healthier, upcountry planters were more inclined to take up permanent residence on their properties and maintain close contact with their labor force. Finally, because the region was not initially settled as a plantation region, white Carolinians outnumbered slaves for a considerable portion of this period, thus making everyday contact between white and black far more likely. Subsequently, whatever autonomy slaves had carved out for themselves in the absence of an observant white population in the Lowcountry dissipated in the more intimate quarters of the upcountry.[64]

In addition to the new social landscape, the physical environment that slaves encountered in the backcountry was also vastly different. In the Lowcountry, slaves lived in dense swamps and marshes that, while unhealthy and deadly, had become recognizable. The rivers and creeks, marshes and swamps that generations of slaves had painstakingly altered and subsequently come to know differed greatly from the forests and cotton fields that they found in the backcountry. Unlike the Lowcountry's curving, meandering streams, South Carolina's backcountry rivers were frequently broken by falls and inaccessible in places. Swamps and marshes could be found in the Piedmont, but not nearly so commonly as in the coastal plain. Slaves' sociospatial practices in part revolved around the Lowcountry's waterways. Differences in the physical landscape therefore directly affected slaves' everyday experiences.[65]

Meanwhile, the slaves who remained in the coastal plain also experienced dramatic changes in their lives. As planters developed their new properties and expanded their operations, they supplemented their labor force with new slave purchases, relocated their slaves to different plantations, and increasingly intensified their exploitative demands. The brutal reality of life on a tidewater rice plantation caused numerous slaves to take flight upon their arrival in the coastal plain. This was true for recent arrivals as well as for slaves who had always lived in the Lowcountry but for whom plantation labor was wholly alien. For example, in 1792, Paul left the Wassamasaw plantation, whose owner had recently purchased him, to return to Charleston, where he had previously labored as a carpenter. Paul's father and mother lived in the city, and he had made it known that he had no desire "to live in the country." Similarly, Isaac left his new master, Claude Guillaud, in 1788. Guillaud thought that Isaac would return to "Georgia, from whence he lately came, and where he had been two years before, at the plantation of William Bryan."[66]

Importantly, however, neither Paul nor Isaac absconded simply because they were averse to labor. Rather, both wanted to return to the places where they had previously resided, and where they had established social and economic ties. This was a familiar theme among black Carolinians in the early national era. One planter in Goose Creek Parish complained that two of his recently purchased slaves, Scipio and November, had run away shortly after arriving at his plantation. Scipio was "brought up at Black Mingo" in Georgetown District but had been sent to Charleston to learn the carpenter trade before being purchased by the Goose Creek planter. November, on the other hand, was "brought into this country when very young, from the coast of Africa." He too lived in Charleston, where he was "employed as a fisherman." It is no surprise that Scipio and November absconded from the Goose Creek plantation. They were skilled laborers who had lived and worked in Charleston. As a "house carpenter" by trade, Scipio would be hard pressed to find similar working conditions in the countryside, and most likely he left behind friends and perhaps family. November, on the other hand, had seemingly only known Charleston and, it seems, the coastal life. To be moved from the city to Goose Creek, though they were not remarkably distant from one another, would have marked a radical change in the lives and livelihoods of both men.[67]

Importantly, then, when Isaac, November, and countless other slaves absconded, they were not running toward freedom—no such space existed yet. Although the institution of slavery was fading in portions of the country, it was still firmly entrenched in the new nation. There was no underground railroad; there was no notion that the North represented a contrasting region of "freedom." Rather, in the first decades of the nineteenth century, slaves ran to spaces of familiarity. Isaac and November left their owner because they found plantation labor brutal and loathsome, but fled to Charleston, not because it was a haven from the brutalities of slavery but rather because it was a known world. Their intimate relations resided there, and they knew where to find work as carpenters and fishermen along the harbor and in the city streets. Thus, while this movement may have represented a form of resistance to their owner's proprietary claims to their bodies and labor, it also signified how slaves defined the landscape and privileged certain spaces. By returning to their former urban haunts, Isaac and November reinforced black Carolinians' representations of those spaces.[68]

In Charleston and Georgetown, on riversides and canals, and at their former plantations, slaves had woven religious, economic, and social connections into the landscape, and maintained an intimate knowledge of the space that they accrued through years of labor. Slaves knew the worlds they left behind—gravesites and spirits, friends and family—and many actively sought to return to the spaces they were forced to vacate. But if black Carolinians returned to these sites because they were woven into slaves' varied conceptualizations of the coastal plain, white Carolinians saw such movement only as evidence of increased intransigence. In particular, they conflated illicit trade, running away, and maroonage with designs against the plantation complex. This is not to say that they had nothing to fear. In 1800, slaves murdered a "Mr. Brown" in Colleton District. In 1804, as mentioned above, slaves on Charles Drayton's Jehossee Island plantation murdered their overseer. Two decades later, Thomas Deliesseline was shot while trying to apprehend a boat filled with black Carolinians "supposed to be runaways." And in 1821, George Ford was shot and killed while trying to apprehend a group of runaway slaves, led by Forest Joe, who were reportedly killing and stealing his livestock.[69]

The case of Deliesseline provides a window through which we can better understand how this violence was not necessarily the action of bloodthirsty, vengeful slaves—as planters feared—but was rather the consequence of white Carolinians' attempts to control and constrain the everyday movement of the enslaved, movement that was both the source of and unintended consequence of state development. On February 10, 1820, "Mr. John Deliesseline reported to his father, that he had seen a boat land at his place, full of Negroes, supposed to be runaways." John then suggested to "his brother Thomas, and Mr. Laval, (a French gentleman) who were present, that they should go in pursuit of them." Neither the Deliesselines nor Laval knew who the slaves were or what they were doing. John noted that he saw the boat approaching the plantation at 7 P.M., making it highly probable that the slaves were visiting their neighbors to socialize or participate in a trade network, or perhaps to hunt in the plantation's uncultivated fields—unsanctioned yet common activities nonetheless. But the white men did not stop to ask. Immediately upon arriving at the slaves' boat, "Mr. John Deliesseline seized one, who broke from him." When Deliesseline attempted to fire, "his gun snapped," backfiring before he could kill his target. He and Laval attempted to seize another "by the collar," and in the struggle, "the Negro drew a pistol, fired, and shot Mr. D. through the head, who expired immediately."[70]

Had Deliesseline asked the slaves the purpose of their visit or to see their passes, it is likely that the scenario would have unfolded differently. By 1820, the enslaved knew that an approaching patrol of white men, regardless of the legality of their movement, was to be taken very seriously. An interaction could easily end in violence. Nevertheless, slaves' travels up and down the rivers of the district—movement, plain and simple, and often in the service of their masters—increasingly made white residents nervous. In 1813, the Grand Jury of Colleton District complained of the "numerous assemblies of armed runaway slaves encamped within said district," which made the "navigation of the rivers and creeks therein excessively dangerous owing to the depredations of these banditti furnished as they are with boats." John Deliesseline must have worried that the slaves who landed at his father's plantation were similarly inclined runaway slaves. But Deliesseline did not know, and because of his ignorance and his actions his brother was shot and killed. When white Carolinians bore witness to the everyday activities of the enslaved, outside of their labors, they reacted according to their own narrow understanding of their power and slaves' presumed place within South Carolina's territory. To Deliesseline, Keller's slave patrol mentioned in chapter 3, and numerous others, when slaves transgressed property bounds—coming or going—they were always potentially challenging the dominion that white Carolinians claimed. And perhaps that was true, to some extent. But in acting on their fears, white Carolinians not only limited their (and our) understanding of enslaved movement, they also transformed the state into a violent, contested space.[71]

Throughout the early national era, white Carolinians increasingly sought to constrain the movement of the enslaved and create a landscape completely under their control. But they were regularly reminded that black mobility was essential to the maintenance of the plantation complex, particularly in the Lowcountry, where black Carolinians remained an overwhelming majority throughout the early national and antebellum eras. How could planters prevent slaves from traveling to Charleston markets, transporting goods between plantations, or visiting swamps and forests after their daily labors were complete? In an era that began with the Haitian Revolution and ended with Nat Turner's Revolt, how could they not? Planters, politicians, and yeomen struggled with this dilemma throughout the late eighteenth and early nineteenth centuries—an era that rang with the rising chorus of abolitionists from without, and economic expansionists and proslavery ideologues from within. And while South Carolinians participated in, and often led, the improvement efforts that were sweeping the nation, they simultaneously created and confronted a violent, local landscape that would come to define their vision of modern state praxis.

CHAPTER FIVE

With the Labor of These Slaves
Producing the Modern State

In the early summer of 1821, George Ford, a wealthy South Carolina planter, was shot and killed while attempting to apprehend a small band of runaway slaves who were reportedly stealing his cattle. What authorities quickly deemed a murder marked the beginning of a desperate three-year search for "Forest Joe," the presumed leader of the fugitives. Having captured and interrogated Joe's accomplice Jack, local authorities quickly located the group's encampment on the edge of the Santee River, as well as their upriver camp that lay at the confluence of Thomas's Creek and the Wateree River. White Carolinians, relying on Jack's coerced confession and their own knowledge of the coastal plain, believed that Joe and a third fugitive would head west on the State Road, just below the Santee River, toward McCord's Ferry on the Congaree. The state militia confidently reported to worried locals that Joe had "attempted to ascend the Santee but was so closely pressed" that he had been forced to abandon his canoe and many of his provisions. Scouring the coastal plain, the members of the search party believed that they had cut off all of Joe's possible escape routes, and confidently claimed that they were nearing the capture of the presumed villain.[1]

Despite their efforts, the search did not yield the immediate results for which the white authorities hoped. Rather, the failed search revealed Joe's intimate knowledge of the Lowcountry, and the startling realities of power relations in early national South Carolina. Those in pursuit were well acquainted with the roads, paths, and bridges that snaked around and over the Santee River. But as the search party soon realized, Joe's survival and escape hinged on "the intelligence and support furnished him from some of the neighboring plantations." The knowledge held by Joe and those black Carolinians who aided him differed from and, in many ways, surpassed that of the state militia and local patrols who searched the countryside in pursuit of the runaways— the contours of which slaves had shaped and defined through generations of habitation and labor. Subsequently, the members of the search party only returned with the unsettling realization that they lacked control, over both the landscape and the enslaved population. As one newspaper ominously reported, Joe uses "the most dense and impervious swamps, places himself at the head of fugitive slaves, arms them and has continued a course of depredations."[2]

The failure of the search party, and Joe's ability to remain hidden, did more than simply trouble and perplex planters and state leaders. At the precise moment that Joe and his band of runaway slaves pushed along the edges of the presumed boundaries of white dominion, white Carolinians were in the midst of a rearticulation of their governing praxis. Throughout the early national era but beginning in earnest in 1815, South Carolina's political elites joined their cohorts across the nation—at the levels of both state and national governance—embarking upon an effort to realize and legitimize their visions of the state. In South Carolina, this included familiar efforts that had long stood at the center of the state building enterprise: the creation of a new state map; the construction of roads, canals, bridges, and causeways; the improvement of rivers, streams, and harbors; and the erection of courthouses, jails, schools, and hospitals. These public works, however, were intimately connected to a robust reform movement that sought to expand the state's role in the everyday lives of South Carolinians. State leaders worked to amend South Carolina's outdated legal system and penal code; provide aid to the state's indigent, ill, and incapacitated; and extend educational opportunities at the primary, secondary, and higher educational levels. Taken as a whole, these internal improvements represented a concerted effort not only to centralize and solidify power in South Carolina but to turn that power toward the creation of a more modern, liberal state. This reflected the profound shift that occurred in state governance at the beginning of the nineteenth century. Unlike during the colonial and Revolutionary eras, when infrastructural designs were primarily focused on external security and establishing commercial traffic, early nineteenth-century state planning focused as much on improving and expanding economic infrastructure as it did on directing the development of an emergent liberal subjectivity.[3]

At the heart of this movement, in South Carolina as across the nation, lay a strategy to redefine landscapes, controlling territory and its inhabitants. Immense in proportion, early national public works—broadly construed as the political, economic, and cultural efforts to produce and define the state's territory and governing praxis—promised not only to solidify the claims of South Carolina's elites but to alter radically the future trajectory of statecraft, as well as the experience and conduct of the governed. Altogether, the envisioned reforms and infrastructural projects sought to bring into being a centralized governmental entity that promised to provide economic opportunity, political stability, bodily security, individual freedom, and moral guidance. As

Samuel Farrow, a member of the General Assembly from the Upstate and a leading advocate of moral reform and internal improvements, argued, the state was to act as a guardian for all of its citizens, "to inform their minds, to repress their vices, to assist their labors, to invigorate their activity and to improve their comforts." In 1821, Governor Thomas Bennett emphatically seconded these bold assertions, arguing that through the state government "the virtues and intelligence of the people are promoted, the public morals regulated and refined, and the character of the state established." State leaders sought to define and secure the rights, freedoms, and responsibilities of the citizens whom they nurtured, and at the same time reshape the territory to which they belonged. These projects, while different from earlier efforts, were similar in that they could not be made real without slaves.[4]

This chapter closely explores South Carolina's developmental policy and reform agenda in the post–War of 1812 era, arguing that public works and the labor of state slaves were part of a broader project seeking to produce not only the state but also liberal subjectivity. South Carolinians, like their peers in other states, crafted their developmental policies in response to new economic and political circumstances, but they did so in the context of an expansive global effort to redefine governing praxis, territoriality, and the maintenance and meaning of power relations. Like their British, French, Russian, and Northern peers, South Carolinians used legal, bureaucratic, cartographic, statistical, architectural, and engineering innovations not only to solidify their claims to authority but to create the very liberal spaces and self-governing subjects that they sought to oversee. As I'll make clear below, South Carolinians were ardently committed to this postwar project of state development. They sought to consolidate ever more authority within the hands of a centralized government that would become the primary conduit of power and of the people's welfare, and in so doing embraced the most up-to-date techniques of statecraft. Besides committing extraordinary funds to infrastructural development, South Carolinians were also among the first Americans to transition to the more familiarly modern—if still unrefined—practices of governance: creating institutional bureaucracies, relying upon expertise and moral authority to legitimize the state's positive claims to power, and actively seeking to shape and define the state's territory through cartography and infrastructural development.[5]

This emergent governing rationality, however, was defined not simply by the broader global discourse of statecraft or the developmental and reform agendas of elite Carolinians but also by the everyday practices of the enslaved majority in South Carolina—from their labors on plantations and infrastructural projects to the maroonage of Forest Joe. Slaves were essential to internal improvements in the early national era, providing indispensable labor and revenue for the state's projects. But, as discussed in chapters 3 and 4, black Carolinians also used the state's modern infrastructure for their own purposes, weaving their own meanings into the landscape; in doing so, they challenged the presumption that a space built for freedom—free movement, free exchange—could have limited access. In order for elite Carolinians to make real their idealized visions for the state, themselves, and the self-governing subjects they sought to create, planners and planters necessarily had to consider and address black Carolinians—not simply the labor they provided, which most took for granted, but also the challenges slaves and slavery posed to the very project of liberal modernity. Accordingly, white leaders refocused their developmental agenda, reconciling their vision of the modern state with the realities of an enslaved black majority that they absolutely feared but could not live, or be free, without. Alongside an active state that sought to nurture, educate, and provide economic opportunities for its citizens, South Carolinians presciently reoriented governing practices to accommodate the brutal maintenance of the economic and racial status quo, providing a model of liberal governance built around institutionalized racism not just for the South but for the nation as a whole. Such internal improvements rested not simply on infrastructural development, reform, and the expansion of governing bureaucracy but also on the brute exertion of racialized physical violence and close policing of enslaved men and women.[6]

Producing the Modern State

On February 4, 1817, South Carolinian John C. Calhoun, who would become the most well-known defender of slavery and Southern states' rights, stood before Congress and delivered his strongest oration to that date. Calhoun's speech, however, did not touch on the themes of tariff policy or federal overreach, nor did it seek to champion the institution of slavery. Rather, his speech sought to solidify the union, expand the powers of the federal government, and create a more powerful nation-state. A few months prior to his speech, Calhoun had offered to Congress the Bonus Bill, a plan to use the government's proceeds from the rechartered Bank of the United States—a charter he championed through committee—to fund the development of a series of internal improvement projects designed to connect the expansive territory west of the Appalachian Mountains to the Atlantic Coast. Calhoun argued to his colleagues that whatever "impedes the intercourse of the extremes with this, the centre of the Republic weakens the union." Elaborating on the argument, he added that the "more enlarged the sphere of commercial circulation, the more extended that of social intercourse; the more strongly are we bound together; the more inseparable are our destinies." Calhoun was concerned that the young nation's rapid geographic growth hastened its undoing. "Those who understand the human heart best," Calhoun noted, "know how powerfully distance tends to break the sympathies of our nature. Nothing, not even dissimilarity of language, tends more to estrange man from man." But Calhoun offered a solution to the potential dangers confronting the nation as it expanded territorially: "Let us then bind the Republic together with a perfect system of roads and canals. Let us conquer space!" While Calhoun's efforts at establishing a national system of internal improvements were largely unsuccessful, his ideas make clear that South Carolinians stood at the center of this important moment of national development.[7]

South Carolinians had enthusiastically embraced the technologies and practices of spatial state development from the state's earliest moments of existence. For example, as discussed earlier, on the eve of the Revolution, white Carolinians seized upon cartography and canal development to improve provincial and early state infrastructure. After the Revolution, elite Carolinians remained fully immersed within the intellectual circles that informed state-based spatial discourse, engaging with and sharing ideas with natural historians, botanists, and geographers in Europe and Spanish America. Elites across the globe privileged this type of knowledge, this way of seeing and writing about the world, perceiving through it the means by which territorial stability and power could be accrued and maintained. From the botanical studies and natural history of Governor John Drayton to the *Statistics of South Carolina* penned by Board of Public Works member Robert Mills, white Carolinians continually turned to the techniques of control used by their colonial forebears to assert their dominion over South Carolina, using natural philosophy, geography, history, and botany to order, understand, and control their universe.[8]

Stephen Elliott noted the continued significance of such techniques of power to his fellow Carolinians at an 1814 meeting of Charleston's Literary and Philosophical Society. Lecturing on a variety of topics, Elliott urged white Carolinians to focus their energies on the science of statecraft, particularly noting its spatial discourse: cartography and infrastructural improvement. "In the topography of our country we are miserably deficient, in our geography very incorrect. We have no maps of our country, on which we can place any reliance; no surveys, except of our sea coast, which have any pretensions to accuracy." This, of course, was not entirely accurate. The British and their European and Native rivals had long produced maps of South Carolina, but Elliott desired a new iteration of this knowledge, not one that gazed from Britain or one that privileged the spatial conceits of their Cherokee or Catawba neighbors, but rather one that favored the view from Columbia and Charleston. Elliott continued, "The exertions of improved and opulent communities" are employed "overcoming, by science and labour, the obstacles of nature." Examples, near and far, made this more than mere speculation. The British were in the midst of their canal- and road-building boom, and the French had long provided an example of state-sponsored infrastructural development following the construction of the Canal du Midi. If South Carolinians hoped to achieve any of their promise, Elliott made clear, then they too would have to embrace a similar agenda.[9]

State leaders agreed. In 1815, in the first stage of their post–War of 1812 internal improvement movement, legislators in Columbia approved the petition of South Carolina College astronomy professor George Blackburn, who requested funds for his unprecedented astronomical, topographical, and trigonometric survey of the state. Blackburn was already well known to state leaders, as just a few years earlier he had been called upon by Governor Joseph Alston to survey and establish the western edge of the border between North and South Carolina. Blackburn promised that his new work would produce an accurate map of South Carolina, and argued that a project of such magnitude and importance should occur only under the direction of the state: "The map of a state ought to be constructed by order of the government, and under its immediate inspection, since it requires unremitted attention, and considerable skill in science." The committee charged with hearing Blackburn's petition highlighted South Carolina's aspirations. In its statement of approval for Blackburn's request, the committee noted that the state hoped to follow the lead of "all enlightened nations in their efforts to extend the bounds of knowledge and science." Blackburn's map, the committee argued, would provide important information to "every portion of our citizens" and would give to the militia "a minute knowledge of the surface of the ground." "But above all," it would present the legislature with the knowledge necessary for "superintending and controlling all the arrangements of the State, both civil and military." In his petition, Blackburn noted that his map could be "calculated to answer all the topographical purposes of the geographer, the historian, the legislator and the states man." The project was deemed of such importance that the General Assembly eventually appropriated over $90,000 for the project, including funds for the construction of a new observatory on the campus of the state college.[10]

Blackburn promised knowledge to white Carolinians—knowledge the state's leaders could transform into real power. Indeed, the importance of such a project in the creation and legitimation of South Carolina as a state, its developmental schemes, and its leaders' conceits to power cannot be overlooked. Across the globe and throughout the United States, the most aspirational of states, as well as the most established, solidified their modern self-realization through survey and cartography. As Blackburn noted in his petition, in "France, in England, and in almost every country of Europe, no pains or expense have been spared for this purpose." Through Blackburn's map, South Carolina's political elite could conjure into being their ideal territory—bounded and whole, knowable and yet still full of promise. The map illuminated South Carolina's landscape, rendering even the dense swamps and marshes of the Lowcountry legible. From the safe confines of the state house, the General Assembly could now, they assumed with the same shared confidence of sovereigns around the globe, supervise the conduct of their subjects and knowledgably debate their plans for political economic development. The map, which would be completed by John L. Wilson and made into an atlas by Robert Mills, naturalized the assembly's spatial conceits, giving their sense of South Carolina's territory the dint of historical permanence.[11]

Importantly, however, Blackburn's map hid from view, through their absence, the grievous conflicts, exploitation, and violence that accompanied the production of South Carolina's modern state space—Joe and his band of runaways; the tens of thousands of slaves who did virtually all of the state's labor; as well as the sites where black Carolinians traded, loved, and fought together. All of these sites were absent from Blackburn's map. As a representation of states, nations, and empires, maps forcefully legitimated the political and economic claims of their benefactors by articulating the body politic within the confines of a bounded territory, free of any competing claims. Because of the purported reliability of surveying technology and techniques in this era, all of which were used by Blackburn, cartographic representations of the state were accepted as objective depictions of space. White Carolinians subsequently believed, and through the map had their beliefs legitimated, that their claims superseded those of tens of thousands of enslaved men and women who presumably had no spatial discourse of their own. And yet, as Joe and other black Carolinians would prove, such a notion required a great deal more work and violence to be made real.[12]

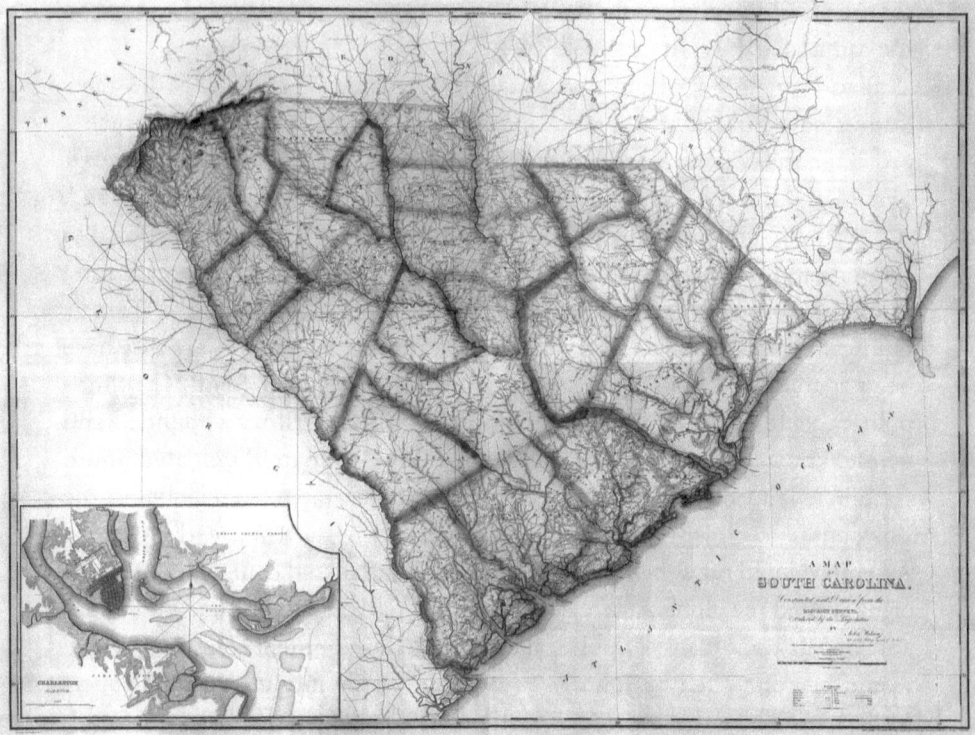

John L. Wilson, *A Map of South Carolina*, 1822. David Rumsey Map Collection, www.davidrumsey.com.

Nevertheless, the map provided state leaders with a device through which they could perceive their unchallenged will stretched out across the landscape of South Carolina. Such a perspective loosened their developmental imaginations. To make their will and ideas material, however, required that the state undertake vast infrastructural projects. Just one year after approving Blackburn's survey, South Carolina governor David R. Williams pressed the General Assembly to embark on this very endeavor, calling on state legislators in his annual message to "consider maturely the expediency of commencing on a large scale, works of internal improvement." For early national South Carolinians, as for most of the nation, such improvements focused overwhelmingly on developing their watercourses. To that end, the governor argued, "no state presents more inviting opportunities for improving inland navigation than our own." Williams encouragingly concluded that the "state is possessed of ample materials; public spirit, enterprise, perseverance are not wanting, and nothing is required for the accomplishment of every desired object in this respect but the patronage of the legislature." It went without saying, that the state also possessed the ample labor power of its slaves, who by then constituted half of South Carolina's total population.[13]

In 1817, the General Assembly heeded the governor's call, appropriating funds and establishing the initial agenda of its ambitious program of internal improvements. John L. Wilson was given charge of public works and tasked with the completion of Blackburn's survey. That Wilson, a professional surveyor and engineer—rather than the politicians or planters, who typically made up local infrastructural administrative bodies—was charged with oversight signaled the state's evolving approach to governance and development. To that end, with the appointment of Wilson, the state created the position of state civil and military engineer. The state had long relied on engineers for military purposes, including road and canal building. Recall that South Carolinians had turned to Othniel Beale and William Gerard de Brahm to plan their colonial fortifications, Antoine Jean Baptiste to erect their Revolutionary-era defenses, and Johann Christian Senf to enact their elaborate plans for inland navigation following the Revolution. But civil engineers were a relatively recent phenomenon, and as such were vital to modern infrastructural development. As one historian of early modern England has recently argued, it was the sole function of the civil—as opposed to the military—engineer to promote, design, and develop a permanent infrastructure that was broad in scope, rather than local, and the purpose of which extended well beyond wartime exigencies. Though Wilson's new position bound together both functions, it was clear that his primary goals would be of the civil variety. Wilson's initial tasks required that he tour the state: traveling over its hardscrabble roads, essaying the impassable rivers that poured down from the mountains to the west, scouting possible routes for canals, and appraising local courthouses and jails. Wilson returned to the assembly in 1818 with a dire report. Many of the public buildings that he encountered were serviceable and would stand temporarily, but most were like the courthouse and jail in Pendleton, which required "considerable repair." His review of the condition of the public roads was more damning. "The actual state of all the public roads is so very bad as to preclude the necessity of describing the defects of each." Wilson's report on the single major transportation innovation completed in the post-Revolutionary era was no better. The Santee-Cooper Canal, privately financed with state backing and completed in 1800, was meant to bind the interior of the state with Charleston by connecting the Santee and Cooper Rivers. But by the second decade of the nineteenth century, its engineering had proven flawed—the consequence, it seems, of private influence during the planning process—and as a result of the drought of 1816–17, the canal had gone completely dry, slowly grinding traffic to the coast to a near halt.[14]

The failures of the Santee-Cooper Canal Company, the Catawba Company, and the Charleston Bridge and Turnpike Company, all privately funded public works, had long signaled the difficulties that confronted infrastructural development in South Carolina, and were at least part of the reason that the state took charge of internal improvement following the War of 1812. Wilson's tour of the state and subsequent report made state leaders aware of the sheer magnitude of the impediments that the government faced in enacting their plans, but the General Assembly did not then shy away from public works. Instead, it furthered its commitment, allocating $1,000,000 to internal improvements over the next four years. This appropriation alone was one of the largest state investments in public works anywhere in the nation, and by the time South Carolina's enthusiasm for fully state-funded public works ebbed in the late 1820s, the General Assembly had spent nearly double that amount. Backed by this financial promise, legislators charged Wilson with clearing the rivers and streams of the state, constructing roads, carving out canals, and "such other works as will facilitate the transportation of the productions of the soil to market." In addition, Wilson was responsible for improving the condition and often completely replacing public buildings—primarily jails and courthouses—in each of South Carolina's counties. Wilson was given broad powers to accomplish these tasks, including the ability to purchase private lands, use nearby materials at will, divert water courses, and hire the engineers and laborers—mostly slaves—necessary to complete such works.[15]

After just a few months, though, it quickly became clear that Wilson alone, no matter the extravagant backing of the state, could not complete the planned improvements. There was simply too much to do, and the work that needed to be done was too widespread for a single person to manage. Wilson's position was dissolved and at the end of 1819 the General Assembly created a five-man Board of Public Works. The creation of the board marked an important transition in the internal improvements movement in South Carolina. In establishing this nascent bureaucratic body to oversee the implementation of public works, South Carolinians signaled the state's further embrace of modern governing techniques. Bureaucracy, in this case the Board of Public Works, not only promised to aid in the planning and implementation of the state's plans but also gave developmental policy-making the imprimatur of disinterest: its sole goal the improvement of the state as a whole. In South Carolina, it was assumed that board members would transcend the local self-interest that so often derailed developmental schemes. More importantly, the makeup of the board provides us with important insights into the broader aspirations of the state. Board members were experts, as far as they could be in the early nation, in their chosen fields. Nicholas Herbemont, for example, was a leading agricultural and social reformer in the state, whose reputation for agronomy and viticulture spread well beyond South Carolina. These were not men, at least on the surface, who simply wanted to aggrandize power, add to their own wealth through the manipulation of improvements, or make a name for themselves. They were uniformly men who were invested in the practice and promise of public works, who desired the legitimization of state power, and who wished to see South Carolina move forward with the reforms I will discuss at more length below.[16]

Abram Blanding, whose tenure as superintendent of public works would continue even after the board was eventually dissolved, was a logical choice to provide the direction South Carolina's reformers desired. A lawyer and statesman, Blanding was instrumental in South Carolina's Constitutional Reform of 1808, helping to draft important reapportionment amendments, while leading the effort to defeat general suffrage. His exploits in the assembly, as well as his participation in the systematization of South Carolina law, meshed well with the overall aim of modernizing state reformers. As Laura Edwards has pointed out in her examination of early national legal culture, South Carolina jurists were busy in this era attempting to supplant the primacy of local judicial power through the codification of statutes and legal decisions at the state level. South Carolina's judicial reformers sought to create a rationalized legal code that would facilitate their vision of economic and political progress and, importantly, centralize legal power in Columbia. Internal improvements were meant to achieve much the same ends. They would solidify the claims of the state through the design of iconic buildings that reflected the state's role in people's everyday lives, while simultaneously directing, shaping, and controlling social and economic intercourse through infrastructural development.[17]

While Blanding reflected the move to the centralization of state power, Robert Mills lent the board an air of modern development born out of his long experience in engineering and planning in Philadelphia, Baltimore, and Washington. Mills also importantly embraced the spirit of reform that stood at the center of South Carolina's post–War of 1812 development. The General Assembly was well aware of what it meant to have Mills as a member of the board. A Charlestonian by birth, Mills left South Carolina at an early age to begin his professional architectural training under Thomas Jefferson and the preeminent Philadelphia-based architect and engineer Benjamin Henry

Latrobe. By the end of his career, Mills would be responsible for the design of numerous public buildings and public works throughout the nation—customs houses, prisons and jails, courthouses, and public monuments. Under Jefferson's and Latrobe's tutelage, Mills honed his opinions concerning the modern state, his ideas of morality and reform, and his belief in the built environment as the physical actualization of such beliefs. As Mills's biographer notes, the "fervor" of Mills's designs conveyed his belief in architecture and the built environment "as an agent of social reform" and expressed his profound belief in the relationship between "form and import" that was evident throughout his work.[18]

In 1806, Mills brought these ideas to South Carolina when he provided the state with a plan for a new penitentiary. As part of the response to the local movement to reform the penal code in South Carolina, Mills presented Governor Paul Hamilton his designs for a new prison and engaged the governor, President Thomas Jefferson, and Benjamin Latrobe in a series of correspondences regarding the promise of modern prisons. Mills argued to Jefferson that the "establishment of a penitentiary house" in South Carolina was meant to "reclaim the vicious and to nourish industry and virtue," as well as unburdening the "state or community at large of the expense and inhumanity of punishing criminals otherwise." His design—premised on Latrobe's plan for the Virginia penitentiary and the broader national and international prison reform movement—was meant to eradicate terror and physical vengeance from the penal system, to be replaced by industry and moral development. The design he presented to Governor Hamilton and the General Assembly represented a practical articulation of these ideas, which he proposed should be stated clearly on the edifice's cornerstone: "Wisdom, which while it punishes would reform the criminal." Despite Mills's inspired design and his argument in favor of the new prison, the General Assembly did not approve the construction of the new penitentiary. A decade later, though, when public support for internal improvements surged again, this well-regarded native son was a seemingly perfect choice to sit on South Carolina's Board of Public Works.[19]

The state granted the board the same broad powers as Wilson before them, and their responsibilities remained largely the same. At the heart of their efforts, as was true for many liberalizing states in the early nineteenth century, was an attempt to remove all obstacles to, while still directing, free exchange and self-governance. As Stephen Elliot argued earlier, improved and opulent communities busied themselves removing the natural impediments to commerce. The board looked to open inland navigation along the Great Pee Dee

River north to the state line. The same was to be done for the Santee, the Wateree-Catawba system, and the Broad River. The General Assembly requested that they also clear the Savannah River in cooperation with the state of Georgia. In addition, the board was meant to open a communication between the rivers along the coast. Such a massive effort required that the board do more than simply remove river obstructions; they also had to build elaborate canal systems that could circumvent the dangerous shoals, rocks, boulders, and long-fallen trees that impeded commerce. In addition, they had to take into consideration the sudden rise of steamboat traffic, which was a boon to commercial transportation but required that rivers be surveyed and dredged to an appropriate depth.[20]

The state also allocated funds and board expertise in the construction and improvement of South Carolina's roads. The state lent aid in the erection of bridges and causeways, and took full responsibility for the construction of a new turnpike that would stretch from Charleston to Columbia and on to western North Carolina through the Saluda Gap. Despite its commitment to the State Road, it was obvious from the start that roads were not to be a priority for the board, as road construction remained under the local oversight of the commissioners of roads. This was hardly a boon to the small, and mostly poor, farmers with little to no river access, who did not possess nearly enough power to dictate infrastructural policy. As one editorialist noted wryly, "The roads have been sacrificed to the rivers." Importantly, however, while the state did not press for the same dedicated improvement of the roads as it did the rivers, it did transfer ultimate oversight of road maintenance to the board. In doing so, the state diluted some of the power of local administrators who had previously been in charge of parish, district, and county roads. As extensions of the board, the commissioners of roads became focal points for the state's overall control of development, rather than remaining their own centers of power. This diminution and transformation of parochial oversight was one of the key ways that the state through the board attempted to realize the centralization of state power. Taking charge of a practice that had once been a primarily communal responsibility transformed the state's abstract dominion into real mastery. Public works projects and the bureaucratic structures created to see them through, then, were more than merely utilitarian; they were manifestations of the state's new governing logic. It made sense for the board to take charge of road improvements even if direct oversight remained in the commissioners' hands, for as Blackburn's map and Blanding's legal reforms sought to establish, the state was a single body, a whole within which only the state—the sovereign—wielded power.[21]

This was made particularly evident in the construction of public buildings. Earlier courthouses and jails were made of weak materials and were poorly designed. This was in part because South Carolina's county seats were relatively new. It was also due, though, to the fact that many residents of the state did not prioritize the construction of such public buildings. To be sure, the adjudication of local justice mattered to residents, but in a pinch a tavern, a church, or the local judge's home would do. Consequently, as board member Thomas Baker noted in his report to the General Assembly, the local courthouses he encountered throughout the state were made of "flimsy material," and the "buildings also appear to me to have been defectively planned." Prisoners regularly escaped from the structures, while those who remained faced horrendous conditions. And the courthouses, when they stood, lacked space for record storage or even regular hearings—"a great inconvenience to the citizens." If, as Abram Blanding and his peers wanted, the state was to enact legal reforms, its local courthouses and jails would have to be more imposing and durable—a visible reminder to residents of who controlled and administered justice throughout South Carolina. To that end, the board tasked Robert Mills with the design and construction of public buildings. Although somewhat limited by local conditions and the availability of materials, Mills's designs lent the buildings the dignity and security they previously lacked. He adorned them with vaulted masonry, porticos that framed the façades, and lateral staircases—elements more typical of his designs for the new national Capitol and the Bank of Philadelphia, not of a small local courthouse. The state may not have (yet) totalized its monopolistic control of the body politic, but the buildings Mills designed provided the perfect setting for such an effort to occur. Whenever South Carolinians walked into these structures, some of which still stand, to purchase property, settle their disputes, or interact with state officials, they could not help but note the centrality of the state in their lives. More importantly, because walking into government structures to complete such everyday tasks was an essential performative act for self-governing subjects, individual freedom and the state increasingly seemed mutually constitutive in the broader social imaginary—one could not exist without the other.[22]

This merger is key to understanding the shifts in governing praxis that occurred in South Carolina and around the Anglo-American world in the early nineteenth century. As historian Patrick Joyce convincingly argues, the raison d'être of modern states was the creation of the liberal subject. South Carolina and other Anglo-American states accomplished this in part through the expansion of their economic infrastructures, but commerce was never their

Robert Mills, *Design for Kershaw County Courthouse*, 1825. South Carolina Historical Society. Drawing of the Kershaw [Camden] Co. Courthouse. From the Robert Mills Papers Collection at the South Carolina Historical Society.

only goal. Alongside the call for economic expansion was an equally powerful demand for moral reform, reflected in South Carolina, as throughout the nation, through changes to penal and legal policy, an expansion of educational opportunities, and a call for social welfare. That such sentiments would infuse the decision-making of state leaders in this era is not surprising. As a number of historians have demonstrated, evangelical Christianity and seismic shifts in the discourse of race, humanity, and morality changed how people interacted with and understood the world around them. These same ideas also clearly influenced state leadership, which sought to dictate and direct the habits and morals of its citizen-subjects. Local and state leaders throughout the early nation were preoccupied with creating and maintaining what one historian has called the "well-regulated society," whereby the practice of governance provided for the general welfare—economic but also moral—of its inhabitants. As William Crafts, the famed orator, lawyer, and one of the key legislative promoters of internal improvements and reform, argued, "the characteristic of the age in which we live is a growing sense of the necessity of adapting the administration of government to the public good." This sentiment, as noted earlier, lay at the heart of Robert Mills's designs. Still, who the public was and what was best for them were highly contested ideas. Just as canals benefited some but not all, and purposefully directed ostensibly open and free commerce to specific locations, the reforms that South Carolina's leadership implemented hardened the borders around the idea of the public, and subtly dictated the acceptable behavior and requisite abilities of South Carolina's self-governing subjects. These reforms were bound together, then, with infrastructural expansion, as the state labored to transform both the landscape and its inhabitants.[23]

In an 1816 editorial stressing the importance of public works, William Langley pushed for not just roads and canals but also the need for improvements in educational facilities, asylums for the insane, "deaf and dumb," and a reformation of state prisons and their disciplinary practices. That Langley and others focused on these institutions is important, for it was in these spaces—educational and sumptuary—that South Carolinians were to be made aware of the boundaries to their subjectivity. This, Langley and other reformers argued, could best be accomplished through education, if made more widely available to even the poorest of white Carolinians, and through the segregation of those incapable of citizenship—the insane, incapacitated, and criminal. Langley noted that the General Assembly had already made one successful improvement to this end: the "establishment of the South Carolina College reflects immortal credit upon its earliest advocates. The clouds of ignorance, superstition, and I might say barbarism, are giving way to the light of literature and science." The establishment of the state college in 1801 and the passage of the Free Schools Act in 1811—which provided primary education at public expense—were indeed important landmarks in the state's improvement. As supporters of the Free School system had argued prior to the passage of the 1811 act, education was "essential to the preservation of independence. As they argued, "The general diffusion of knowledge is essential to the existence of freedom, and the best means of securing to posterity all the blessings resulting from a free and independent government." In other words, through the Free Schools system and the College of South Carolina, "the understandings of the citizens" were greatly improved. To be sure, the benefits and beneficiaries of South Carolina's public education system were limited. As William Johnson noted, by 1822 the system had provided free education to only "about seven thousand" children, the consequence of parental prerogatives, limited funds, and the "scattered state" of South Carolina's population, most of which did not live in close proximity to established schools. Nevertheless, the Free School system at least offered the possibility of education to a broad section of the public, and established the idea that the state government was responsible for producing and shaping South Carolina's citizenry.[24]

Still, as Langley and other reformers made clear, South Carolina was "far short of perfection." Stephen Elliott agreed, and, echoing the arguments of Langley, Crafts, and Farrow, made it clear that he believed it was the state's unique responsibility to transform South Carolina: "Make it, for you have the power to make it, the land of science as well as of courtesy and honour, the land of art as well as the home of patriotism and virtue." Planters, merchants, and yeoman alike all looked to benefit from the state's infrastructural improvements, but as Crafts argued, the general welfare was conceived of more broadly than simple economic opportunity. At the very least, he believed, the market should not be the state's sole concern: "We cut canals through mountains to facilitate commerce, and we make roads and turnpikes for the benefit of trade.... Shall we not cut the canals of joy? Shall we not labour to remove the obstacles of nature, when suffering man call for our relief?"[25]

South Carolina's political elite heeded the editorials, grand jury presentments, and petitions offered by reformers, and for a time embraced their agenda. For example, Crafts and Samuel Farrow convinced the General Assembly to construct the lunatic asylum that they believed would provide a haven for the state's mentally ill population, simultaneously removing or isolating what many would deem impossible subjects from the body politic. The hospital, Farrow argued, would protect these "hapless victims themselves from the dangers of life and from the selfish contempt of our unruly world." The state appropriated $30,000 for the building's construction, Robert Mills provided the design, and Board of Public Works member Nicholas Herbemont was chosen as the first presiding officer of the institution. That Mills and Herbemont were intimately connected to the project highlights the close ties that existed between economic improvements and the moral reform spirit at the highest levels of the state. At the occasion of the building's groundbreaking, Crafts reflected on what he believed to be his adopted state's commitment to compassion and mercy: "Welcome then be this day and this solemnity, which consecrates another effort of South-Carolina in the cause of humanity." The asylum, Crafts argued, "assures every individual amongst us of the guardian sympathy of the State."[26]

Robert Mills, *Design for Lunatic Asylum, Columbia, SC*, 1822. South Carolina Historical Society. Drawing for Lunatic Asylum, Columbia, SC. From the Robert Mills Papers Collection at the South Carolina Historical Society.

Slavery and Liberal Governance

Crafts's assertion was bold, but in keeping with the efforts of state planners across the nation and around the world. Of course, South Carolina's leadership confronted a profound dilemma that their peers were able to ignore: slavery and the everyday practices of the enslaved. And this meant much more than simply reconciling the incongruity of outdated labor practices in a world increasingly designed for freedom. Black Carolinians were, as they had been in the colonial and Revolutionary eras, essential to the production of South Carolina's planned state. Without slaves' labor, or the revenues generated through taxes on both their persons and their daily toils, none of the state's bold experiments in liberal governance were possible. But, as Forest Joe made clear as he eluded state authorities along the banks of the Santee-Cooper Canal precisely at the moment that the state government sought to implement many of their plans, slaves' everyday practices were never as pliable as white Carolinians hoped or imagined. Rather than simply providing labor, as noted in chapter 4, slaves imbued South Carolina's landscape with their own meanings. And as the state extended and expanded South Carolina's infrastructural system, slaves were afforded more opportunities and more spaces in which they could press against white Carolinians' expectations. As Blackburn's map demonstrates, many state leaders sought simply, in the face of this reality, to ignore slaves and slavery in their visions of South Carolina. But the on-the-ground reality of the institution, its centrality to the state's economic and social materiality, and the everyday practices of the enslaved made this impossible.[27]

Which leads us to an important question. Beyond labor, in what ways did slavery intersect with state planners' postwar developmental agenda? How did the Board of Public Works and reformers intend to deal with the issue of unfreedom, the status of more than half of South Carolina's population, and simultaneously create a space for freedom? More immediately, did Crafts and other reformers imagine that the state would safeguard the humanity of the enslaved as well? The short answer to this last question, perhaps surprisingly, is yes. Of course, such efforts had little to do with slaves themselves, and everything to do with, again, actively shaping the appropriate habits and customs of South Carolina's liberal subjects. South Carolina's reformers actively sought to ameliorate the harsh conditions of the state's peculiar institution and increasingly saw slavery as an impediment to improvement. Some, like Mills and Herbemont, suggested improvement schemes to the public that eased the state toward abolition; but these efforts were reflective of other antislavery activities across the early nation, concerned more with creating exclusively white spaces than ending slavery. For the most part reformers simply sought to ensure the humane treatment of the enslaved. Of course, there was little that the state could do in terms of how specific planters controlled their slaves, but officials did attempt to dictate how the enslaved were treated by whites more generally.[28]

This is nowhere more clearly seen than in the state's penal reform, and more specifically the movement to change the punishment for the murder of a slave by a white man. Reform-minded white Carolinians consistently highlighted the incongruity between their sense of self and morality and their outdated criminal justice system, and sought to rehabilitate South Carolina's image and strengthen the state's claim to power through the improvement of its penal code. Reformers saw in the state's outdated punishments, its lack of judicial uniformity, and its decrepit prisons cause for serious alarm. Perhaps surprisingly, the punishment for the cold-blooded murder of slaves, or lack thereof, was one of their primary concerns. In his final message to the General Assembly, Governor John Geddes noted, "No law exhibits a greater disproportion of punishment, than that which relates to the offence of killing a slave by a white man." The law according to Geddes and other reformers was "so very inadequate to the demands of Justice, that the state has suffered in its reputation for humanity." As he made clear, "the rule of reason, Justice, and religion require that the punishment for willful and deliberate murder should be the same in all cases." To be sure, while Geddes and the legislature sought to influence the conduct of white Carolinians, they did not believe that the enslaved were equal subjects under the law. As the governor made clear in his justification for the law's alteration, slaves deserved the state's protection because they were intrinsically deprived of the "natural right of self-defense against a white man." As was the case with internal improvements, education, and the insane asylum, the General Assembly eventually heeded Geddes's call and in its next session passed a new law making the murder of a slave a capital crime.[29]

Of course, one should read this law and its passage, in part, as the state privileging the property claims of slaves' white owners, shielding the enslaved—as property—from unjustified violence. This perspective is most clear in the Constitutional Court's 1819 decision in a suit brought by Lewis Hogg against a "Mr. A. Keller," mentioned in chapter 3, in which Keller was found by the Constitutional Court to have wrongfully assaulted Hogg's slave. The court, remember, had clarified the slave pass system in its decision, arguing, "The law does not require a master to state in every pass, to what place the negro shall be permitted to go. It is sufficient if it express a leave of absence." For many white Carolinians, who witnessed an increase in slave mobility as the state built more roads and canals, this decision was, to say the least, disheartening. But many planters, who absolutely relied on their slaves' mobility, felt differently. This decision not only granted them broad leeway in terms of enslaved movement—removing yet another obstacle for the free economic exchange necessary for a liberal political economy—but also extended and protected their property claims well beyond the limits of the plantation. Still, the Constitutional Court's decision and the state's legislation concerning slave murder must also be seen within the context of the moral reforms of which they were a part: as explicit efforts to limit racial violence within the state, thereby dictating the conduct of white Carolinians. In doing so, however, the state ran headlong into the central conflict of development in early national South Carolina: between white Carolinians' evolving techniques of control, both over the landscape and the enslaved population, and black Carolinians' everyday practices.[30]

At the heart of white Carolinians' concerns lay black mobility. The movement of slaves was an absolute necessity for the sustainability of the plantation enterprise and the growth of the state, but such mobility also provided slaves with countless opportunities to stake their own claims to the landscape. Whether transporting goods to and from Charleston, laboring on their owners' multiple plantations, or performing their mandated work on the state's infrastructure, slaves created their own spaces throughout South Carolina. And in this era of dramatic economic expansion and infrastructural development, such opportunities abounded. In checking violence against the enslaved, the state may have replaced local power with its own, defined the proper deportment of its self-governing subjects, and protected the property of its most powerful constituents. But it then confronted a much more difficult obstacle: controlling and minimizing the spatial practices and claims of the enslaved population. How were state leaders supposed to control impossible liberal subjects, without whom their liberal project would be impossible?[31]

From the outset of the improvement era, it was clear that confronting the everyday practices of black Carolinians was to be an integral aspect of white Carolinians' state-building endeavors. In the same message to the General Assembly in which he expressed the importance of internal improvements, Governor Williams noted that "during the present year," events occurred "which required a resort to military force." The first was the uninterrupted "petty plunderings" of an increasingly large group of slaves who were encamped between the Ashepoo and Combahee Rivers in Colleton District. Led by two men known as Mowby and Dunmore, the group's robberies had become "too serious to be suffered with impunity," forcing Governor Williams to send the militia to disperse or destroy the group. In July of the same year, the militia was called out again, this time to aid Camden's town council—which at the time included Abram Blanding and William Langley—in quelling a rumored slave insurrection. The state militia who responded to the events in Colleton District eventually reported that they "captured, or destroyed, the whole body" of runaways, but this victory would come to seem ephemeral. Any actions the militia, slave patrols, or state planners took that would truly have limited slaves' mobility could at best only be temporary. There was little that the state could do to eliminate the possibility of maroonage or the fears of insurrection so long as white Carolinians continued to depend upon slaves to create and maintain their prosperity.[32]

Here, then, we return to the dilemma that Forest Joe presented to the state: in order for elite Carolinians to realize their state-building efforts, and to create the liberal spaces they desired, they relied on the labor of the enslaved. But slaves took advantage of this and created their own vibrant, if circumscribed, world, which could not be ignored. Exacerbating this dilemma was the fact that slaves' troublesome practices were not confined to runaways like Joe but instead were the products of everyday labor, which were absolutely necessary for the maintenance of the plantation enterprise and, more importantly, the state's development and economic expansion. Blackburn's map, the board's infrastructural improvements, and the erection of public buildings all assumed a space defined exclusively by and for its white population. Even the 1821 legislation that made slave murder a capital crime was primarily concerned with carefully crafting the white state's image and dictating the actions of its white subjects. But this was an imagined reality, and one that could not be implemented without confronting the hard truth of a territory overwhelmingly occupied by black Carolinians. Answering the question of how the ideal would become real in this context was fraught, for it necessarily brought the future of slavery to the forefront of governing discourse. This was made most clear to South Carolinians in the aftermath of the Denmark Vesey Conspiracy.

In May 1822, the mayor of Charleston was informed of the rumored slave insurrection. What information authorities were able to ascertain led them to believe that Denmark Vesey, a former slave who had purchased his own freedom and was now a leading member of Charleston's free black community, planned to lead an uprising against slavery set to begin in early July. The insurrectionists were reportedly going to first set fire to the city, and in the subsequent confusion begin their attack on Charleston's white residents. Upon learning of the plan, the mayor immediately ordered city officials to begin making arrests of the supposed conspirators. Officials headed directly to the well-known centers of black Carolinians' social world. For instance, they arrested several of Thomas Bennett's slaves, who labored at his busy mill on the Ashley River—a prominent site, as discussed in chapter 4, within the socioeconomic world of Lowcountry black Carolinians. According to Edward Pearson's account of the conspiracy, the Bennett slaves lived and worked in the Harleston neighborhood, which lay on the outskirts of Charleston where Denmark Vesey and several of his alleged co-conspirators also lived. These sites may have been the locus of a planned conspiracy; they were without question central to the everyday spatial lives of the enslaved. White Carolinians took the opportunity of the scare to unmake, as much as they could, many of these spaces that black Carolinians had built for themselves. For example, in 1820, prominent residents of Charleston petitioned the General Assembly to lodge a complaint about the recently opened African Methodist Episcopal (AME) Church on Charleston Neck. The petitioners argued that the church was a great evil, as it was solely for the use of enslaved and free black Charlestonians, and unnecessary since white churches were supposedly open to their use. But despite their complaints the church remained open, as in many ways the religious institution was the embodiment of the reform effort that still held sway in the General Assembly. As soon as the Vesey Conspiracy came to light, however, white residents were freed to let loose their accumulated frustrations and fears upon the black religious community, razing the AME church, which for many was the presumed center of the insurrection.[33]

Between June and late July, courts of magistrates and freeholders gathered and heard over 100 cases related to the suspected insurrection. The city, white and black, remained on edge, as city officials began punishing the accused on July 2. Of the black Carolinians arrested in connection to the affair, twenty-seven were tried and acquitted, thirty-one were permanently transported out of the state, and thirty-five were executed. On the line that separated Charleston Neck from the city, the convicted were hung, and their bodies left suspended from the gallows to mark the boundary into and out of the city.[34]

The Vesey Conspiracy, alongside the continued search for Forest Joe, and the general apprehensiveness of black movement led to a heightened state of fear throughout South Carolina. Members of the Board of Public Works, of course, recognized how such matters complicated the state's improvement efforts. They subsequently provided direct responses to the Vesey Conspiracy, as well as what some board members perceived to be the more pressing underlying problems confronting the state, in a series of developmental schemes presented to the public and the General Assembly. Board members argued that the state would never reach its development goals, nor free itself from the fears of slave rebellion, if it did not find some way to diminish black claims to South Carolina's territory. Nicholas Herbemont stated their position: "It has frequently been asserted, and probably with truth, that slavery is an obstacle to improvements." Given that it was the board's task to remove nature's obstacles, this was an important assertion. Did the Board of Public Works desire to dispatch slavery and slaves as they would the boulders, sediment, and timber that impeded water-borne traffic?[35]

The board members were products of their time and place, so any antislavery positions they maintained revolved around a broader antiblack sentiment. But that did not stop them from alerting their legislative audience to the dangers of inaction. Robert Mills, in a pamphlet focusing on internal improvements specifically for the Lowcountry, asked bluntly, "Shall we willingly consent to yield this fine portion of our state to be inhabited only by our slaves? I trust not. And yet will not this be virtually the case if we take no measures to put it in a condition suitable to our own residence?" Even Abram Blanding, the least radical member of the board, felt compelled in the wake of the Denmark Vesey scare to remind the General Assembly of the specter that haunted so many of white Carolinians' thoughts, arguing that if the inland swamps of the coastal plain were not improved, then "this whole region will be deserted by the white population and become the resort of the banditti of the black."[36]

Blanding's fear of black bandits and his overall assessment of a spatial cession through neglect resonated with many Lowcountry residents in 1823. Besides the residual apprehensiveness left in the wake of the Vesey affair, the state militia and local residents were still searching for Forest Joe. And during their search, white Carolinians came face-to-face with black Carolinians' intimate knowledge and use of the coastal plain. As one newspaper reported, "We have learned from some of our respectable citizens, who have been engaged in this unpleasant though essential duty, that they never witnessed stronger evidences of long existing licentiousness and want of subordination than were apparent on some of the plantations visited by them." Joe's white pursuers were disturbed by the practices they observed, but dumbfounded, as noted earlier, when they discovered that Joe had received "intelligence and support" from some "of the neighboring plantations." Joe was not merely an outlier, but symptomatic of something much more far-reaching and dangerous.[37]

As board members would make clear, white Carolinians' problems were not simply issues of mastery but also of demography. The 1820 Census revealed to state leaders the reality that most South Carolinians, particularly in the Lowcountry, already knew: South Carolina was the nation's first state with an enslaved majority. The 1820 Census not only revealed this new reality but also highlighted South Carolina's relatively moribund demographic growth, as well as its corresponding declension in national political influence through legislative apportionment. Other states across the nation experienced significant population booms following the War of 1812, but South Carolina's growth remained relatively slow. Between 1810 and 1820, Pennsylvania's population nearly doubled, New York's grew by 70 percent, and states like Ohio and Kentucky, formerly on the periphery of the nation, grew exponentially. Meanwhile, white Carolinians increasingly migrated out of their state to the fertile cotton fields of Georgia, Alabama, and Mississippi. As a result, South Carolina's total population rose by less than 20 percent, from 415,000 to 490,000, and most of that growth was among the enslaved. As a consequence, while South Carolina remained static with its nine seats in

Congress, New York and Pennsylvania gained, respectively, seven and three seats. Even more worrisome to South Carolinians, new western states were making substantial gains in legislative power. Tennessee and Kentucky accrued a combined five seats; the only recently created state of Maine entered Congress with seven seats; and Ohio added eight seats in Congress, pushing its total well beyond South Carolina's. For South Carolinians, who were already growing more concerned with the general government's policy proposals and legislative agenda following the Missouri Compromise of 1820, such shifts in power were nettlesome, if not deeply distressing.[38]

To members of the Board of Public Works, the source of South Carolina's demographic and impending political problems lay in the Lowcountry—in its fertile but unworked fields, its unhealthy environment, and its black majority. In 1820, there were 123,000 slaves residing in the districts that constituted the coastal plain, and only 33,000 white residents. Including the more than 4,000 free persons of color who resided along the coast, black Carolinians made up 81 percent of the Lowcountry's total population. As Mills argued, while considering what he perceived to be the sickliness and subsequent barrenness of the Lowcountry, "whilst things continue thus, we cannot anticipate an increase of its [South Carolina's] prosperity, but must unwillingly see it retrograde in population and political importance until it shall lose its interest entirely in the councils of the nation." Ever the optimist, Mills maintained that through internal improvements, specifically in the Lowcountry, the loss of national influence could be reversed, or at least balanced, by the strengthening of South Carolina's fortunes. As he argued, developing the coastal plain "might truly defy any act of policy, domestic or foreign, to affect our prosperity." Transform the Lowcounty into a salubrious site, the board argued, and the fortunes of the state would immediately turn. Indeed, "no country on the habitable globe, offers the same advantages to the cultivator of the soil." If the state completed its improvements, South Carolina would prove "to possess equal health with any part of the Union" and would immediately "increase rapidly in population, wealth, and political power." As Mills saw it, the reclamation of the Lowcountry "would be the consummation of Internal Improvements of the state which would realize immense wealth and prosperity to the country," for the coastal plain's swamps were "the gold mines of our state, far superior to those of Ophir or Peru. They are more valuable to us than the gems of Golconda, provided we improve their natural advantages."[39]

Board members, then, presented the General Assembly with elaborate plans to reverse both this discomfiting demographic reality and their lingering fears following the Vesey Conspiracy and continued search for Forest Joe. Nicholas Herbemont had closely studied the dangers associated with slavery, providing South Carolinians with the first English translation of Jean-Louis Dubroca's *Vie de Toussaint Louverture*. As South Carolinians considered any number of ways to respond to the possibility of insurrection, Herbemont made a plea for a measured response. From his study of the "revolution of St. Domingo," he reasoned that "great severity is the surest means of keeping slaves in due subjection." But Herbemont the reformer and state planner recoiled at such a thought. "God forbid that such a plan be adopted! Humanity forbids it." Yet something, he argued, had to be done. For Herbemont, Mills, and Blanding, the best solution was to find a means by which the "white population would be considerably augmented." Not surprisingly, given the board's emphasis on infrastructural development, all of its plans sought to radically alter the landscape itself, literally transforming it into a territory fit for "the permanent residence of a white population."[40]

The members of the board, then, argued that if South Carolinians wanted to truly ameliorate their fears of insurrection, and maintain or augment their national political power, then they would have to transform the state into one "thickly inhabited by an industrious class of white people." Such specificity—the new inhabitants were expected to be "industrious"—revealingly highlighted the liberal order to which the board continued to aspire. This important effort, Herbemont explained to state leaders, would require "some exertions on our part and some money judiciously expended." As remarkable an understatement as this was, Herbemont's plan proved to be the *least* radical and expensive of the proposals offered by the board, as Herbemont simply wanted the state to actively encourage the immigration of Europeans to South Carolina, a policy that had mixed results in the eighteenth century. These white families, Herbemont hoped, would move to the Piedmont for the express purpose of developing new uses for state land. White immigrants, Herbemont suggested, would focus their efforts on the production of "olive oil, wool, silk, and wine," all of which he argued were well suited for South Carolina's climate and soil. By encouraging immigration and the cultivation of these new products, Herbemont argued, South Carolina could revel in "the great security we should enjoy as the natural consequence of so great an increase of our white population."[41]

Mills similarly focused on increasing the white populace, but he turned his attention not on the Piedmont but rather to the Lowcountry, where so many of the state's enslaved labored and lived. When Mills ventured into and through the region to complete George Blackburn's survey, examine the state's public buildings, and appraise South Carolina's roads and canals, he did not find the culmination of a century's worth of development, but instead abandoned fields, rotting vegetation, and the fear of death. As he noted, "During the most enchanting season of the year, how desolate appears our low country! The rich glow of colors from a thousand flowers, bloom in vain to catch the admiring eye of intelligent man." Of course, the region was not deserted. Some planters and yeoman farmers still resided in the area, and thousands of slaves continued to labor in and around the swamps. But to Mills and other board members, the inland swamp region of the coastal plain appeared unnecessarily forsaken. This perceived desolation—the absence of a robust, settled white populace—was the sole result of the unhealthiness of the Lowcountry and the long-standing techniques of absentee plantation management, which had direct repercussions for the standing and security of the state. Mills noted, "Whilst things continue thus, we cannot anticipate an increase of its prosperity, but must unwillingly see it retrograde in population and political importance until it shall lose its interest entirely in the councils of the nation." Presaging the efforts of later Boards of Public Health, South Carolina's Board of Public Works designed plans that would specifically address this issue of unhealthiness in the Lowcountry, draining the swamps of both miasmatic fevers and the dangers they imagined black Carolinians represented. In doing so, Mills and Blanding advanced a radical new vision of the South Carolina Lowcountry. To make real the changes that internal improvements promised, to transform South Carolina into a modern state, this landscape—which had previously been the source of the state's wealth—would have to be fundamentally altered.[42]

Abram Blanding suggested to the General Assembly that the state's problems could be resolved if the state followed through with one of its long-standing development schemes, the construction of the Edisto Canal. Completing this canal promised to simultaneously ease commodious traffic bound for Charleston, supply clean water to the city via an aqueduct, and provide irrigation and drainage for the inland swamps that lay idle. The canal would begin on the Edisto near Giveham's Ferry, flowing thirty-five miles northeast to the Ashley River at Charleston Neck. As Blanding made clear, the Edisto Canal would ease the traffic of boats and rafts that "now reach Charleston by a circuitous route, which carries them along Dawho river, to North Edisto inlet, and by Wadmalaw to Stono river, and thence by Wappo Cut to Charleston." This route, which was used by Charles Drayton's boatmen and countless others, typically took ten days to travel if conditions were perfect. Blanding's canal offered to shorten that journey to just three.[43]

More importantly, Blanding asserted that the canal would provide irrigation and drainage for the inland Stono and Cacaw swamps, making them safe for cultivation and healthy resettlement. Public drains, constructed by planters for their mutual benefit, had provided much-needed water control for ricelands throughout the colonial era. But following the Revolutionary War, as planters left to pursue their interests in cotton or tidal rice cultivation, the cuts that drained the inland rice fields were ruined, leaving in their wake, it was believed, stagnant waters and deadly diseases. Situated thusly, Blanding noted, "it often proves fatal to a resident of Charleston to stay one night in it during the months of July, August, September and October." Blanding believed that the Edisto Canal could be put to use both as irrigation for inland fields during dry seasons and as a public drain, thus reopening the fields for cultivation and increased white settlement. Such a plan, it was believed, would reinvigorate much of the coastal plain.[44]

Mills, on the other hand, called for "*a general system of embanking, draining, and reclaiming our river and swamp lands, rending them fit for cultivation and capable of becoming the permanent residence of a white population.*" To accomplish this expensive, dangerous, and backbreaking task, Mills thought that the General Assembly alone "should have control and execution of the work," a further aggrandizement of state power, and to that end suggested that the government purchase unused inland swamps from their owners as well as "a number of able bodied negroes, say 1500, who would be able to reclaim, at least 64,000 acres of swamp land in two years." This was a plan of epic proportions. And, perhaps most importantly, like all other plans in South Carolina, it relied on the very black laborers whom Mills hoped to displace. Mills argued that the "period has now arrived when it is our best policy and true interest to begin a work with the labor of these slaves (for they only can effect it with any probability of success) that shall make it no longer necessary to retain." Once the land was reclaimed from the enslaved by the enslaved, Mills suggested that the state should resettle the Lowcountry with white farmers, and then market the state's now unnecessary slaves to western states "to place their lowlands in a state fit for the residence and labor of a white population." What Mills was suggesting was, in a way, quite revolutionary. The state, he thought, should own slaves and task them with developmental labor; but, more strikingly, he thought that such developments should be oriented to the gradual end of slavery. This was an idea born out of the still-prominent belief that slavery was a necessary evil, bestowed on Americans by the British, and maintained only because of the presumed susceptibility of whites to dangerous diseases harbored in the swamps and forests of the South. Once slaves drained and embanked the coastal plain's swamps, Mills argued, South Carolina could resell the land to white farmers, making a profit and providing for the increase of the state's white population at the same time.[45]

Given the scale of South Carolina's other internal improvements, as well as those taking place across the nation, Mills's plan—economically and physically—was not all that far-fetched. Rendering the rocky rivers of the Upstate passable was a task of enormous proportions, but one that the state enthusiastically undertook. At the same time that the board made its suggestions, New York was in the middle of completing the Erie Canal, a project that would span 363 miles, requiring dozens of difficult-to-construct locks. And in South Carolina, slaves had transformed the swamps and marshes into productive plantations that they painstakingly maintained for over a century, and had long been responsible for the state's infrastructure. But Mills's plan was too radical, as he sought to fundamentally alter South Carolina not just physically but socially, transforming the Lowcountry into a site primarily inhabited by white men and women. In the minds of many South Carolinians, such plans threatened all that they stood for. Of course, planters, just as much as planners, were deeply troubled by the degree to which the enslaved used the coastal plain for their own purposes. But whereas members of the board sought to dilute the power of, if not completely remove, black Carolinians, planters and their allies in the General Assembly sought other, more physically violent means of reconciling the creation of a modern, liberal state with their absolute dependence on enslaved bodies, labor, and knowledge, and the ever-present threat of slave insurrection and black transgression. State leaders rejected the audacious and expensive aspirations of state planners. But they did not jettison the idea of economic expansion or a liberal polity. Instead, they began to clamor for the state to embrace new policies, focusing primarily on the overt and brutal policing of the state's black populace.[46]

A State of Violence

Two events during the second week of October 1823 reflected the multiple directions internal improvements and governmental practice would take across the country in the decades to come. On Wednesday the eighth, hundreds of spectators gathered in Albany, New York, to celebrate the completion of the first section of the Erie Canal. Dewitt Clinton watched as a boat bearing his name slowly pushed through the canal opening into the Hudson River. Cannons were fired, speeches were made, and doves with poetry festooned to their necks were released to the sky. At the end of the festivities, Samuel L.

Mitchell, New York's great orator, rose to speak and make a symbolic offering. Into the great canal, Mitchell poured water from the Pacific and Atlantic Oceans, symbolizing the connections that the Erie Canal promised to make.[47]

Two days before Mitchell's symbolic offering, something very different was spilled into the waters of South Carolina's Santee-Cooper Canal. After two years of frustrated and futile searches, the Pineville Police Association—aided by an enslaved boatman named Royal—finally caught and killed the fugitive slave Forest Joe and his band of runaway slaves. The volunteer white Carolinians, hidden in Royal's boat, were taken to Joe's encampment in the swamps "just above the canal." When the slaves saw the approaching boat with Royal at its helm, "they came up to the bank of the river, and ordered the boat to come to or they would fire upon them." Royal obeyed, and floated the white men close to Joe and his party. As soon as they were near enough, the search party "showed themselves and fired." Three of the "banditti were killed and fell into the Canal, and the fourth jumped overboard, who was shot and immediately sunk." And so the bodies of four black Carolinians descended into the waters of South Carolina's first major infrastructural project, making clear that improvement in South Carolina was to be forever joined with the brutal coercion of the state's black population. Immediately after their surprise attack, the search party violently descended upon Joe's maroon encampment, sparing no one. They fired haphazardly, killing men, women, and even a three-year-old child. Stephen, one of the fugitives captured during the attack, "was hung close by the Canal Bridge." And as for Forest Joe, "his head was cut off and stuck on a pole at the mouth of the creek, as a solemn warning to vicious slaves."[48]

The display of Joe's and Stephen's mangled bodies at the intersection of the Santee-Cooper Canal and the State Road should be read as more than "a solemn warning," however. By publicly punishing Forest Joe and his band and leaving their withered remains in full view, white Carolinians, and in particular the planters who made up the Pineville Police Association, illuminated both the means by which they intended to reclaim and govern the contentious space along the Santee River that Joe had successfully hidden in for nearly three years, and the direction that modern development would take in South Carolina. Despite the activities of Joe's band and the state's anxious pursuit of this presumed villain, the lives of those who labored and lived in and around the canal never ceased. As enslaved boatmen navigated their flats down the Santee, into the canal, and onward to Charleston, they received a message from white authorities that would spread through black neighborhoods across the Lowcountry. Joe's severed head and Stephen's mangled form were meant as declarations of spatial control—both over the bodies of the enslaved and over the area that lay beyond and around the canal's entrance. The remains of the fugitive slaves also conveyed an important message to the coastal plain's white populace. Certainly, many in the area would be pleased to learn that Joe had been killed. But as travelers on the State Road and the canal passed by the remains, or smelled their decomposition from a distance, their sense of the space was forever marked by the brutality visited upon Joe's band—a profound political statement in an era when legislators and religious leaders were prodding for the more humane treatment of the enslaved population. When commercial and social travelers, black and white, passed the entrance to the canal and saw Joe's head, or traveled on the roads to and from Charleston that passed through the Neck and saw the remains of the Denmark Vesey conspirators, they could not help but understand that South Carolina's modern development revolved around the violent policing of black Carolinians.

It is important to make clear in closing, then, that as the state made violence a cornerstone of its governing praxis, its intentions were in no way meant to undermine the project of modern state-building. As members of the police associations that formed in the wake of the Denmark Vesey insurrection regularly reminded their fellow Carolinians, they had "but one object, namely, to aid in the enforcement of such of our laws, as relates to the '*government* and *discipline* of our colored population.'" Importantly, the prominent planters, merchants, and statesmen who made up the associations—including Stephen Elliott, perhaps the loudest and most learned advocate of the state's improvement project—continually pledged their allegiance to the state, claiming that they were "not an association of individuals," but instead, "a society of well-informed citizens, most of them owners of the soil, and all of them ready to bow with reverence to the supremacy of the laws." This they agreed to, so long as the laws remained subservient to their seemingly narrow needs. And those needs, it seems, were best served through the brutal policing of enslaved and free black Carolinians.[49]

The Pineville Police Association that caught and killed Forest Joe also signaled through its actions, however, that the association, like state planners, would have to rely upon the enslaved to realize many of its aspirations. At one of the first meetings of the association, prominent planter William Dubose made this clear. He argued to his fellow members that if they made "secret offers of Reward to certain negroes, their agency and assistance might so far be obtained, as to enable a party judiciously posted to surprise and take them." The association turned to Royal, a black boatman, whose mobility symbolized both the source of white Carolinians' wealth and their accumulated fears. By relying on Royal, the Pineville Police Association let it be known that white Carolinians' continued prosperity, their security, and even their freedom were to forever be facilitated by the enslaved.[50]

These planters-turned-policemen did not, then, make statecraft impossible in early national South Carolina; they merely altered its direction and impetus. Humane reforms, expert bureaucracies, and expensive infrastructural improvements were now to be paired with a governing praxis that focused substantial energy on violently maintaining the unfree status of more than half of the territory's inhabitants, coercing their labor to secure the freedom and economic opportunities of the state's white population. But even as South Carolinians reinforced the importance of violence to their continued existence, they revealed their sustained reliance on the labor of enslaved black Carolinians for the maintenance and protection of their modern state.

Nowhere was the marriage between violence and improvement more obvious than on the railroad, that most modern of infrastructural developments. South Carolina was among the first states to construct a long-distance railroad, and it did so by callously extracting deadly labor from black Carolinians. As one former slave remembered of his time laboring on the Hamburg and Charleston Rail Road, "Every hour in the day we could hear the whip going. They did not use brine there. After we were whipped we had to go straight back to our work. They did not care whether we got well or not, because we were other people's niggers." Relying upon the enslaved in this manner, of course, did come at a cost. One night, after realizing that he "could not be worse treated than I was on the rail road" the slave secretly boarded the train. This anonymous slave sought his own freedom on the very infrastructure that was designed to free white Carolinians' commercial enterprise. Hiding among bales of cotton, the global economy's most prized possession, he made his way to Charleston. Once there, he visited the sites of economic exchange that he had come to know in the course of his everyday labors, going first "to the tavern where I used to stop when I carried eggs and peaches and other things to market." Shortly after his arrival, he found work on Charleston's wharves, loading cotton onto vessels bound for the Atlantic's buzzing textile mills. Eventually, he buried himself in these northward-bound bales, losing himself again in the circuits of commerce that he had helped construct, until he emerged, untethered from his bonds, in Boston.[51]

The anonymous slave who escaped his bondage through railroad and steamship was not alone in his travels in and around South Carolina and across the state's borders. Throughout the 1810s and 1820s, slaves and free blacks regularly were transported to or traveled into South Carolina for a variety of reasons. In response to this movement and the fears that such mobility inspired, South Carolinians passed a number of acts, issued prominent protests, and gathered together as violent mobs, all with the goal of securing the racial borders of their state. In 1822, during the crisis provoked by the Denmark Vesey Conspiracy and in the midst of the search for Forest Joe, South Carolinians passed a law now commonly referred to as the Negro Seamen Act, which barred black sailors from entering the state. While historians have rightfully made clear that this law reflected the overwhelming fears associated with the Vesey plot, many have lost sight of the way this statute fit into a longer trajectory of legislative action designed to augment the racial boundaries of the state.[52]

The 1822 act was preceded by a statute passed in 1816, which prohibited the importation of slaves into South Carolina. In 1817, lawmakers clarified the 1816 law after receiving numerous petitions from South Carolinians who were prevented from bringing their property to their homes, as well as from those who simply wished to transport slaves through the state on their way to points west. The amended law also took into consideration the everyday movement of slaves, particularly those who lived on the Savannah River and near the North Carolina border, whose everyday labor included crossing and recrossing the state's boundaries. In 1820, well before Denmark Vesey alerted South Carolinians to the dangers of a growing free black population, the General Assembly passed an act strictly forbidding individual acts of manumission, rendering emancipation possible only through legislative action. The 1820 statute also forbade "free persons of color from entering into the state." The 1822 act, then, was not only a reaction to Vesey but also a clarification and strengthening of previous laws that were specifically designed to prohibit black immigration or importation into the state. Further statutes were passed in 1823 and 1825 that continually sought to make black entry into South Carolina, manumission, and certain types of black movement more difficult, if not wholly impossible.[53]

The provisions of the cumulative laws not only sought to preclude African American entry into the state but also sought to constrain the possibilities of freedom for black Carolinians. Beyond making manumission an exclusively legislative responsibility, the General Assembly also imposed a tax on newly freed black men of "fifty dollars per annum," an impossible amount for most free blacks to pay. If they could not pay the tax, they faced the possibility of arrest and enslavement for a period not exceeding five years. Such rules not only kept free blacks from entering South Carolina but also forced many black Carolinians to emigrate out of the state rather than face reenslavement. Those who remained were allowed to do so only if they fostered relationships with prominent white men, as they were "compelled" by the General Assembly "to have a guardian" who would vouchsafe their "good character and correct habits."[54]

These laws, like the designs of early national planners, Revolutionary leaders, and provincial officials before them, were implemented to produce a very specific vision of South Carolina—one that reinforced and re-created the racial status quo, and one that continued to rely upon the labor of the enslaved for its maintenance. These laws sought to do much the same work as the developmental designs presented by Robert Mills, Abram Blanding, and Nicholas Herbemont: produce a modern state whose freedoms were meant exclusively for white Carolinians. Though South Carolina rejected the ideas of the Board of Public Works, state leaders and individual Carolinians went to great lengths—through both violence and legislation—to guarantee that the blessings of the liberal state were bestowed exclusively on the white population. As the anonymous runaway made clear in his reminiscences of laboring on the railroad, however, such a state continued to rely upon the labor of the enslaved. Subsequently, as his memoir illuminated, regardless of the sharp limits and boundaries that South Carolinians placed around the state or the meaning of freedom, enslaved men and women challenged, reshaped, and imposed their own meanings on such spaces and ideas. And in doing so, they asserted a particular vision of a state built for freedom that was itself revolutionary. By using the state's (and nation's) infrastructure to liberate themselves—freeing their actions, if not completely demolishing their condition as slaves—enslaved men and women articulated an idea of the liberal state that extended well beyond economic access and disciplinary subjectivity. Theirs was a conceptualization of freedom that was radically egalitarian and emancipatory. In this way, black Carolinians not only reshaped the meaning of South Carolina's early governing praxis but also created a unique vision of freedom that would continue to shape the idea of the liberal state for generations.

Conclusion

Slaves made the state. To understand this—slaves' role in the production of the modern state—is not simply to add another historical actor to our narration of early American political development; it is also to reimagine how we contemplate the state itself. In the first place, this is about moving our analysis of statecraft from the courthouses, governors' mansions, and legislative halls that have for so long preoccupied our analysis of governance and, instead, center our focus more closely on the everyday drudgery and meanness of the state's on-the-ground creation. For generations, South Carolina's state leaders, local administrators, private contractors, engineers, militia commanders, governors, legislators, and city officials called upon the labor of thousands of unfree black Carolinians to construct and maintain South Carolina's physical infrastructure. The enslaved gathered together in large and small groups—sometimes near their homes and sometimes at considerable distances—building roads, carving out canals, raising public buildings, and hastily constructing fortifications. Their jobs were dangerous, dirty, unrelenting, and often deadly. Slaves cut down whole forests, removed acres and acres of earth by hand, built elaborate edifices, and all the while cooked, and cleaned, and cared for themselves and the white men for whom they labored. Their work was not glamorous, and for the most part it is forgotten. Nevertheless, their significant and essential labors remain hidden in plain view among the newspaper advertisements, accounting slips, petitions, governors' reports, administrative orders, and legislative debates that together constitute the early record of state governance. The relative invisibility of slave state labor has a lot to do with the early states', particularly Southern states', elision from our historical memory. But it is also a consequence of the normalization of unfree labor to state development. In South Carolina, it became almost an afterthought that slaves would be laboring on roads, canals, bridges, public buildings, and fortifications. State leaders did not debate if slaves should labor on public works; they simply sought to determine how they would procure their labor, what the work would look like, and the means through which they would compensate slave owners.[1]

Even as the analysis of slave state labor pulls our imagination away from the centers of state power and toward the swamps and forests of the transforming countryside, an analysis of enslaved Carolinians' role in the production of the state also allows us to reconsider our analysis of the content and contours of early governing discourse. The debates and discussions surrounding slave state labor, which occurred regularly in the statehouse, at meetings of local road commissioners, among army and militia commanders and their subordinates, and in the private correspondence, newspaper articles, and petitions of individual South Carolinians, placed slaves at the center of the earliest discourse of state development. Whenever South Carolinians considered infrastructural development, the erection of public buildings, the defense of the province and then state, and the repayment of their soldiers, they invariably turned to the topic of the state's enslaved population. In this way, slaves often lay at the center of the most mundane aspects of early governing praxis: the everyday interactions between citizens and government that underlay the production of the state. Black Carolinians, then, were often essential to the dialogue that tethered together political elites in the colonial and then state assembly, local administrators of roads and fortifications, and the individual white men who claimed ownership over their bodies. Amid the conversations, debates, and correspondence regarding the appropriation, compensation, and supervision of slave state labor, South Carolinians worked out governing hierarchies, administrative procedures, and the meaning of citizenship and duty. To be sure, slave state labor was not the only thing that state leaders discussed, but enslaved labor was the rare topic that occurred at all levels of governance, from governors' messages and comptroller's reports to local grand jury presentments, individual petitions, and corporate reports.

Importantly, such discussions did not focus exclusively on the labors that slaves performed for the state. The bulk of slaves' lives revolved around the work they did for their masters. In the colonial and early national eras, such work was as important to the early creation of the state as the roads and canals that they painstakingly constructed and the procedures and policies that such labor entailed. South Carolina was on the cutting edge of infrastructural development throughout the colonial and early national eras, producing what travelers often described as some of the finest roads, causeways, and bridges in all of Britain's North America, as well as constructing innovative waterworks and even the nation's first long-distance railway. But without traffic, roads, rivers, and cuts lacked meaning and significance. Enslaved boatmen, skilled slaves, midwives, drivers, and field hands—all of whom were in one way or another, and to varying degrees, on the move throughout the eighteenth and early nineteenth centuries—provided much of the meaning that transformed a contested space on the southern edge of the North American

Atlantic Coast into both province and state. While state planners, cartographers, and government officials may have imagined South Carolina's infrastructure as an interconnected web of economic activity, it was often slaves, in the course of their everyday labors, who turned agendas, schemes, and ideas into material realities. Acknowledging the significance of movement to infrastructural development requires that we stretch our analytical framework in our assessments of governing praxis and political development.[2]

Of course, slaves produced the state not only through their day-to-day labors but also through their everyday activities on their own behalf—mundane and rebellious alike—which occurred in the interstices, margins, and even sometimes at the center of state space. Black Carolinians took advantage of their access to South Carolina's territory to create their own places of significance—religious, economic, social, and political. Such spaces regularly challenged and reshaped the meaning of state space, as well as the practices of government—be they maroon communities on hidden river islands or economic entrepôts at the edges of plantations. South Carolina's territory and its earliest governing praxis were formed out of the dynamic interplay between state leaders' and slave owners' labor demands, and the practices that constituted black Carolinians' everyday lives.

Unfree state labor remained important well beyond the early national era, and in states across the American South and beyond. As one historian argues, throughout the antebellum era, states like Mississippi, Georgia, and Louisiana relied on slaves to labor on a variety of public works, from railroads in Mississippi to roads in Georgia. Such labor allowed Southern governments, including South Carolina's, to continue to promote the creation of modern states, even as they distanced themselves from and challenged the sovereignty of the general government. As Stephanie McCurry has argued, the forced labor of slaves was also considered a cornerstone of the Confederate state-building project. In addition, while slave state labor was mostly centered in the South in the United States, it was vital to development in slaveholding societies like Cuba and Brazil. And even though Northern and Western states eschewed slavery in their developmental schemes, as Ryan Dearinger has shown, they were unexceptional in their exploitation of marginalized labor for the construction of railroads and canals; such work was vital for the production of infrastructure in empires, nations, and states around the world. This remained true well after emancipation as governments and states depended on and continue to rely upon unfree and marginalized labor for the material construction and maintenance of their developmental agendas. Such truths are recognizable whether one examines the exploitation of prison labor in the United States throughout the long twentieth century to the more recent development of World Cup venues in Qatar.³

As I have tried to illuminate throughout, however, black Carolinians did much more than simply provide labor for early infrastructural development. Through their laboring movement and day-to-day practices, they imbued the state's territory with everyday significance and, more importantly, directly and indirectly challenged South Carolina's narrow vision of the modern state. White South Carolinians imagined into being an expansive, if increasingly isolated, state that provided economic opportunity, security, and individual freedoms exclusively for its white residents. That vision, however, depended on enslaved men and women who consistently undermined and challenged the presumed limits and boundaries of that state. Consequently, white Carolinians integrated surveillance, overt violence, and brutal racial policing into their vision and practice of liberal governance. Just as the exploitation of unfree labor remained vital to modern governing practices, so too these practices continue to endure as integral aspects of the contemporary state. Importantly, however, we must also remember that while slaves constructed the state's infrastructure and reshaped its governing policies, black Carolinians also enacted their own vision of state space. By using the state's infrastructure to survive and resist slavery, and even to escape to freedom, they provided a vision of the state and its infrastructure that was at once egalitarian, emancipatory, and without racial limits.

Notes

Abbreviations

CUSC   Clemson University Special Collections
DH   Drayton Hall
GHS   Georgia Historical Society
LOC   Library of Congress
NARA   National Archives
SCDAH   South Carolina Department of Archives and History
SCHS   South Carolina Historical Society
SCL   South Caroliniana Library, University of South Carolina
SHC   Southern Historical Collection, University of North Carolina

Introduction

1. Mills, *Internal Improvement of South-Carolina*, 18.

2. Mills made clear that both of these issues lay at the center of his argument. Mills, *Internal Improvement of South-Carolina*, 3, 11–12. For population estimates, see Social Explorer, accessed July 11, 2017, https://www.socialexplorer.com/6f4cdab7a0/.

Throughout this book I have made reference to both Charleston and Charlestown, the former being the post-Revolutionary rendering of the latter. I've chosen to use the colonial spelling when making any reference to Charleston prior to the name change.

3. Governor William Bull, "Representation of the Present State of Religion, Polity, Agriculture, and Commerce," in Smith, *Stono*, 31; Quintana, "Planners, Planters, and Slaves."

4. For the association of states with maps, see Winichakul, *Siam Mapped*, 16–17; Brenner et al., "State Space in Question," 1–2. For an introduction to state space, see Lefebvre, "Space and the State"; Elden, "Land, Terrain, Territory"; Ballve, "Everyday State Formation"; Agnew, "Territorial Trap." My idea of the influence of everyday practices on the production of states and state space is heavily influenced by Mitchell, "Limits of the State," and Mitchell, "Society, Economy, and the State Effect."

5. Lefebvre, "Space and the State," 224–25.

6. The question of "how" the state is made possible is shaped by recent work in early modern European history, especially Joyce, *State of Freedom*; and Guldi, *Roads to Power*. For a small sample of recent work that confronts governance and space in early U.S. history, see Balogh, *Government Out of Sight*; Saler, *Settlers' Empire*; Downs, "Three Faces of Sovereignty"; and Alvarez, "Inventing the US-Mexico Border." For an excellent examination of the social production of national state space, see St. John, *Line in the Sand*.

7. Novak, *People's Welfare*; Balogh, *Government Out of Sight*. For an excellent review of the literature on the state and American political development, see Sugrue, "Reconfiguration of Political History"; and Novak, "Beyond Stateless Democracy." For an excellent introduction into studies of race and American political development, see Lowndes, Novkov, and Warren, *Race and American Political Development*. For sovereignty and jurisdiction, see Ford, *Settler Sovereignty*.

8. My idea of the everyday practices of the state is informed by Joyce, *State of Freedom*, 1–27. For an interesting analysis of South Carolina's state from the perspective of the law, see Edwards, *People and Their Peace*.

9. Hahn, *Nation under Our Feet*, 13–61; Brown, "Social Death and Political Life."

10. Mukerji, *Impossible Engineering*, 36–59.

11. Bellucci, "Introduction."

12. For an example of an excellent recent study of the national state, see Rao, *National Duties*.

13. Freehling, *Prelude to Civil War*; Sinah, *Counterrevolution of Slavery*; Ford, *Deliver Us from Evil*.

14. Greene, *Quest for Power*; Mercantini, *Who Shall Rule at Home?*; Klein, *Unification of a Slave State*. For a more specific focus on development, see Hewitt, "Expansion and Improvement."

15. Sinah, *Counterrevolution of Slavery*; Ford, *Deliver Us from Evil*.

16. Rockman, "Unfree Origins of American Capitalism"; Bellows, "'Insanity Is the Disease of Civilization'"; Marrs, *Railroads in the Old South*.

17. For more on the technologies of government, see Joyce, "Material Powers"; and Joyce and Bennett, *State of Freedom*, 1–52.

18. Social Explorer, accessed July 11, 2017, https://www.socialexplorer.com/6f4cdab7a0/.

Chapter One

1. Morgan, *Slave Counterpoint*, 152, 162; Otto, "Origins of Cattle Ranching"; Edelson, "Nature of Slavery"; McCord, *Statutes at Large of South Carolina*, 9, 66.

2. Bull, "Representation of the Present State of Religion, Polity, Agriculture, and Commerce," 31. For more on the Stono Rebellion, see Wood, *Black Majority*, 271–320; Thornton, "African Dimensions of the Stono Rebellion"; Pearson, "'Countryside Full of Flames.'" From petitions to the assembly, Supreme Court decisions, and anecdotal evidence gleaned from newspapers and plantation diaries, I make the assumption that the enslaved regularly purchased goods on behalf of themselves and their masters. For example, see "Petition from the Inhabitants of Camden to the General Assembly," Petitions to the South Carolina General Assembly, ND01854/ND01855, SCDAH; "Petition from the Inhabitants of Georgetown to the General Assembly," 1810, no. 75, SCDAH; "The State vs. Francis Anone," in Nott and McCord, *Reports of Cases Determined in the Constitutional Court of South Carolina*, 27–34. For more on law and society in eighteenth- and nineteenth-century South Carolina and interpreting statutes, see Edwards, *People and Their Peace*, 26–54.

3. Some historians argue that since the colonial assembly did not mention increased vigilance for road construction in the subsequent, harsh slave laws passed following the rebellion, it is unlikely that the rebellion grew out of road construction. See Lockley, *Maroon Communities in South Carolina*, 12. In fact, however, the colonial assembly did pass new regulations for road construction, increasing the fines for white men who did not participate in road duty or spent the time drunk; penalizing commissioners of the roads who failed to do their duty; and legislating that "no more than 30 slaves be suffered to work upon the High Roads together; and that there be one Overseer appointed to each Gang." While such regulations would be implemented only haphazardly, what is in fact clear is that the Stono Rebellion led to a dramatic shift in infrastructural policy, if not practice. Easterby, *Journal of the Commons House of Assembly, 1741–1742*, 236–37. In discussing the "mundane" activities of state development, I follow the lead of historian Patrick Joyce. Joyce, *State of Freedom*, 1–52.

4. Specific infrastructural laws will be discussed throughout the chapter. For a list of most of South Carolina's early developmental laws, see McCord, *Statutes at Large of South Carolina*, 9; and McCord, *Statutes at Large of South Carolina*, 7: 475–588.

5. April, 17, 1756, William de Brahm to Commissioners of Fortifications, Journal of the Commissioners of Fortifications, 1755–1770, ser. 164001, SCDAH.

6. Ramsey, *Yamasee War*; Beck, *Chiefdoms, Collapse, and Coalescence*; Gallay, *Indian Slave Trade*, 40–100, 199–258.

7. Lawson, *New Voyage to Carolina*, 14. Gallay, *Indian Slave Trade*, 157; Beck, *Chiefdoms, Collapse, and Coalescence*, 137–80.

8. Edelson, *Plantation Enterprise in Colonial South Carolina*, 13–52.

9. The 1702 act is not listed in the edited collection of statutes, but the act was buttressed in 1703. The 1703 statute quoted from the original. McCord, *Statutes at Large of South Carolina*, 9: 1.

10. McCord, *Statutes at Large of South Carolina*, 9: 24–25, 65.

11. Weir, *Colonial South Carolina*, 80, 117–18, 265–75; Smith, *Stono*, xi–xv; McCord, *Statutes at Large of South Carolina*, 9: 2, 6, 11.

12. Gallay, *Indian Slave Trade*, 259–354; Beck, *Chiefdoms, Collapse, and Coalescence*, 137–222.

13. Roper, *Conceiving Carolina*, 132–57; McCord, *Statutes at Large of South Carolina*, 9: 43.

14. McCord, *Statutes at Large of South Carolina*, 9: 50.

15. Ibid.

16. Morgan, "Black Society in the Lowcountry," 85–92; Wood, *Black Majority*, 142–66.

17. Edelson, *Plantation Enterprise in Colonial South Carolina*, 126–65; Meriwether, *Expansion of South Carolina*.

18. Minutes of the South Carolina Commissioners of the High Roads, St. John's Parish, Berkley County, folder 2, SCHS; St. Stephen's Parish, Commissioners of the Roads, Minutes of the Commissioners of the Roads, ser. L 60001, no. 60, SCDAH.

19. Cooper, *Statutes at Large of South Carolina*, 3: 122–24, 255, 272; Meriwether, *Expansion of South Carolina*, 17–33; Hewitt, "State in the Planters' Service," 49–73.

20. Petition of Several of the Inhabitants of the Parish of St. James Santee in Craven County, May 5, 1743, in Easterby, *Journal of the Commons House of Assembly, 1742–1744,* 437–38.

21. McCord, *Statutes at Large of South Carolina,* 7: 503–4, 489–91.

22. Petition of Residents Residing near Congaree and Wateree River, in Easterby, *Journal of the Commons House of Assembly, 1751–1752,* 137.

23. Woodmason, "Remonstrance Presented to the Common's House of Assembly," 215–18; Klein, *Unification of a Slave State,* 19.

24. Hooker, *Carolina Backcountry on the Eve of the Revolution,* 215.

25. Minutes of the Commissioners of the Roads, 1783–1839, St. Paul's Parish, Commissioners of the Roads, ser. L58001, SCDAH; Minutes of the Commissioners of the Roads, 1817–1858, All Saints Parish, Commissioners of the Roads, ser. L47001, SCDAH; Minutes of the Commissioners of the Roads, St. Stephen's Parish, Commissioners of the Roads, ser. L 60001, SCDAH; Minutes of the Commissioners of the Roads, St. John's Parish, Berkley County, folder 1, SCHS. For British infrastructural policy, see Guldi, *Roads to Power,* 25–78. For examples of other colonial road-building practices, see Mitchell, *Statutes at Large of Pennsylvania,* 68–70.

26. August 24, 1789, Minutes of the Commissioners of the Roads, St. Stephen's Parish, Commissioners of the Roads, SCDAH; *South Carolina Gazette,* September 3, 1733; Minutes of the Commissioners of the High Roads, St. John's Parish, Berkley County, folder 1, SCHS.

27. Joyce, "Material Powers," 1–22; Mukerji, *Impossible Engineering,* 36–59; Joyce, *State of Freedom,* 53–185.

28. McCord, *Statutes at Large of South Carolina,* 7: 397–418; Cooper, *Statutes at Large of South Carolina,* 3: 556–62, 593–94, 739–42; Easterby, *Journal of the Commons House of Assembly, 1741–1742,* 236–37; Wax, "Great Risque We Run."

29. Lanning, *St. Augustine Expedition of 1740,* 12, 93; Easterby, *Journal of the Commons House of Assembly, 1741–1742,* 563–77.

30. Easterby, *Journal of the Commons House of Assembly, 1742–1744,* 42, 117–34, 80–81.

31. Easterby, *Journal of the Commons House of Assembly, 1742–1744,* 81. Interestingly, John Laurens's insistence on enlisting enslaved men in the Revolutionary army forced South Carolinians to revisit this debate during the Revolution. Then, as before, South Carolina's assembly voted down the proposal, despite Laurens's insistence that he would labor "to transform the timid Slave into a firm defender of Liberty and render him worthy to enjoy it himself." John Laurens to Henry Laurens, February 17, 1779, in Chesnutt, *Papers of Henry Laurens,* 15: 60, 60n3. For more on compensating slave informants, see McCord, *Statutes at Large of South Carolina,* 7: 420–25.

32. Easterby, *Journal of the Commons House of Assembly, 1742–1744,* 15, 99–102.

33. Ibid., 100–102.

34. Ibid., 273, 281.

35. September 1 and November 17, 1755, February 2, 1756, Journal of the Commissioners of Fortifications, 1755–1770, South Carolina, Commissioners of Fortifications, ser. S164001, SCDAH. For more on South Carolina and the Seven Years' War, see Hatley, *Dividing Paths,* 105–40; Weir, *Colonial South Carolina,* 265–75, 287–89.

36. April 17, 1756, Journal of the Commissioners of Fortifications, SCDAH; Hamer, "Fate of the Exiled Acadians in South Carolina." For another example of the use of Acadian labor, see Hodson, "'Bondage So Harsh.'"

37. September 8, 1755, April 17, 1756, Journal of the Commissioners of Fortifications, SCDAH.

38. Henry Laurens to James Cordes Jr., August 30, 1765; Laurens to Cordes, August 31, 1765, in Rogers Jr., et al., *Papers of Henry Laurens*, 4: 670–71; November 28, 1765, Minutes of the Commissioners of the Roads, St. John's Parish, SCHS.

39. Henry Laurens to James Cordes Jr., August 30, 1765, Henry Laurens to James Cordes Jr., August 31, 1765, Henry Laurens to James Marion, August 31, 1765, in Rogers, *Papers of Henry Laurens*, 4: 670–72.

40. Henry Laurens to James Cordes Jr., August 31, 1765, in Rogers, *Papers of Henry Laurens*, 4: 670–71.

41. Henry Laurens to James Marion, August 31, 1765, in Rogers, *Papers of Henry Laurens*, 4: 671–72. For a biography of Laurens, see Wallace, *Life of Henry Laurens*; and Edelson, *Plantation Enterprise in Colonial South Carolina*, 200–254.

42. Petition from Samuel Harris and Others Asking that Harris Receive Compensation for a Skilled Slave Who Was Accidentally Killed, 1802, no. 174, ser. S165015, SCDAH.

43. Petition from William McCants Asking Payment for His Slave Daniel Who Was Killed, November 18, 1807, no. 124, ser. S165015, Legislative Papers, SCDAH; Petition from William Baker Asking Remuneration for a Slave Accidentally Killed, 1825 c., no. ND1696, ser. S165015, Legislative Papers, SCDAH.

44. "Journal of the Second Council of Safety," 167, 172.

45. McCord, *Statutes at Large of South Carolina*, 7: 358; Lipscomb, *Journal of the Commons House of Assembly, November 20, 1755–July 6, 1757*, 29–30, 96, 180, 274.

46. Lipscomb, *Journal of the Commons House of Assembly*, 418.

47. *South Carolina Council Journal*, April 4, 1769, SCDAH.

48. "Ranger's Report of Travels with General Oglethorpe," 223.

49. Bartram, "Diary of a Journey through the Carolinas, Georgia, and Florida," 22.

50. Ibid.

Chapter Two

1. *Charleston Evening Gazette*, October 1, 1785.

2. Ibid.

3. Olwell, *Masters, Slaves, and Subjects*, 221–70.

4. For more on the runaways on Sullivan's Island, see Olwell, "'Domestick Enemies,'" 40–46; Journal of the Second Council of Safety, 167, 95, 126.

5. *South Carolina Gazette*, December 11, 1775. The initial advertisement mentioned also appears in the *South Carolina Gazette* on November 7, 14, 21, and 28; McCord, *Statutes at Large of South Carolina, Edited under Authority of the Legislature*, 7: 428–29.

6. McCord, *Statutes at Large of South Carolina, Edited under Authority of the Legislature*, 7: 429.

7. Ibid. For South Carolina and the oath of allegiance, see Piecuch, *Three Peoples, One King*, 93–108.

8. Hemphill, *Journals of the General Assembly and House of Representatives, 1776–1780*, 270; Piecuch, *Three Peoples, One King*, 124–227.

9. Hemphill, *Journals of the General Assembly and House of Representatives*, 250–51, 253–55; Chesnutt and Taylor, *Papers of Henry Laurens*, 15: 234–35 note 4; de Brahm, "Journal of the Siege of Charleston by the English, in 1780," 273.

10. Salley, *Journal of the Commissioners of the Navy of South Carolina*, 9, 79, 119.

11. Lander, "Iron Industry in Ante-Bellum South Carolina," 339; *Gazette of the State of South Carolina*, November 24, 1779.

12. *Gazette of the State of South Carolina*, November 24, 1779; Salley, *Col. William Hill's Memoirs of the Revolution*, 8.

13. Petition of William Ancrum, March 1, 1785, item no. 62, Petitions to the General Assembly, 1776–1883, ser. 165015, Legislative Papers, SCDAH; Thompson, *Journals of the House of Representatives, 1783–1784*, 11; Liles, "Thomas Sumter's Law," 106–46.

14. Liles, "Thomas Sumter's Law," 228–37.

15. Salley, *Journal of the House of Representatives of South Carolina, January 8, 1782–February 26, 1782*, 46.

16. Liles, "Thomas Sumter's Law," 228–37. Also see Weir, "'Violent Spirit'"; and Brannon, "Reconciling the Revolution," 85–108; Salley, *Journal of the Senate*, 82–84.

17. Salley, *Journal of the Senate*, 124; Liles, "Thomas Sumter's Law," 242; Morgan, "Black Society in the Lowcountry, 1760–1810," 110–11; Salley, *Journal of the House of Representatives*, 57; Edwards, *Journals of the Privy Council*, 13.

18. Salley, *Journal of the House of Representatives*, 72.

19. Ibid. For Kershaw, Robinson, and Ferguson (respectively): Kirkland and Kennedy, *Historic Camden*, 11–12; Culler, *Orangeburg District, 1768–1868*, 331; McCord, *Statutes at Large*, 9: 211.

20. Salley, *Journal of the House of Representatives*, 77.

21. Ibid., 127; Cooper, *Statutes at Large of South Carolina*, 4: 515–22; Brannon, "Reconciling the Revolution," 140–249; Sales of Land & Negroes, Negroes for Public Service, box 2-1, Commissioners of Forfeited Estates, Comptroller General Papers, SCDAH.

22. "Gov. Matthews to Col. P. Horry, May 27, 1782," in Gibbes, *Documentary History of the American Revolution*, 2: 182.

23. Sales of Land & Negroes, Negroes for Public Service, box 2-1, Commissioners of Forfeited Estates, SCDAH.

24. Ibid.; Cooper, *Statutes at Large of South Carolina*, 4: 522.

25. "Governor John Matthews to General Francis Marion, March 4, 1782," "General Francis Marion to Col. P. Horry, March 13, 1782" and "General Francis Marion to Col. P. Horry, March 29, 1782," in Gibbes, *Documentary History of the American Revolution*, 2: 263, 280.

26. McCord, *Statutes at Large*, 9: 274. Even after commissioners were elected or appointed following the war, road maintenance remained a work in progress. For example,

road commissioners in Pendleton District complained that they did not even have copies of the existing road laws, making it difficult to fulfill their duties. Commissioners of Roads for Pendleton District, Report Recommending That the Present Plan to Repair Roads be Retained, 11/27/1807, item no. 23, Misc. Reports to the General Assembly, ser. S165029, Legislative Papers, SCDAH; Petition of John Rutledge and Others, February 7, 1786, item no. 5, Petitions to the General Assembly, ser. S165015, Legislative Papers, SCDAH.

27. *South Carolina Gazette*, January 18, 1770. For more on the Santee Canal, see Kapsch, *Historic Canals & Waterways of South Carolina*, 21–53. For the Regulator movement, see Klein, *Unification of a Slave State*, 78–108.

28. *South-Carolina Gazette*, January 18, 1770; July 4, 1774.

29. David Ramsay to Benjamin Rush, April 8, 1784, in Ramsay, *Transactions of the American Philosophical Society: David Ramsay, 1749–1815*, 77.

30. Kapsch, *Historic Canals and Waterways of South Carolina*, 41.

31. *City Gazette and Daily Advertiser*, September 3, 1792; *South Carolina State Gazette & Timothy & Mason's Daily Advertiser*, October 20, 1794.

32. Webber, "Col. Senf's Account of the Santee Canal," 9.

33. Webber, "Col. Senf's Account of the Santee Canal (Continued)," 126, 127; Diary of Henry and Rene Ravenel 1785–1851, Thomas P. Ravenel Collection, SCHS.

34. Petition of the President and Directors of the Santee Canal Company, December 12, 1793, Petitions to the General Assembly, ser. S165015, 129, Legislative Papers, SCDAH; South Carolina Commissioners of the High Roads, St. John's Parish, Berkley County, folder 2, SCHS; October 9, 1794, St. Stephen's Parish, Commissioners of the Roads, Minutes of the Commissioners of the Roads, ser. L 60001, no. 60, SCDAH; South Carolina Commissioners of the High Roads, St. John's Parish, Berkley County, folder 2; St. Stephen's Parish, Commissioners of the Roads. Minutes of the Commissioners of the Roads, SCDAH.

35. *City Gazette and Daily Advertiser*, February 26, 1796; *Supplement to the City Gazette and Daily Advertiser*, March 7, 1796; Chesnutt, *Papers of Henry Laurens*, 15: 304–5, note 1.

36. *Philadelphia Gazette*, June 12, 1801; *South-Carolina State Gazette*, August 15, 1801.

37. *South-Carolina State Gazette*, August 15, 1801.

38. Petition of Adam Gilchrist and Other Members of the Santee Canal Company, ND, no. 1095, Petitions to the General Assembly, S165015, Legislative Papers, SCDAH.

39. McCord, *Statutes at Large*, 9: 550.

40. Kapsch, *Historic Canals and Waterways of South Carolina*, 54–55; Petition of the Incorporated Catawba Company, ND, no. 1671, Petitions to the General Assembly, S165015, Legislative Papers, SCDAH.

41. Kapsch, *Historical Canals and Waterways of South Carolina*, 61–62.

42. McCord, *Statutes at Large*, 9: 556–57; Daniel Stevens, For the Commissioners Appointed for the Opening of Walls Cut, Report on the Completion of their Work, ND, no. 5, Report to the General Assembly, S165029, Legislative Papers, SCDAH.

43. Petition of Richard Proctor and Supporting Papers, December 10, 1794, no. 122, Petitions to General Assembly, S165015, Legislative Papers, SCDAH.

44. Commissioners of Columbia Letters to Governor Charles Pinckney, May 29–October 29, 1789, no. 511, Governor's Messages, S165009, Legislative Papers, SCDAH; Petition of James Brown, Carpenter, December 12, 1793, no. 130, Petitions to the General Assembly, S165015, Legislative Papers, SCDAH.

45. *South Carolina Gazette; And General Advertiser,* June 11, 1811.

46. *Charleston Courier,* August 11, 1804.

47. Commissioners of Roads for St. James Goose Creek, Report Regarding the System for Repairing Roads, October 3, 1807, item no. 23, Misc. Reports to the General Assembly, ser. S165029, Legislative Papers, SCDAH. Commissioners of Roads for Lower District of St. George's Parish, Report Enumerating the Miles of Road to Be Kept in Repair and the Number of Persons Liable for Road Duty, December 2, 1807, item no. 11, Misc. Reports to the General Assembly, ser. S165029, Legislative Papers, SCDAH.

48. Commissioners of Roads for St. John's Berkley Parish, Report of the Miles of Road to Be Maintained and Number of Persons Liable for Road Duty, ND, item no. 91, Misc. Reports to the General Assembly, ser. S165029, Legislative Papers, SCDAH; Commissioners of Roads Saint Peters Parish, Report of the Miles of Road to Be Maintained and Number of Persons Liable for Road Duty, November 27, 1807, item no. 17, Misc. Reports to the General Assembly, ser. S165029, Legislative Papers, SCDAH.

49. McCord, *Statutes at Large,* 9: 474–75; Charleston Bridge Company, Petition Asking Legislative Aid in Rebuilding a Bridge Destroyed by a Storm, ND, no. 1498, Petitions to the General Assembly, ser. S165015, Legislative Papers, SCDAH; Petition of Inhabitants of the Parishes of St. George Dorchester, St. James Goose Creek, and St. Andrews, Requesting the Appropriation of Funds to Maintain the Roads from Givhans Ferry to Charleston, ND, no. 1213, Petitions to the General Assembly, S165015, Legislative Papers, SCDAH.

50. Governor William Moultrie, Message Concerning Negroes Sold to John Taylor, March 22, 1785, no. 349, Governor's Messages, ser. S165009, Legislative Papers, SCDAH; Edwards, *Journals of the Privy Council, 1783–1789,* 13; Olwell, *Masters, Slaves, and Subjects,* 267.

51. *South-Carolina Gazette; And General Advertiser,* April 29, 1783; *South-Carolina Gazette,* August 30, 1785.

52. General Francis Marion to Col. Peter Horry, Gibbes, *Documentary History of the American Revolution,* 266–67; Memorial of William Bull Jr., February 1788, Loyalists, microfilm, 57. Quoted in Olwell, *Masters, Slaves, and Subjects,* 267.

53. *South-Carolina Gazette,* December 8, 1779; *Charleston Gazette & Daily Advertiser,* March 14, 1800.

54. Diouf, *Slavery's Exiles,* 190; *Gazette of the State of Georgia,* October 19, 1786.

55. *Gazette of the State of Georgia,* October 19, 1786.

56. *Charleston Morning Post,* October 26, 1786; Diouf, *Slavery's Exiles,* 192.

57. Diouf, *Slavery's Exiles*, 192; "The State vs. Lewis a Negroe," in Georgia Slavery Trials, Telemon Cuyler Collection, Hargrett Library, University of Georgia; *Columbian Herald*, May 28, 1787.

58. *Gazette of the State of Georgia*, May 10, 1787; Thomas Pinckney Letterbook, 1787–1789, SCDAH; Letter from Lieutenant Governor William Bull to Colonel George Jackson, December 30, 1765, South Carolina Commons House of Assembly Journals, 2–4, NARA. Quoted in Lockley, *Maroon Communities in South Carolina*.

59. De Vorsey, *Georgia–South Carolina Boundary*, 21–50.

60. Governor Thomas Pinckney Message with Enclosures, Regarding the Right of Citizens to Navigate the Savannah River, January 26, 1788, Governor's Messages, no. 448, S165009, SCDAH.

61. Winichakul, *Siam Mapped*, 16–17.

62. Mitchell, "Society, Economy, and the State Effect," 76–97.

63. General James Jackson to Governor Thomas Pinckney, December 2, 1786, Joseph Valance Beven Papers, GHS.

64. *Columbian Herald*, May 28, 1787.

65. Ibid.

66. Ibid.

Chapter Three

1. Charles Drayton Diary, January 12–17, 1791, DH.

2. Ibid.

3. My focus on movement developed out of theoretical pieces on everyday practice, space, and movement: Henderson, "South of the North, North of the South"; McKittrick, *Demonic Grounds*. For more on changes in the plantation landscape in the late colonial and early national eras, see Edelson, *Plantation Enterprise in Colonial South Carolina*, 92–165 and 200–254; Chaplin, *Anxious Pursuit*, 187–355; and Mendenhall, "History of Agriculture in South Carolina."

4. For more on the necessity of slave movement and planters' attempts to control that movement, see Schermerhorn, *Money over Mastery, Family over Freedom*; Wood, *Black Majority*, 95–270; Otto, "Origins of Cattle-Ranching in Colonial South Carolina," 117–24; Edelson, "Nature of Slavery"; Edelson, "Affiliation without Affinity"; Morgan, *Slave Counterpoint*, 146–243; Olwell, *Masters, Slaves, and Subjects*, 17–56; Hadden, *Slave Patrol*, 105–66; Camp, "Pleasures of Resistance"; Franklin and Schweninger, *Runaway Slaves*; Buchanan, *Black Life on the Mississippi*, 101–48; Cecelski, *Waterman's Song*, 25–118.

5. See, for example, Cecelski, *Waterman's Song*, 25–57. To be sure, while slaves found opportunity in their mobility, the spaces they carved for themselves were heavily policed, and they remained vulnerable to the violent whims of the market, governing officials, and individuals. For example, see Schermerhorn, *Money over Mastery, Family over Freedom*, 134–63.

6. Charles Drayton Diary, 1791–1818, DH. My idea of the possibilities inherent to the lived experience of space comes from Certeau's *The Practice of Everyday Life* and in particular his analysis of spatial practices in the chapter, "Walking in the City," 91–110.

7. Bartram, *Travels*, 373.

8. Ibid. For more on the construction of the plantation enterprise on the northern fringes of South Carolina's coastline, see Edelson, *Plantation Enterprise in Colonial South Carolina*, 126–65; Morgan, *Slave Counterpoint*, 27–101, 146–203.

9. Bartram, *Travels*, 373.

10. Ibid. Population estimates come from Morgan, *Slave Counterpoint*, 40–101.

11. For more on the early construction of the plantation enterprise, see Wood, *Black Majority*, 35–130; Coclanis, *Shadow of a Dream*, 48–110; Edelson, *Plantation Enterprise in Colonial South Carolina*, 53–165; Chaplin, *Anxious Pursuit*, 92–186.

12. Chaplin, *Anxious Pursuit*, 190.

13. Edelson, *Plantation Enterprise in Colonial South Carolina*, 200–254.

14. Ibid. July 29, 1777, John Lewis Gervais letter to Henry Laurens, John Lewis Gervais Collection, SCHS; Letter from Mr. Loocock, July 12, 1786, Margaret Colleton Papers, SCL.

15. July 2, 1778, John Lewis Gervais letter to Henry Laurens, John Lewis Gervais Collection, SCHS; Samuel Mathis, Unbound Plantation Journal Notes, Samuel Mathis Papers, SCL.

16. Charles Drayton Diary, 1791–1793, DH. See, for example, the following entries: February 23, 1791, February 28, 1793, March 3, 1793, and December 16, 1798.

17. Charles Drayton Diary, March 3, 1793, and December 16, 1798, DH.

18. Chaplin, *Anxious Pursuit*, 228–30.

19. Ramsay, *Ramsay's History of South Carolina*, 2: 292–93; Chaplin, *Anxious Pursuit*, 229.

20. Drayton, *View of South Carolina*, 28; Charles Drayton Diary, February 23, 1796, DH.

21. Chaplin, *Anxious Pursuit*, 232–34.

22. Ibid., 232–34; American, *American Husbandry*, 1: 373–74.

23. Edelson, *Plantation Enterprise in Colonial South Carolina*, 200–254.

24. Ibid., 126–65.

25. Ibid. The idea of South Carolina's colonial settlements being devised into core and periphery comes from Edelson, *Plantation Enterprise in Colonial South Carolina*, 126–65.

26. Rogers, *Papers of Henry Laurens*, 4: 319; Charles Drayton Diary, September 16, 1792; J. J. Hales to Isaac Ball, September 6, 1817, Ball Family Papers, SCL.

27. Charles Drayton Diary, March 14, 1792, DH. Drayton's diary is in part defined by the comings and goings of his slaves. For more on skilled labor, including estimates, see Chaplin, *Anxious Pursuit*, 227–76; and Morgan, *Slave Counterpoint*, 217.

28. February 9, 1817, John J. Hales to Isaac Ball, Ball Family Papers, box 2, SCL.

29. Chaplin, *Anxious Pursuit*, 227–76.

30. July 2, 1778, Gervais to Laurens, John Lewis Gervais Collection, SCHS; Morgan, *Slave Counterpoint*, 237–44.

31. July 16, 1778, Gervais to Laurens, John Lewis Gervais Collection, SCHS. Georgetown District Grand Jury Presentment, no. 7, 1818, SCDAH; Georgetown District Grand Jury Presentment, no. 11, 1823, SCDAH; Charles Drayton Diary, March 19, 1796, DH.

32. Governor David R. Williams, Governor's Message to the General Assembly, 1816, SCDAH.

33. Ibid.

34. Message from Lieutenant Governor William Bull, December 30, 1765, South Carolina Commons House of Assembly Journals, SCDAH.

35. Lieutenant Governor William Bull to Col. George Jackson, December 30, 1765, South Carolina Commons House of Assembly Journals, SCDAH.

36. See, for example, Petition to the General Assembly, Williamsburg District, November 21, 1820, no. 144, SCDAH, discussed in more detail below; Petition to the General Assembly from Godin Guerard, December 3, 1793, no. 151, SCDAH—Guerard sought compensation for four slaves killed by the state militia; Petition to the General Assembly from Matthew O'Driscoll, 1814, no. 119, SCDAH—O'Driscoll sought compensation for two of his slaves who were shot because they were considered runaways according to the militia law; Petition to the General Assembly from Edward Brailsford, November 26, 1816, no. 100, SCDAH—Brailsford sought compensation for two of his slaves who were killed by the patrol in St. George Parish while the patrol was in pursuit of runaway slaves.

37. Petition to the General Assembly, David L. Rodgers, November 21, 1820, no. 144, SCDAH. For another example of slave patrols, militias, confused killings, and compensation claims, see Brophy, "Nat Turner Trials," 1830–1836.

38. Petition to the General Assembly, David L. Rodgers, November 21, 1820.

39. Ibid.

40. Ibid. For more on hiring out as a practice, see Martin, *Divided Mastery*, 17–43; Morgan, *Slave Counterpoint*, 204–44.

41. Petition to the General Assembly from David L. Rodgers, November 21, 1820, no. 144, SCDAH. For more on property rights in the South Carolina Lowcountry, see McCurry, *Masters of Small Worlds*, 5–36. McCurry highlighted the notion of "rights" and "private property" that William Elliott articulated in relation to the Lowcountry. Elliott, *Carolina Sports by Land and Water*.

42. Petition to the General Assembly from inhabitants of Georgetown, 1810, SCDAH. Georgetown residents' fears were somewhat overblown, but they were surrounded by what they believed was evidence that supported their anxieties. For example, on June 13, 1796, Charleston erupted in flames. By the time the flames were extinguished, nearly a quarter of the city had burned, including many of the city's iconic structures. Charles Drayton noted in his diary, "At D[rayton] hall I saw the smoke soon after it began & at night saw the very flames." Two days later he noted, "The fire has made great devastation. It is said 300 houses forming the lines of the streets have been destroyed." Once the smoke cleared, Charlestonians looked to the cause, but as one

correspondence from the city noted, "People seemed afraid to inquire into it—some would whisper their opinion that the negroes of the place were the authors—others that the French negroes were, and that they certainly intended to make a St. Domingo business of it." Authorities eventually arrested several slaves, who confessed to being hired by several white men who sought to use the conflagration as a cover for a planned robbery. Events like this lingered in the collective memory of white Carolinians; and in combination with slave rebellions—rumored and real—informed their perceptions, tinged as they were with tangible fears and anxieties, of black Carolinians' spatial practices. Charles Drayton Diary, June 14 and 16, 1796, DH; "Extract of a Letter Dated Charleston, June 19," *Moral and Political Telegraphe or Brookfield Advertiser*, July 27, 1796.

43. Petition to the General Assembly from the Black Swamp Association, 1823, no. 147, SCDAH; Pineville Police Association Secretary Book, vol. 1, 1823–1840, SCHS. The Charleston association that members of the Black Swamp Association were making reference to was the South Carolina Association, a vigilance society formed the same year. For more on the association, see January, "South Carolina Association"; Ford, *Deliver Us from Evil*, 282–96.

44. Social Explorer, accessed July 11, 2017, https://www.socialexplorer.com/6f4cdab7a0/.

45. O'Neall, *Negro Law of South Carolina*, 36; Hadden, *Slave Patrols*, 105–36.

46. O'Neall, *Negro Law of South Carolina*, 36; Hadden, *Slave Patrols*, 105–36.

47. O'Neall, *Negro Law of South Carolina*, 36.

48. Hadden, *Slave Patrols*, 41–136; Henry, "Police Control of the Slave in South Carolina," 28–50.

49. Henry, "Police Control of the Slave in South Carolina," 28–50. John Drayton, Governor's Message to the General Assembly, no. 768, 1800, SCDAH; John Geddes, Governor's Message to the General Assembly, no. 1271, 1820, SCDAH.

50. Hadden, *Slave Patrols*, 41–136; Henry, "Police Control of the Slave in South Carolina," 28–50.

51. Hadden, *Slave Patrols*, 41–136; Henry, "Police Control of the Slave in South Carolina," 28–50.

52. Charles Drayton Diary, October 10, 1796, October 21, 1796, DH.

53. Charles Drayton Diary, April 12, 1798, DH.

54. Nott and McCord, *Reports of Cases Determined in the Constitutional Court*, 113–14.

55. *Daily Telegraph*, November 4, 1848, quoted in Henry, "Police Control of the Slave in South Carolina," 30.

Chapter Four

1. *City Gazette and Morning Daily Advertiser*, July 18, 1825. For the possibility of black politics, see Hahn, *Nation under Our Feet*, 13–61; and Brown, "Social Death and Political Life in the Study of Slavery." For more on the economic possibilities present in Charleston, see Thompson, *Working on the Dock of the Bay*.

2. For more on the laboring movements of black Carolinians, see chapter 3.

3. For more on enslaved boatmen, see Buchanan, *Black Life on the Mississippi*, 16–80; Cecelski, *Waterman's Song*, 25–56; Schermerhorn, *Money over Mastery, Family over Freedom*, 63–98.

4. For more on the varied way that slaves experienced space, see Kaye, *Joining Places*; Camp, "Pleasures of Resistance"; Camp, *Closer to Freedom*; Blassingame, *Slave Community*; Morgan, *Slave Counterpoint*; Wood, *Black Majority*; Edelson, "Nature of Slavery"; Gomez, *Exchanging Our Country Marks*; Young, *Rituals of Resistance*; Creel, *Peculiar People*; Brown, *African-Atlantic Cultures and the South Carolina Lowcountry*; Brown, "'Walk in the Feenda'"; Rucker, *River Flows On*, 91–121; Schermerhorn, *Money over Mastery, Family over Freedom*.

5. Slaves across North America made similar choices throughout the eighteenth and nineteenth centuries. See, for example, Schermerhorn, *Money over Mastery, Family over Freedom*; and Maris-Wolf, *Family Bonds*. For more on runaways and maroons in South Carolina, see Franklin and Schweninger, *Runaway Slaves*; Camp, *Closer to Freedom*; Camp, "Pleasures of Resistance"; Lockley, *Maroon Communities in South Carolina*.

6. For more on the ramifications of white perceptions of black practices in South Carolina, see Ford, *Deliver Us from Evil*, 207–98; Young, *Domesticating Slavery*, 161–92; Freehling, *Prelude to Civil War*, 1–86.

7. For more on white perceptions of black practices, see Lichtenstein, "'That Disposition to Theft, with Which They Have Been Branded.'" For an analysis of the historical essentialization of black practices, see Johnson, "On Agency."

8. Davison McDowell Plantation Journal, September 4, 1826, Davison McDowell Papers, SCL; Georgetown District Grand Jury Presentment, no. 11, 1823, SCDAH. For the possibilities of bodily politics through running away, see Allewaert, *Ariel's Ecology*, 85–113.

9. J. J. Hale to Isaac Ball, February 26, 1817, Ball Family Papers, SCL. For more on the knowledge that slaves gained while laboring away from the plantation, see Otto, "Origins of Cattle-Ranching in Colonial South Carolina"; Edelson, "Nature of Slavery"; Edelson, "Affiliation without Affinity."

10. Charles Drayton Diary, March 19, 1796, DH; Morgan, *Slave Counterpoint*, 340. For more on enslaved boatmen, see Cecelski, *Waterman's Song*, 25–56; Buchanan, *Black Life on the Mississippi*, 19–80; Morgan, *Slave Counterpoint*, 237–44.

11. Henry Laurens, Letter to John Smith, June 4, 1765, Rogers, Chesnutt, Clark, and Edgar, *Henry Laurens Papers*, 4: 633. Davison McDowell Plantation Journal, May 3, 1827; Drayton, *View of South Carolina*, 28; Charles Drayton Diary, June 2, 1796, DH; Lichtenstein, "That Disposition to Theft."

12. Henry Laurens, August 15, 1765, *Henry Laurens Papers*, 5: 661–62. Charles Drayton Diary, August 27, 1813, DH; Charles Drayton Diary, October 30, 1798, DH; Charles Drayton Diary, July 11, 1808, DH.

13. Henry Laurens to Abraham Schad, April 30, 1765, in Rogers, Chesnutt, Clark, and Edgar, *Papers of Henry Laurens*, 4: 616. See, for example, the complaints that led to

the creation of the Charleston Bridge and Turnpike Company, *Charleston Courier*, August 11, 1804.

14. Josiah Smith to George Austin, January 31, 1774, Josiah Smith Letterbook, Josiah Smith Papers, SHC, quoted in Morgan, *Slave Counterpoint*, 338; Charles Drayton Diary, February 26, 1801, DH; "An Addition Act to the Several Acts for Making and Repairing of Highways," in McCord, *Statutes at Large of South Carolina*, 9: 26–28.

15. Morgan, *Slave Counterpoint*, 39–47. See especially Table 3, 43; Social Explorer, accessed July 11, 2017, https://www.socialexplorer.com/6f4cdab7ao/. McCord, *Statutes at Large of South Carolina*, 9: 26–28, 128–29, 162–63, and 397. For the growth of traffic in the early nation, see *Charleston Courier*, August 11, 1804; and Commissioners of Roads for St. James Goose Creek, Report Regarding the System for Repairing Roads, August 3, 1807, item no. 23, Misc. Reports to the General Assembly, ser. S165029, Legislative Papers, SCDAH.

16. Charles Drayton Diary, March 9, 1805, DH; Charles Drayton Diary, March 26, 1805, DH; Morgan, *Slave Counterpoint*, 237–44; Cecelski, *Waterman's Song*, 25–56; Buchanan, *Black Life on the Mississippi*, 101–48; Petition of Nathaniel Heyward and Others Requesting That a Public Landing May Not Be Established on Their Plantations, December 4, 1806, item no. 92, ser. S165015, Legislative Papers, SCDAH.

17. Petition of Nathaniel Heyward and Others Requesting That a Public Landing May Not Be Established on Their Plantations, December 4, 1806, item no. 92, ser. S165015, Legislative Papers, SCDAH.

18. Charles Drayton Diary, January 14, 1803, DH.

19. *City Gazette and Morning Daily Advertiser*, July 18, 1825. See, for example, *State Gazette of South Carolina*, August 10, 1786; *City Gazette*, November 18, 1820; *City Gazette and Daily Advertiser*, June 16, 1788; Petition to the General Assembly, 1818, n.d., no. 2849, SCDAH. See also Schweninger, "Slave Independence and Enterprise in South Carolina, 1780–1865."

20. *City Gazette and Daily Advertiser*, July 7, 1796; Charles Drayton Diary, May 4, 1800, DH; *Charleston Morning Post*, October 26, 1786; Petition to the General Assembly, Colleton District, 1813, no. 2, SCDAH.

21. Davison McDowell Plantation Diary, August 1, 1832, Davison McDowell Papers, SCL; Letter from James Gordan to Elias Ball, November 18, 1793, Ball Family Papers, SCL; *City Gazette and Daily Advertiser*, February 22, 1800.

22. Petition to the General Assembly, Saint James Santee Parish, 1785, no. 100, SCDAH; Charles Drayton Diary, March 23, 1801, DH; Morgan, *Slave Counterpoint*, 339.

23. Dawson, "Enslaved Swimmers and Divers in the Atlantic World"; Charles Hately to John Ball, August 6, 1792, Ball Family Papers, SCL.

24. For more on mortality and plantation labor, see McCandless, *Slavery, Disease, and Suffering in the Southern Lowcountry*, 3–148; Dusinberre, *Them Dark Days*, 48–83; Davis, *Inhuman Bondage*, 138.

25. For more on the lives of slaves in the slave market and the market itself, see Johnson, *Soul by Soul*; and Deyle, *Carry Me Back Home*. For an excellent depiction of the travel experience from barracoon to North American plantation, see Gomez, *Exchanging Our Country Marks*, 154–85; Smallwood, *Saltwater Slavery*.

26. Wallace, *History of South Carolina*, 378. For more on plantation construction, see Chaplin, *Anxious Pursuit*, 227–355.

27. Several historians are participating in an ongoing conversation concerning the role of West Africans in the development of Lowcountry rice production. Their debate revolves around the primacy of African practices in the construction of rice as a commodity crop. My work is less concerned with this debate, and simply interested in the extent to which rice fields were familiar to the recently imported African slaves. Littlefield, *Rice and Slaves*; Carney, *Black Rice*; Edelson, *Plantation Enterprise in Colonial South Carolina*, 53–91; Fields-Black, *Deep Roots*; Eltis, Morgan, and Richardson, "Agency and Diaspora in Atlantic History."

28. Charles Drayton Diary, April 30, 1804, DH; *Charleston Courier*, March 9, 1805; *South-Carolina State Gazette*, August 10, 1786.

29. Gomez, *Exchanging Our Country Marks*, 154–85. See also Young, *Rituals of Resistance*; Brown, "Crossing Kalunga"; Brown, *African-Atlantic Cultures and the South Carolina Lowcountry*; Creel, *Peculiar People*.

30. *South-Carolina Gazette*, "Letter from a Stranger," September 17, 1772.

31. *City Gazette and Daily Advertiser*, June 16, 1788; *City Gazette and Daily Advertiser*, August 2, 1812; *City Gazette and Daily Advertiser*, May 20, 1813. For more on black lives in Charleston and on Charleston Neck, see McCinnis, *Politics of Taste in Antebellum Charleston*, 66–89; Myers, *Forging Freedom*, 21–36; Powers, *Black Charlestonians*, 9–72.

32. *City Gazette and Daily Advertiser*, December 19, 1791; *City Gazette and Daily Advertiser*, June 22, 1798.

33. "Recollection of Slavery, by a Runaway Slave," *Emancipator*, October 18, 1838.

34. *Charleston Courier*, April 22, 1805. For more on drivers in South Carolina, see Morgan, *Slave Counterpoint*, 218–24. For more on West Africans in South Carolina, see Young, *Rituals of Resistance*; Brown, *African-Atlantic Cultures and the South Carolina Lowcountry*.

35. *Charleston Courier*, April 22, 1805; *City Gazette and Daily Advertiser*, January 27, 1808.

36. For more on West and West-Central African perceptions of the Lowcountry, see Young, *Rituals of Resistance*; Brown, *African-Atlantic Cultures and the South Carolina Lowcountry*, 189–280; Gomez, *Exchanging Our Country Marks*, 154–290.

37. Brown, "Crossing Kalunga," 98–103, 312–29; Brown, *African-Atlantic Cultures and the South Carolina Lowcountry*, 198–250. Also see MacGaffey, *Religion and Society in Central Africa*; Slenes, "Great Porpoise-Skull Strike," 183–208; MacGaffey, "Twins, Simbi Spirits, and Lwas."

38. The Trans-Atlantic Slave Trade Database, Emory University, accessed March 5, 2017, slavevoyages.org/assessment/estimates; Pollitzer, *Gullah People and Their African Heritage*, 60.

39. Brown, "Crossing Kalunga," 326; Brown, *African-Atlantic Cultures and the South Carolina Lowcountry*, 198–250; Matthew, *Agriculture, Geology, and Society in Antebellum South Carolina*, 164–67.

40. Young, *Rituals of Resistance*, 66; Brown, *African-Atlantic Cultures and the South Carolina Lowcountry*, 198–250.

41. Creel, *Peculiar People*, 288–90; Brown, "Crossing Kalunga," 317–28; Brown, *African-Atlantic Cultures and the South Carolina Lowcountry*, 198–250.

42. Ibid. Quote from Brown, "Crossing Kalunga," 325. Brown's historico-linguistic research reveals the retention of names and terms associated with *kimpasi* in the Lowcountry. He notes, "Evidence of this link may be found in the retention of the name *Nganga*, the male *kimpasi* names *Lumbu* and *Bangula*, and the female *kimpasi* names *Beya* and *Senga* in the Lowcountry. Additionally, the connection of the *kimpasi* initiation enclosure with the process of purification may be reflected in the term *tunia*, which meant 'cleanness, whiteness, purity' in Kongo and 'very clean' in the Core Lowcountry African Lexicon. The possibility that *kimpasi* may have remained important to West-Central African captives underscores the larger significance of local spirits in the formation of community in the early Lowcountry." Brown, "Crossing Kalunga," 325.

43. For an interesting analysis of Central African initiation societies in the Atlantic Diaspora, see Miller, *Voices of the Leopard*; and Brown, *African-Atlantic Cultures and the South Carolina Lowcountry*, 218–21.

44. *City Gazette and Daily Advertiser*, June 27, 1796.

45. J. J. Hale to Isaac Ball, August 10, 1817, Ball Family Papers, SCL; Charles Drayton Diary, March 9, 1793, DH.

46. John Peyre Thomas Diary, February 24, 1829, Thomas Family Papers, SCL. Also see Fett, "Consciousness and Calling"; White, *Ar'n't I a Woman*, 110–14; Marshall, "They Are Supposed to Be Lurking about the City."

47. Brown, "Interwoven Traditions," 107. See also Brown, "Material Culture and Community Structure"; Leone and Fry, "Conjuring in the Big House Kitchen"; Ferguson, *Uncommon*; Ferguson, "This Cross Is a Magic Sign"; Vlach, *Back of the Big House*; Guthrie, *Catching*; and Thompson, *Flash of the Spirit*.

48. On the importance of burial sites, see Brown, "Crossing Kalunga," 97–100; Brown, *African-Atlantic Cultures and the South Carolina Lowcountry*; Hugh McCauley to Isaac Ball, April 25, 1814, Ball Family Papers, SCL.

49. Hugh McCauley to Isaac Ball, June 2, 1814, Ball Family Papers, SCL; Hugh McCauley to Isaac Ball, August 9, 1814, Ball Family Papers, SCL.

50. Hugh McCauley to Isaac Ball, December 19, 1816, Ball Family Papers, SCL. McCauley was replaced by overseer John J. Hales. John J. Hales to Isaac Ball, January 13, 1817, Ball Family Papers, SCL.

51. Charles Drayton Diary, January 18, 1800, January 28, 1800, DH.

52. Charles Drayton Diary, March 7, 1800, March 21, 1800, April 8, 1800, DH.

53. Charles Drayton Diary, October 23, 1800, December 30, 1800, DH.

54. Charles Drayton Diary, January 25, 1802, January 30, 1804, March 27, 1807, February 11, 1808, January 14, 1803, December 11, 1801, DH.

55. While a great deal has been written on the Denmark Vesey affair, little has been offered until recently concerning the Camden or Georgetown insurrection. For the Denmark Vesey conspiracy, see Johnson, "Denmark Vesey and His Co-Conspirators." For more on the Camden insurrection, see Ford, *Deliver Us from Evil*, 173–79. For more

on the Georgetown scare, see Freehling, *Prelude to Civil War*, 62–64. For white reaction to insurrection scares, see the above and Young, *Domesticating Slavery*.

56. Freehling, *Prelude to Civil War*, 1–86; Ford, *Deliver Us from Evil*, 269–96; Young, *Domesticating Slavery*, 161–92; Faust, "Culture, Conflict, and Community."

57. Freehling, *Prelude to Civil War*, 1–86; Ford, *Deliver Us from Evil*, 269–96; Young, *Domesticating Slavery*, 161–92; Faust, "Culture, Conflict, and Community."

58. For more on the shifting plantation complex, see chapter 3; and Chaplin, *Anxious Pursuit*, 277–355.

59. Mr. Loocock to Mrs. Margaret Colleton, July 12, 1786, Margaret Colleton Papers, SCL; *City Gazette and Daily Advertiser*, November 10, 1796. Quoted in Morgan, "Black Society in the Lowcountry, 1760–1810"; *Charleston Morning Post*, October 26, 1786.

60. Joyce Chaplin argues that South Atlantic planters transformed the plantation complex in part as a response to the tumultuous Atlantic economy of which they were a part. When war decreased demand or disrupted labor on plantations, planters attempted to shift production or develop new commodity crops. Each of these changes deeply affected the everyday practices of the enslaved majority, who were sold or transported to new plantations or forced to construct the infrastructure for commodity production. Chaplin, *Anxious Pursuit*, 187–355. For more on the dramatic downturn in the postwar South Carolina economy, see Wallace, *History of South Carolina*, 177; Ramsay, *Ramsay's History of South Carolina*, 2: 292–93; Morgan, "Black Society in the Lowcountry," 85–87; Coclanis, *Shadow of a Dream*, 111–60. Many planters responded to the economic downturn by moving their slaves to western lands, or selling them in the nascent internal slave market. For more on the migration and the domestic slave trade, see Brady, "Slave Trade and Sectionalism in South Carolina, 1787–1808"; Deyle, "Irony of Liberty"; Shugerman, "Louisiana Purchase and South Carolina's Reopening of the Slave Trade in 1803."

61. Chaplin, *Anxious Pursuit*, 187–355; Ramsay, *Ramsay's History of South Carolina*, 2: 292–93. For the economic difficulties following the Revolution and the redevelopment of the plantation South, see Spooner, "Origins of the Old South."

62. Governor William Moultrie, Governor's Message to the General Assembly, 1785, SCDAH; *City Gazette*, November 18, 1820.

63. For the differences in Upcountry and Lowcountry plantations, see Chaplin, "Creating a Cotton South in Georgia and South Carolina, 1760–1815"; Ford, *Origins of Southern Radicalism*, 5–43.

64. Chaplin, "Creating a Cotton South in Georgia and South Carolina, 1760–1815"; Ford, *Origins of Southern Radicalism*, 5–43; Edelson, *Plantation Enterprise in Colonial South Carolina*, 92–155; and Morgan, *Slave Counterpoint*, 27–254.

65. For more on the way that black and white interacted with the physical environment in the eighteenth and nineteenth centuries, see Silver, *New Face on the Countryside*; Stewart, *"What Nature Suffers to Groe."*

66. *City Gazette and Daily Advertiser*, May 18, 1792; *City Gazette and Daily Advertiser*, August 20, 1788.

67. *State Gazette of South Carolina*, October 16, 1792.

68. They may also have sought the economic opportunities afforded them in Charleston. Egerton, "Slaves to the Marketplace."

69. Governor John Drayton, Governor's Message to the General Assembly, 1800, SCDAH; *City Gazette and Daily Advertiser*, February 10, 1820, February 11, 1820, February 17, 1820; *Charleston Courier*, June 1, 1821: Petition to the General Assembly from the Inhabitants of Clarendon, Claremont, St. Johns, St. Stephens, and Richland District, no. 1874, n.d., SCDAH.

70. *City Gazette and Daily Advertiser*, February 17, 1820.

71. Colleton District Grand Jury Presentment, 1813, no. 2, SCDAH.

Chapter Five

1. October 2, 1823, Pineville Police Association, 1823–1840, vol. 1, Secretary Book, SCHS; "Georgetown, June 9," *Camden Gazette*, June 21, 1821. The sources concerning Joe, including the above, can be found in Lockley, *Maroon Communities in South Carolina*, 93–120.

2. "Georgetown, June 9," *Camden Gazette*, June 21, 1821; *Southern Chronicle*, September 17, 1823; Petitions, item 1874, n.d., Legislative Papers, SCDAH.

3. The idea of the modern, liberal state is debated across disciplines. Here I follow, in part, the argument that Patrick Joyce articulates in his recent work on the nineteenth-century British state. See Joyce, *State of Freedom*, 1–53; Smith, *Economic Readjustment of an Old South Cotton State*. For more on the white construction of the South Carolina plantation complex and the frailty of those claims, see Edelson, *Plantation Enterprise in Colonial South Carolina*. A citation of all the works that deal with internal improvements in the early nation would be exhaustive. A partial list includes Larson, *Internal Improvement*; Larson, "'Bind the Republic Together'"; Goodrich, "Revulsion against Internal Improvements"; Goodrich, "Internal Improvements Reconsidered"; Baker, "Washington National Road Bill"; Way, *Common Labor*; Sheriff, *Artificial River*. For the broader context of internal improvements in the early nation, see Sellers, *Market Revolution*; and Howe, *What Hath God Wrought*.

4. "Report on the Lunatic Asylum," 1822, General Assembly Committee Reports, SCDAH; quoted in Bellows, "'Insanity Is the Disease of Civilization,'" 264; "Governor's Message," Columbia (SC) *South Carolina State Gazette*, November 29, 1822, 1–2. The highly active, centralized state in the early nineteenth century reflects the findings of two recent and important works: Balogh, *Government Out of Sight*; and Novak, *People's Welfare*. For more on the project of centralization in early national South Carolina, see Edwards, *People and Their Peace*, 26–54 and 203–85; Klein, *Unification of a Slave State*, 238–68; and Ford, *Origins of Southern Radicalism*, 1–96. For recent works on the project of modernization in South Carolina, see Marrs, *Railroads in the Old South*; Downey, *Planting a Capitalist South*.

5. Gordon, "Governmental Rationality"; Foucault, "Governmentality"; Joyce, *State of Freedom*. Most of the literature on internal improvements in the United States focuses on the legal, economic, and political contexts and consequences of development. This chapter seeks to add to that literature by examining the spatial discourse and practice

of the modern state, and by placing African American social and political history within that conversation. In doing so, I am using several models borrowed from European, Latin American, Southeast and South Asian, and Native American history, the history of cartography and geography, and political theory. Partial lists of these works include Scott, *Seeing like a State*; Chatterjee, *Empire and Nation*, 241–66; Edney, *Mapping an Empire*; Craib, *Cartographic Mexico*; Burnett, *Masters of All They Surveyed*; Winichakul, *Siam Mapped*; Hudson, *Creek Paths and Federal Roads*; Barr, "Geographies of Power"; and Hannah, *Governmentality and the Mastery of Territory in Nineteenth-Century America*. For more on internal improvements and the liberal state in the South, see Heath, *Constructive Liberalism*. For an excellent historiographical overview of slavery's place in the scholarship on national political economy, see Rockman, "Unfree Origins of American Capitalism." For older scholarship on the topic, see Bensel, *Yankee Leviathan*; McCoy, *Elusive Republic*; Taylor, *Transportation Revolution*; and Novak, *People's Welfare*. The historiography on the relationship of slavery to the political economy of American capitalism has shifted dramatically in the last several years toward a re-centering of the institution in the nation's past. For examples of this, see Johnson, *River of Dark Dream*; Rothman, *Slave Country*; Rockman, *Scraping By*; Rothman, *Flush Times and Fever Dreams*; Baptist, "Toxic Debt, Liar Loans, and Securitized Human Beings."

6. Hahn, *Nation under Our Feet*, 1–115; McCurry, *Confederate Reckoning*, 11–37 and 218–309. For an excellent discussion of the role the institution of slavery played in the development of state praxis and politics in South Carolina, see Freehling, *Prelude to Civil War*, 49–176; Ford, *Deliver Us from Evil*, 207–98; Edwards, *People and Their Peace*, 203–87.

7. John C. Calhoun, "Speech on Internal Improvements," in Meriwether, *Papers of John C. Calhoun*, 401.

8. Drayton, *View of South Carolina*; Mills, *Statistics of South Carolina*; Withers, "Geography, Natural History and the Eighteenth-Century Enlightenment"; Harley, "Deconstructing the Map"; Harley, "Maps, Knowledge, and Power."

9. Elliott, *Address to the Literary and Philosophical Society of South-Carolina*, 13 and 14. For more on the English and French examples, see Joyce, *State of Freedom*; Guldi, *Roads to Power*; and Mukerji, *Impossible Engineering*.

10. Petitions, item 2276, Legislative Papers, ND, SCDAH; Petitions, item 118, Legislative Papers, 1815, SCDAH; South Carolina, *House Journal*, December 13, 1815, 128–29, quoted in Ristow, *American Maps and Mapmakers*, 207–8. For total appropriations, see Ristow, *American Maps and Mapmakers*, 210. For an overview of the shifts in cartographic surveys and techniques in the late eighteenth and early nineteenth centuries, see Edney, *Mapping an Empire*, 39–120.

11. Petitions, item 118, Legislative Papers, 1815 SCDAH; Waddell, "Robert Mills, Cartographer," ii; Ristow, *American Maps and Mapmakers*, 207–8; Winichakul, *Siam Mapped*, 20–61; Harley, "Maps, Knowledge, and Power," 277–312.

12. Winichakul, *Siam Mapped*, 20–61. For more on the belief, maintained by modern geographers until recently, that African Americans lacked a concrete spatial discourse of their own, see McKittrick, *Demonic Grounds*, ix–xxiv.

13. Annual Report of the Comptroller General, 1800–1838, Legislative Papers, SCDAH; "Governor's Message," *Camden Gazette*, December 5, 1816.

14. John L. Wilson, "Report of the Civil and Military Engineer, of the State of South-Carolina for the year 1818," in Glenn and Kohn, *Internal Improvement in South Carolina*, A19. For the creation of Wilson's position: McCord, *Statutes at Large*, 6: 58–60. For more on the emergence and importance of the civil engineer, see Guldi, *Roads to Power*, 46–53. For more on the early internal improvement movement, see Downey, *Planting a Capitalist South*, 101–3; Ford, *Origins of Southern Radicalism*, 16; Edgar, *South Carolina*, 282.

15. McCord, *Statutes at Large*, 6: 91–92 (quotation, 92); Glenn and Kohn, *Internal Improvement in South Carolina*, xii–xiii.

16. Glenn and Kohn, *Internal Improvement in South Carolina*, xii–xiii; Chatterjee, *Empire and Nation*, 241–66; Scott, *Seeing Like a State*, 9–52; Guldi, *Roads to Power*, 75–76 and 80–88; Edwards, *People and Their Peace*, 38; O'Neall, *Biographical Sketches of the Bench and Bar of South Carolina*, 2: 236–46; Shields, *Pioneering American Wine*, 2–5; Bryan, *Robert Mills, Architect*.

17. Edwards, *People and Their Peace*, 26–63.

18. Bryan, "Robert Mills, Benjamin Henry Latrobe, Thomas Jefferson, and the South Carolina Penitentiary Project." For more on Mills's engagement with national internal improvements, see Bryan, *Robert Mills*, 57–58; Rao, *National Duties*, 6.

19. Bryan, *Robert Mills*, 1–34. The letters from Mills to Thomas Jefferson and Paul Hamilton, as well as an analysis of his design, can be found in Bryan, "Robert Mills, Benjamin Henry Latrobe, Thomas Jefferson, and the South Carolina Penitentiary Project."

20. "Report of the Board of Public Works for 1820," in Glenn and Kohn, *Internal Improvement in South Carolina*, 17–68.

21. John L. Wilson, "Report of Civil and Military Engineer for 1819," in Glenn and Kohn, *Internal Improvement in South Carolina*, A19–A22; "Report of the Board of Public Works to the Legislature of South-Carolina, for the Year 1821," in Glenn and Kohn, *Internal Improvement in South Carolina*, 126–28; Abram Blanding, "Report of the Superintendent of Public Works for the year 1824," in Glenn and Kohn, *Internal Improvement in South Carolina*, 254–364; and "The Edisto Canal," *Charleston Courier*, January 20, 1826. For more on local governments as the focal point for centralized power, see Joyce, *Rule of Freedom*, 98–143.

22. Thomas Baker, "Report of the Board of Commissioners, for the Department of Public Buildings to the Board of Public Works, for the Year 1820," in Glenn and Kohn, *Internal Improvement in South Carolina*, 25–38; For more on Abram Blanding, Robert Mills, and the intellectual world of early national internal improvements, see Bryan, "Robert Mills, Benjamin Henry Latrobe, Thomas Jefferson, and the South Carolina Penitentiary Project"; Bryan, *Robert Mills*; O'Neall, *Biographical Sketches of the Bench and Bar of South Carolina*, 236–46; and Edwards, *People and Their Peace*, 203–17.

23. Patrick Joyce argues that the raison d'être of nineteenth-century liberalism, when understood as governmentality, was the creation of the liberal subject. Joyce, *Rule of*

Freedom, 117; Novak, *People's Welfare*, 2; Crafts, *Oration on the Occasion of Laying the Cornerstone of the Lunatic Asylum at Columbia*, 19. For more on humanitarianism and the rise of planter paternalism, see Chaplin, "Slavery and the Principle of Humanity"; Young, *Domesticating Slavery*, 91–192.

24. *Camden Gazette*, July 25, 1816; Petition from the Inhabitants of St. Stephens Parish Asking for the Establishment of Schools in the Election Districts of the State, Petitions, item no. 12, 1811, Legislative Papers, SCDAH; Harrison, "South Carolina's Educational System in 1822."

25. *Camden Gazette*, July 25, 1816; Elliott, *Address Delivered at the Opening of the Medical College in Charleston*, 4–5; Crafts, *Oration on the Occasion of Laying the Cornerstone of the Lunatic Asylum at Columbia*, 19. For more on South Carolina College and the Free School System, see Klein, *Unification of a Slave State*, 240–44; Allston, *Report on the Free School System in South Carolina*, 5–8.

26. Report on the Lunatic Asylum, General Assembly Committee Reports, Legislative Papers, 1822, SCDAH, cited in Bellows, "Insanity Is the Disease of Civilization," 263–72; Crafts, *Oration on the Occasion of Laying the Cornerstone of the Lunatic Asylum*, 15; Leone, "Historical Archaeology of Capitalism."

27. For more on the revenue generated by the enslaved, see Annual Report of the Comptroller General, 1800–1838, Legislative Papers, SCDAH.

28. Herbemont, *Observations Suggested by the Late Occurrences in Charleston*; Mills, *Statistics of South Carolina*, 294–325; and Mills, *Internal Improvement of South-Carolina*.

29. *Pendleton Messenger*, December 6, 1820. For the debate on this legislation in 1821, see "The Penal Code, No. 1," *Charleston Courier*, November 6, 1821; and "The Penal Code—No. 2," *Charleston Courier*, November 7, 1821, cited in Michael P. Johnson, "Denmark Vesey and His Co-Conspirators," 966.

30. Nott, *Reports of Cases Determined in the Constitutional Court of South Carolina*, 113–14; *Daily Telegraph*, November 4, 1848, cited in Henry, "Police Control of the Slave in South Carolina," 30.

31. Edelson, "Nature of Slavery"; Edelson, "Affiliation without Affinity."

32. Governor David R. Williams, Governor's Message to the General Assembly, 1816, SCDAH. For more on the Camden insurrection scare, see Ford, *Deliver Us from Evil*, 173–206.

33. Petition to the General Assembly from inhabitants of Charleston, 1820, no. 123, SCDAH; Pearson, *Designs against Charleston*, 49–52.

34. Ibid. Johnson, "Denmark Vesey and His Co-Conspirators." Johnson's article, intended as a review of Douglas R. Egerton's and Edward A. Pearson's books on the Vesey conspiracy and trial, sparked a heated debate among historians concerning the rumored conspiracy. This debate primarily focuses on the veracity of white Charlestonians' claims that Denmark Vesey and his co-conspirators planned a rebellion against Charleston's white inhabitants. I am less concerned with proving the veracity of such claims as I am concerned with understanding white fears and the state's violent reaction to the rumors. See Wade, "Vesey Plot"; Gross, "Forum: The Making of a Slave Conspiracy, Part I"; Gross, "Forum: The Making of a Slave Conspiracy, Part II"; Paquette and Egerton, "Of Facts and Fable"; and Paquette, "From Rebellion to Revisionism."

35. Herbemont, *Observations Suggested by the Late Occurrences*, 5.

36. Mills, *Statistics of South Carolina*, 321; Abram Blanding, "Report of the Superintendent of Public Works on the Edisto Canal," in Glenn and Kohn, *Internal Improvement in South Carolina*, 379.

37. *Camden Gazette*, June 21, 1821.

38. Social Explorer, accessed July 11, 2017, https://www.socialexplorer.com/6f4cdab7a0/.

39. Mills, *Statistics of South Carolina*, vii, 61, 320–21, 323; Glenn and Kohn, *Internal Improvement in South Carolina*, 199–225; and Blanding, "Report of the Superintendent," 369–86.

40. Herbemont, *Observations on the Late Occurrence*, 7 and 9; Mills, *Internal Improvement of South-Carolina*, 4.

41. Herbemont, *Observations on the Late Occurrence*, 9 and 16.

42. Mills, *Statistics of South Carolina*, 321 and 322. For another, similar board perspective, see Blanding, "Report of the Superintendent," 369–86. For more on Boards of Public Health in the context of governmentality, see Shah, *Contagious Divides*.

43. Blanding, "Report of the Superintendent," 371.

44. Ibid., 379.

45. Mills, *Internal Improvement of South-Carolina*, 4, 14, 18; Mills, *Statistics of South Carolina*, 317.

46. Sheriff, *Artificial River*, 27–78. The shift in South Carolina's governing praxis away from reform and toward a defense of the institution of slavery is best captured in the laws the state passed in the shadow of the Denmark Vesey scare, including harsher restrictions on the free black and enslaved mobility, and most famously, the Negro Seamen's Act, which required that black sailors be jailed upon entry to Charleston harbor. See Ford, *Deliver Us from Evil*, 207–96; and Freehling, *Prelude to Civil War*, 89–300.

47. *Watch-Tower*, October 20, 1823.

48. *City Gazette*, October 8, 1823, 2; *Southern Chronicle*, October 29, 1823; *Southern Chronicle*, October 8, 1823. Interestingly, but not surprisingly, Royal is not mentioned in the newspaper reports. That and several details of the final encounter between the state and Joe are from a petition for Royal's manumission: Petitions, item 1874, Legislative Papers, n.d., SCDAH.

49. *City Gazette and Commercial Daily Advertiser*, August 5, 1825. For the South Carolina Association, January, "The South Carolina Association."

50. October 2, 1823, Pineville Police Association Secretary Book, SCHS.

51. *A Runaway Slave*, 1838, *Recollection of Slavery by a Runaway Slave* serialized in *The Emancipator*, Documenting the American South, University Library, University of North Carolina at Chapel Hill, 2003.

52. Ford, *Deliver Us from Evil*, 207–97.

53. McCord, *Statutes at Large of South Carolina*, 7: 451–54, 459–60, 461–63, 466–67.

54. Ibid., 459–61.

Conclusion

1. For an interesting analysis of the on-the-ground production of infrastructure more broadly, see, for example, Dearinger, *Filth of Progress*. For more on the role of slaves and the creation of infrastructure in the antebellum era, see Hall, "Slaves of the State."

2. Ballve, "Everyday State Formation."

3. Dearinger, *Filth of Progress*; Hall, "Slaves of the State"; McCurry, *Confederate Reckoning*, 11–37 and 218–309; Graham, "Slavery and Economic Development"; Donoghue and Jennings, *Building the Atlantic Empires*; Lichtenstein, *Twice the Work of Free Labor*; Thompson, "Why Mass Incarceration Matters." For Qatar, see, for example, "Migrant Workers Suffer 'Appalling Treatment' in Qatar World Cup Stadiums, Says Amnesty," *The Guardian*, March 30, 2016, accessed March 5, 2017, https://www.theguardian.com/global-development/2016/mar31/migrant-workers-suffer-appaling-treatment-in-qatar-world-cup-says-amnesty.

Bibliography

Unpublished Manuscripts

Clemson University Special Collections, Clemson University
    James Edward Colhoun Diaries
Drayton Hall, Charleston, South Carolina
    Charles Drayton Diary
Georgia Historical Society, Atlanta, Georgia
    Joseph Valance Beven Papers
Hargrett Rare Book and Manuscript Library, University of Georgia
    Telemon Cuyler Collection
Library of Congress
    Thomas Jefferson Papers
National Archives, Washington, DC
    South Carolina Commons House of Assembly Journals
South Carolina Department of Archives and History, Columbia, South Carolina
    All Saints Parish, Commissioners of the Roads
    Commissioners of Fortifications
    Comptroller General Papers
    Executive Council of South Carolina, 1763–67
    General Assembly Committee Reports
    Governor's Messages to the General Assembly, 1776–1883
    Grand Jury Presentments, 1776–1883
    John McCrady Plat Collection
    Journal of the Commissioners of Fortifications, 1755–70
    Petitions to the General Assembly, 1776–1883
    Thomas Pinckney Letterbook
    Reports to the General Assembly
    St. John's Parish, Berkley County, Commissioners of the High Roads
    St. Paul's Parish, Commissioners of the Roads
    St. Stephen's Parish, Commissioners of the Roads
    South Carolina Commons House of Assembly Journals
    South Carolina Council Journal
South Carolina Historical Society, Charleston, South Carolina
    R. F. W. Allston Papers
    Allard Belin Papers
    Thomas Bennett Proclamation
    Alexander Garden Papers

John Lewis Gervais Collection
Hutson Family Papers
Lucas Family Papers
Pineville Police Association Secretary Books
Porcher Collection
Thomas P. Ravenel Collection
South Carolina Commissioners of the High Roads, St. John's Parish, Berkley County

South Caroliniana Library, University of South Carolina
R. F. W. Allston Papers
Ball Family Papers
William Blanding Papers
John Ewing Colhoun Papers
Margaret Colleton Papers
William Johnston Papers
Thomas Kirkland Papers
Samuel Mathis Papers
Davison McDowell Papers
Palmer Family Papers
Thomas Pinckney Papers (1750–1828)
Records of the Methodist Episcopal Church, Georgetown, South Carolina, 1818–24
Thomas Family Papers

Southern Historical Collection, University of North Carolina
Josiah Smith Papers

Newspapers & Journals

BROOKFIELD, MASSACHUSETTS
Moral and Political Telegraph or Brookfield Advertiser

CAMDEN, SOUTH CAROLINA
Camden Gazette

CHARLESTON, SOUTH CAROLINA
Charleston Courier
Charleston Evening Gazette
Charleston Morning Post
City Gazette
City Gazette and Daily Advertiser
City Gazette and Morning Daily Advertiser
Columbian Herald
The Columbian Herald, or the Patriotic Courier of North-America

The Daily Telegraph
The Gazette of the State of South Carolina
South Carolina Gazette
South-Carolina Gazette; And General Advertiser
South-Carolina State Gazette
The South Carolina State Gazette & Timothy & Mason's Daily Advertiser
Southern Review
State Gazette of South Carolina

COLUMBIA, SOUTH CAROLINA

Southern Chronicle

COOPERSTOWN, NEW YORK

The Watch-Tower

LONDON

The Guardian

NEW YORK, NEW YORK

Emancipator

PHILADELPHIA, PENNSYLVANIA

Philadelphia Gazette

SAVANNAH, GEORGIA

Gazette of the State of Georgia

Internet Resources

David Rumsey Map Collection, www.davidrumsey.com
Documenting the American South, docsouth.unc.edu
Social Explorer, www.socialexplorer.com
Trans-Atlantic African Slave Trade Database, Emory University, slavevoyages.org

Published Primary Sources

Allston, R. F. W. *Report on the Free School System in South Carolina*. Charleston, SC: Miller and Browne, 1847.
American. *American Husbandry: Containing an Account of the Soil, Climate, Production and Agriculture, of the British Colonies in North-America and the West-Indies; ... By an American. In Two Volumes*. London: J. Bew, 1775.
Bacon-Foster, Corra. *Early Chapters in the Potomac Route to the West*. Washington, DC: Columbia Historical Society, 1912.

Bartram, John. "Diary of a Journey through the Carolinas, Georgia, and Florida, from July 1, 1765 to April 10, 1766." In *Transactions of the American Philosophical Society*. Vol. 33, pt. 1.
Bartram, William. *Travels*. New Haven, CT: Yale University Press, 1958.
Chesnutt, David R., George C. Rogers, and Peggy J. Clark, eds. *The Papers of Henry Laurens*. Vol. 5, *Sept. 1, 1765–July 31, 1768*. Columbia: University of South Carolina Press, 1968.
Chesnutt, David R., and C. James Taylor, eds. *The Papers of Henry Laurens*. Vol. 15. Columbia: University of South Carolina Press, 2000.
Cooper, Thomas, ed. *The Statutes at Large of South Carolina*. Vol. 2, *Containing the Acts from 1682 to 1716*. Columbia, SC: A. S. Johnston, 1837.
———, ed. *The Statutes at Large of South Carolina*. Vol. 3, *Containing the Acts from 1716, Exclusive, to 1752, Inclusive*. Columbia, SC: A. S. Johnston, 1838.
———, ed. *The Statutes at Large of South Carolina*. Vol. 4, *Containing the Acts from 1752, Exclusive, to 1786*. Columbia, SC: A. S. Johnston, 1838.
Crafts, William. *Oration on the Occasion of Laying the Cornerstone of the Lunatic Asylum at Columbia, July 1822*. Charleston, SC, 1822.
Culler, Daniel Merchant, et al. *Orangeburg District, 1768–1868: History and Records*. Columbia, SC: The Reprint Company, 1995.
Davis, Charles S. "The Journal of William Moultrie While a Commissioner on the North and South Carolina Boundary Survey, 1772." *Journal of Southern History* 8, no. 4 (November 1942): 549–55.
de Brahm, Ferdinand. "Journal of the Siege of Charleston by the English, in 1780." In *Engineers of Independence: A Documentary History of the Army Engineers in the American Revolution, 1775–1783*, edited by Paul K. Walker. Washington, DC: Historical Division, Office of the Chief of Engineers, 1981.
De Brahm, John William Gerard. "Philosophico-Historico-Hydrogeography of South Carolina, Georgia, and East Florida." In *Documents Connected with the History of South Carolina*, edited by Charles Jennett Weston Plowden, 159–227. London: Privately printed, 1856.
———. *Report of the General Survey in the Southern District of North America*. Columbia: University of South Carolina Press, 1971.
Drayton, John. *A View of South Carolina, as Respects Her Natural and Civil Concerns*. Spartanburg, SC: The Reprint Company, 1972.
Dubose, Samuel. "Address Delivered at the Seventeenth Anniversary of the Black Oak Agricultural Society." In *A Contribution to the History of the Huguenots of South Carolina*, edited by T. Galliard Thomas. Columbia: University of South Carolina Press, 1972.
Easterby, J. H., ed. *The Colonial Records of South Carolina: The Journal of the Commons House of Assembly, 1741–1742*. Columbia: The Historical Commission of South Carolina, 1953.
———, ed. *The Colonial Records of South Carolina: The Journal of the Commons House of Assembly, 1742–1744*. Columbia: South Carolina Archives Department, 1954.

―――, ed. *The Colonial Records of South Carolina: The Journal of the Commons House of Assembly, 1751–1752*. Columbia: South Carolina Archives Department, 1951.
―――, ed. *The Journal of the Commons House of Assembly, Sept. 12, 1739–March 26, 1741*. Columbia: The Historical Commission of South Carolina, 1952.
Edwards, Adele Stanton, ed. *Journals of the Privy Council, 1783–1789*. Columbia: University of South Carolina Press, 1971.
Elliott, Stephen. *An Address to the Literary and Philosophical Society of South-Carolina, Delivered in Charleston, on Wednesday, the 10th August, 1814*. Charleston, SC, 1914.
―――. *An Address Delivered at the Opening of the Medical College in Charleston on the 13th of November 1826*. Charleston, SC, 1826.
Elliott, William. *Carolina Sports by Land and Water: Including Incidents of Devil-Fishing, Wild-Cat, Deer, and Bear Hunting, Etc*. New York: Arno, 1967.
Ford, Timothy. "Diary of Timothy Ford, 1785–1786." *The South Carolina Historical and Genealogical Magazine*, no. 3 (July 1912): 132–47.
Gallatin, Albert. *Report of the Secretary of the Treasury, on the Subject of Public Roads and Canals: Made in Pursuance of a Resolution of Senate, of March 2, 1807*. Washington, DC: R. C. Weightman, 1808.
Gibbes, R. W., ed. *Documentary History of the American Revolution: Consisting of Letters and Papers Relating to the Contest for Liberty, Chiefly in South Carolina, from Originals in the Possession of the Editor, and Other Sources*. Vol. 1. New York: D. Appleton, 1857.
―――, ed. *Documentary History of the American Revolution: Consisting of Letters and Papers Relating to the Contest for Liberty, Chiefly in South Carolina, from Originals in the Possession of the Editor, and Other Sources*. Vol. 2. Columbia: Banner Steam-Power Press, 1853.
Glen, James. "A Description of South Carolina." In *Colonial South Carolina: Two Contemporary Descriptions by Governor James Glen and Doctor George Milligen-Johnston*, edited by Chapman J. Milling, 3–104. Columbia: University of South Carolina Press, 1951.
Glenn, Bess, and David Kohn, eds. *Internal Improvement in South Carolina*. Washington, DC, 1938.
Hemphill, William Edwin, ed. *Journals of the General Assembly and House of Representatives, 1776–1780*. Columbia: University of South Carolina Press, 1970.
Herbemont, Nicholas. *Observations Suggested by the Late Occurrences in Charleston, by a Member of the Board of Public Works, of the State of South-Carolina*. Columbia, SC, 1822.
Hewatt, Alexander. *An Historical Account of the Rise and Progress of the Colonies of South Carolina and Georgia in Two Volumes*. Vol 1. London: Alexander Donaldson, 1779.
"Journal of the Second Council of Safety, Appointed by the Provisional Congress, November, 1775," in *Collections of the South-Carolina Historical Society*, Vol. 3. Charleston: South Carolina Historical Society, 1859, 35–271.
Lanning, John Tate, ed. *The St. Augustine Expedition of 1740: A Report to the South Carolina General Assembly*. Columbia: University of South Carolina Press, 1954.

Lawson, John. *A New Voyage to Carolina*. Chapel Hill: University of North Carolina Press, 1967.

Lipscomb, Terry, ed. *The Journal of the Commons House of Assembly, November 20, 1755–July 6, 1757*. Columbia: University of South Carolina Press, 1989.

Matthew, William M., ed. *Agriculture, Geology, and Society in Antebellum South Carolina: The Private Diary of Edmund Ruffin, 1843*. Athens: University of Georgia Press, 1992.

McCord, David J., ed. *The Statutes at Large of South Carolina*. Vol. 6. *Containing the Acts from 1814, Exclusive, To 1838, Inclusive*. Columbia: A. S. Johnston, 1839.

———, ed. *The Statutes at Large of South Carolina*. Vol. 9. *Containing the Acts Relating to Roads, Bridges, and Ferries with an Appendix, Containing the Militia Acts Prior to 1794*. Columbia, SC: A. S. Johnston, 1841.

———, ed. *The Statutes at Large of South Carolina, Edited under Authority of the Legislature*. Vol. 7. *Containing the Acts Relating to Charleston Courts, Slaves and Rivers*. Columbia, SC: A. S. Johnston, 1840.

Meriwether, Robert L., ed. *The Papers of John C. Calhoun*. Vol. 1, *1801–1817*. Columbia: University of South Carolina Press, 1959.

Merrens, H. Roy. *The Colonial South Carolina Scene: Contemporary Views, 1697–1774*. Columbia: University of South Carolina Press, 1977.

Mills, Robert. *Internal Improvement of South-Carolina, Particularly Adapted to the Low Country*. Columbia, SC: State Gazette Office, 1822.

———. *Statistics of South Carolina: Including a View of Its Natural, Civil, and Military History, General and Particular*. Charleston, SC: Hurlbut and Lloyd, 1826.

Mitchell, James T., and Henry Flanders, eds. *The Statutes at Large of Pennsylvania from 1682 to 1801*. Vol. 2, *1700–1712*. Philadelphia: State Printer of Pennsylvania, 1896.

Nott, Henry Junius, and David James McCord, eds. *Reports of Cases Determined in the Constitutional Court of South Carolina*. Columbia, SC: Daniel Faust, 1821.

O'Neall, John Belton. *Biographical Sketches of the Bench and Bar of South Carolina*. Vol. 2. Charleston, SC: S. G. Courtenay, 1859.

———, ed. *Negro Law of South Carolina, Collected and Digested by John Belton O'Neall, One of the Judges of the Courts of Law and Errors of the Said State*. Columbia, SC: John G. Bowman, 1848.

Popple, Henry. *American Septentrionalis: A Map of the British Empire in America, with the French and Spanish Settlements Adjacent Thereto*. London: William Henry Toms and R. W. Seale, 1733.

Ramsay, David. *Ramsay's History of South Carolina, from Its First Settlement in 1670 to the Year 1808*. Vol. 2. Newberry, SC: W. J. Duffie, 1858.

———. *Transactions of the American Philosophical Society: David Ramsay, 1749–1815, Selections from His Writings*. Vol. 55, no. 4. Philadelphia: American Philosophical Society, 1965.

A Ranger's Report of Travels with General Oglethorpe, 1739–1742. In *Travels in the American Colonies*, edited by Newton Dennison Mereness. New York: Macmillan, 1916.

Rogers, George C., Jr., David R. Chesnutt, Peggy J. Clark, and Walter B. Edgar, eds. *The Papers of Henry Laurens.* Vol. 4, Sept. 1, 1763–Aug. 31, 1765. Columbia: University of South Carolina Press, 1974.
Salley, A. S., ed. *Col. William Hill's Memoirs of the Revolution.* Columbia: Historical Commissioner of South Carolina, 1921.
———, ed. *Journal of the Commissioners of the Navy of South Carolina, October 9, 1776–March 1, 1779.* Columbia: Historical Commission of South Carolina, 1912.
———, ed. *Journal of the House of Representatives of South Carolina, January 8, 1782–February 26, 1782.* Columbia: Historical Commission of South Carolina, 1916.
———, ed. *Journal of the Senate of South Carolina, January 8, 1782–February 26, 1782.* Columbia: Historical Commission of South Carolina, 1941.
Shields, David S., ed. *Pioneering American Wine: Writings of Nicholas Herbemont, Master Viticulturist.* Athens: University of Georgia Press, 2009.
Thompson, Theodora J., ed. *The State Records of South Carolina: Journals of the House of Representatives, 1783–1784.* Columbia: University of South Carolina Press, 1977.
Webber, Mable L. "Col. Senf's Account of the Santee Canal." *South Carolina Historical and Genealogical Magazine* 28, no. 1 (January 1927): 8–21.
———. "Col. Senf's Account of the Santee Canal (Continued)." *South Carolina Historical and Genealogical Magazine* 28, no. 2 (April 1927): 112–31.
William Johnson to Thomas Jefferson. August 11, 1823, *South Carolina Historical and Genealogical Magazine* no. 3 (July 1900): 206–12.
Woodmason, Charles. "The Remonstrance Presented to the Common's House of Assembly by the Upper Inhabitants—1767." In *The Carolina Backcountry on the Eve of the Revolution*, edited by Richard Hooker. Chapel Hill: University of North Carolina Press, 1953.

Secondary Sources

Agnew, John. "The Territorial Trap: The Geographical Assumptions of International Relations Theory." *Review of International Political Economy* 1, no. 1 (1994): 53–80.
Allewaert, Monique. *Ariel's Ecology: Plantations, Personhood, and Colonialism in the American Tropics.* Minneapolis: University of Minnesota Press, 2013.
Alvarez, C. J. "Inventing the US-Mexico Border." In *Boundaries of the State in US History*, edited by James T. Sparrow, William J. Novak, and Stephen W. Sawyer, 79–100. Chicago: University of Chicago Press, 2015.
Anderson, Benedict. *Imagined Communities: Reflections on the Origins and Spread of Nationalism.* London: Verso, 1991.
Aptheker, Herbert. "Maroons within the Present Limits of the United States." *Journal of Negro History* 24, no. 2 (April 1939): 167–84.
Bachelard, Gaston. *The Poetics of Space.* Boston: Beacon, 1994.
Baker, Pamela L. "The Washington National Road Bill and the Struggle to Adopt a Federal System of Internal Improvement." *Journal of the Early Republic* 22, no. 3 (Autumn 2002): 337–64.

Balinski, Michael L., and H. Peyton Young. *Fair Representation: Meeting the Ideal of One Man, One Vote*. Washington, DC: Brookings Institution Press, 2001.

Ballve, Teo. "Everyday State Formation: Territory, Decentralization, and the Narco Landgrab in Colombia." *Environment and Planning D: Society and Space* 30, no. 4 (2012): 603–22.

Balogh, Brian. *A Government Out of Sight: The Mystery of National Authority in Nineteenth-Century America*. New York: Cambridge University Press, 2009.

Bancroft, Frederick. *Calhoun and the South Carolina Nullification Movement*. Baltimore: Johns Hopkins University Press, 1928.

Baptist, Edward. "Toxic Debt, Liar Loans, and Securitized Human Beings: The Panic of 1837 and the Fate of Slavery." *Common-Place* 10, no. 3 (April 2010). Accessed November 11, 2011. http://www.common-place.org/vol-10/no-03/baptist/.

Barr, Juliana. "Geographies of Power: Mapping Indian Borders in the 'Borderlands' of the Early Southwest." *William and Mary Quarterly* 68 (January 2011): 5–46.

Beck, Robin. *Chiefdoms, Collapse, and Coalescence in the Early American South*. New York: Cambridge University Press, 2013.

Bellows, Barbara. "'Insanity Is the Disease of Civilization': The Founding of the South Carolina Lunatic Asylum." *South Carolina Historical Magazine* 82, no. 3 (July 1981): 263–72.

Bellucci, Stefano. "Introduction: Labour in Transport: Histories from the Global South." *International Review of Social History* 59, no. 22 (December 2014): 1–10.

Bensel, Richard. *Yankee Leviathan: The Origins of Central State Authority, 1859–1877*. Cambridge: Cambridge University Press, 1990.

Blassingame, John W. *The Slave Community: Plantation Life in the Antebellum South*. New York: Oxford University Press, 1972.

Bostick, Douglass W. *Sunken Plantations: The Santee Cooper Project*. Charleston, SC: History Press, 2008.

Brady, Patrick S. "The Slave Trade and Sectionalism in South Carolina, 1787–1808." *Journal of Southern History* 38 (1972): 601–20.

Brannon, Rebecca. "Reconciling the Revolution: Resolving Conflict and Rebuilding Community in the Wake of Civil War in South Carolina, 1775–1860." PhD diss., University of Michigan, 2007.

Brenner, Neil, Bob Jessop, Martin Jones, and Gordon Macleod. "State Space in Question." In *State/Space: A Reader*, edited by Neil Brenner, Bob Jessop, Martin Jones, and Gordon Macleod, 1–26. Malden, MA: Blackwell, 2003.

Brophy, Alfred L. "The Nat Turner Trials." *North Carolina Law Review* 91, no. 2 (2013): 1817–64.

Brown, Kenneth L. "Interwoven Traditions: The Conjurer's Cabins and the African American Cemetery at the Jordan and Frogmore Manor Plantations." In *Places of Cultural Memory: African Reflections on the American Landscape*, 99–114. Washington, DC: U.S. Department of the Interior, National Park Service, 2003.

———. "Material Culture and Community Structure: The Slave and Tenant Community at Levi Jordan's Plantation, 1848–1892." In *Working toward Freedom,*

edited by Larry E. Hudson, Jr, 95–118. Rochester, NY: University of Rochester Press, 1994.
Brown, Ras Michael L. B. *African-Atlantic Cultures and the South Carolina Lowcountry.* Cambridge: Cambridge University Press, 2014.
———. "Crossing Kalunga: West-Central Africans and Their Cultural Influence in the South Carolina–Georgia Lowcountry." PhD diss., University of Georgia, 2004.
———. " 'Walk in the Feenda': West-Central Africans and the Forest in the South Carolina–Georgia Lowcountry." In *Central Africans and Cultural Transformations in the American Diaspora*, edited by Linda M. Heywood, 289–318. Cambridge: Cambridge University Press, 2002.
Brown, Vincent. "Social Death and Political Life in the Study of Slavery." *American Historical Review* 114, no. 5 (2009): 1231–49.
Bryan, John M. *Robert Mills: America's First Architect.* New York: Princeton Architectural Press, 2001.
———. "Robert Mills, Benjamin Henry Latrobe, Thomas Jefferson, and the South Carolina Penitentiary Project, 1806–1808." *South Carolina Historical Magazine* 85, no. 1 (January 1984): 1–21.
———, ed. *Robert Mills, Architect.* Washington, DC: American Institute of Architects Press, 1989.
Buchanan, Thomas C. *Black Life on the Mississippi: Slaves, Free Blacks, and the Western Steamboat World.* Chapel Hill: University of North Carolina Press, 2004.
Burnett, D. Graham. *Masters of All They Surveyed: Exploration, Geography, and a British El Dorado.* Chicago: University of Chicago Press, 2001.
Camp, Stephanie M. H. *Closer to Freedom: Enslaved Women and Everyday Resistance in the Plantation South.* Chapel Hill: University of North Carolina Press, 2004.
———. "The Pleasures of Resistance: Enslaved Women and Body Politics in the Plantation South." *Journal of Southern History* 68, no. 3 (August 2002): 533–72.
Carney, Judith A. *Black Rice: The African Origins of Rice Cultivation in the Americas.* Cambridge, MA: Harvard University Press, 2001.
Carter, Paul. *The Road to Botany Bay: An Exploration of Landscape and History.* Chicago: University of Chicago Press, 1989.
Cecelski, David S. *The Waterman's Song: Slavery and Freedom in Maritime North Carolina.* Chapel Hill: University of North Carolina Press, 2001.
Certeau, Michel de. *The Practice of Everyday Life.* Berkeley: University of California Press, 1988.
Chaplin, Joyce E. *An Anxious Pursuit: Agricultural Innovation and Modernity in the Lower South, 1730–1815.* Chapel Hill: University of North Carolina Press, 1993.
———. "Creating a Cotton South in Georgia and South Carolina, 1760–1815." *Journal of Southern History* 57, no. 2 (May 1991): 171–200.
———. "Natural Philosophy and an Early Racial Idiom in North America: Comparing English and Indian Bodies." *William and Mary Quarterly* 54, no. 1 (January 1997): 229–52.

———. "Nature and Nation: Natural History in Context." In *Stuffing Birds, Pressing Plants, Shaping Knowledge: Natural History in North America, 1730–1860, Transactions of the American Philosophical Society*, edited by Sue Ann Prince, 75–95. Philadelphia: American Philosophical Society, 2003.

———. "Slavery and the Principle of Humanity: A Modern Idea in the Early Lower South." *Journal of Social History* 24, no. 2 (Winter 1990): 299–315.

Chatterjee, Partha. *Empire and Nation: Selected Essays*. New York: Columbia University Press, 2010.

Cippola, Carlo M. *Miasmas and Disease: Public Health and the Environment in the Pre-Industrial Age*. New Haven, CT: Yale University Press, 1992.

Coclanis, Peter A. *Shadow of a Dream: Economic Life and Death in the South Carolina Low Country, 1670–1920*. New York: Oxford University Press, 1988.

Cowan, William Tynes. *The Slave in the Swamp: Disrupting the Plantation Narrative*. New York: Routledge, 2005.

Craib, Raymond B. *Cartographic Mexico: A History of State Fixations and Fugitive Landscapes*. Durham, NC: Duke University Press, 2004.

Creel, Margaret Washington. *A Peculiar People: Slave Religion and Community-Culture among the Gullahs*. New York: New York University Press, 1988.

Davis, David Brion. *Inhuman Bondage: The Rise and Fall of Slavery in the New World*. New York: Oxford University Press, 2006.

Dawson, Kevin. "Enslaved Swimmers and Divers in the Atlantic World." *Journal of American History* 92, no. 4 (March 2006): 1327–55.

Dearinger, Ryan. *The Filth of Progress: Immigrants, Americans, and the Building of Canals and Railroads in the West*. Berkeley: University of California Press, 2015.

De Vorsey, Louis. *The Georgia–South Carolina Boundary: A Problem in Historical Geography*. Athens: University of Georgia Press, 1982.

Deyle, Steven. *Carry Me Back: The Domestic Slave Trade in American Life*. New York: Oxford University Press, 2005.

———. "The Irony of Liberty: Origins of the Domestic Slave Trade." *Journal of the Early Republic* 12, no. 1 (Spring 1992): 37–62.

Diouf, Sylviane A. *Slavery's Exiles: The Story of the American Maroons*. New York: New York University Press, 2014.

Doar, David. *Rice and Rice Planting in the South Carolina Low Country*. Charleston, SC: Charleston Museum, 1970.

Donoghue, John, and Evelyn Jennings, eds. *Building the Atlantic Empires: Unfree Labor and Imperial States in the Political Economy of Capitalism, ca. 1500–1915*. Leiden: Brill, 2016.

Downey, Tom. *Planting a Capitalist South: Masters, Merchants, and Manufactures in the Southern Interior, 1790–1860*. Baton Rouge: Louisiana State University Press, 2006.

Downs, Gregory P. "Three Faces of Sovereignty: Governing Confederate, Mexican, and Indian Texas in the Civil War Era." In *Civil War Wests: Testing the Limits of the United States*, edited by Adam Arenson and Andrew R. Graybill, 118–38. Berkeley: University of California Press, 2015.

Du Bois, W. E. B. *The Souls of Black Folk*. New York: Bantam Books, 1989.
Dusinberre, William. *Them Dark Days: Slavery in the American Rice Swamps*. Athens: University of Georgia Press, 2000.
Edelson, S. Max. "Affiliation without Affinity: Skilled Slaves in Eighteenth-Century South Carolina." In *Money, Trade, and Power: The Evolution of Colonial South Carolina's Plantation Society*, edited by Jack P. Greene, Rosemary Brana-Shute, and Randy J. Sparks, 217–55. Columbia: University of South Carolina Press, 2001.
———. "Clearing Swamps, Harvesting Forests: Trees and the Making of a Plantation Landscape in the Colonial South Carolina Lowcountry." *Agricultural History* 81, no. 3 (Summer 2007): 381–406.
———. "The Nature of Slavery: Environmental Disorder and Slave Agency in Colonial South Carolina." In *Cultures and Identities in Colonial British America*, edited by Robert Olwell and Alan Tully, 21–44. Baltimore: Johns Hopkins University Press, 2006.
———. *Plantation Enterprise in Colonial South Carolina*. Cambridge, MA: Harvard University Press, 2006.
Edgar, Walter B. *South Carolina: A History*. Columbia: University of South Carolina Press, 1998.
Edney, Matthew H. "The Irony of Imperial Mapping." In *The Imperial Map: Cartography and the Mastery of Empire*, edited by James R. Akerman, 11–45. Chicago: University of Chicago Press, 2009.
———. *Mapping an Empire: The Geographical Construction of British India, 1765–1843*. Chicago: University of Chicago Press, 1997.
———. "Mathematical Cosmography and the Social Ideology of British Cartography, 1780–1820." *Imago Mundi* 46 (1994): 101–16.
———. "Reconsidering Enlightenment Geography and Map Making." *Geography and Enlightenment*, edited by David N. Livingstone and Charles W. J. Withers, 165–98. Chicago: University of Chicago Press, 1999.
Edwards, Laura F. *The People and Their Peace: Legal Culture and the Transformation of Inequality in the Post-Revolutionary South*. Chapel Hill: University of North Carolina Press, 2009.
Egerton, Douglas R. *He Shall Go Out Free: The Lives of Denmark Vesey*. Oxford: Rowman and Littlefield, 2004.
———. "Slaves to the Marketplace: Economic Liberty and Black Rebelliousness in the Atlantic World." *Journal of the Early Republic* 26, no. 4 (Winter 2006): 617–39.
———, and Robert Paquette, eds. *The Denmark Vesey Affair: A Documentary History*. Gainesville: University of Florida Press, 2017.
Elden, Stuart. "Land, Terrain, Territory." *Progress in Human Geography* 34, no. 6 (2010): 799–817.
Elkins, Stanley M. *Slavery: A Problem in American Institutional and Intellectual Life*. Chicago: University of Chicago Press, 1959.

Eltis, David, Philip Morgan, and David Richardson. "Agency and Diaspora in Atlantic History: Reassessing the African Contribution to Rice Cultivation in the Americas." *American Historical Review* 112 (December 2007): 1329–58.
Faust, Drew Gilpin. "Culture, Conflict, and Community: The Meaning of Power on an Ante-Bellum Plantation." *Journal of Social History* 14, no. 1 (Autumn 1980): 83–97.
———. *James Henry Hammond and the Old South: A Design for Mastery*. Baton Rouge: Louisiana State University Press, 1985.
Ferguson, Leland G. "This Cross Is a Magic Sign: Marks on Eighteenth-Century Bowls from South Carolina." In *I, Too, Am America: Archaeological Studies of African American Life*, edited by Theresa A. Singleton, 116–31. Charlottesville: University of Virginia Press, 1999.
———. *Uncommon Ground: Archaeology and Early African America, 1650–1800*. Washington, DC: Smithsonian Institution Press, 1992.
Fett, Sharla M. "Consciousness and Calling: African American Midwives at Work in the Antebellum South." In *New Studies in the History of American Slavery*, edited by Edward E. Baptist and Stephanie M. H. Camp, 65–86. Athens: University of Georgia Press, 2006.
———. *Working Cures: Healing, Health, and Power on Southern Slave Plantations*. Chapel Hill: University of North Carolina Press, 2002.
Fields-Black, Edda L. *Deep Roots: Rice Farmers in West Africa and the African Diaspora*. Bloomington: Indiana University Press, 2008.
Ford, Lacy K. *Deliver Us from Evil: The Slavery Question in the Old South*. New York: Oxford University Press, 2009.
———. *Origins of Southern Radicalism: The South Carolina Upcountry, 1800–1860*. New York: Oxford University Press, 1988.
———. "Republican Ideology in a Slave Society: The Political Economy of John C. Calhoun." *Journal of Southern History* 54, no. 3 (August 1988): 405–24.
Ford, Lisa. *Settler Sovereignty: Jurisdiction and Indigenous People in America and Australia, 1788–1836*. Cambridge, MA: Harvard University Press, 2010.
Forrett, Jeff. *Race Relations at the Margins: Slaves and Poor Whites in the Antebellum Southern Countryside*. Baton Rouge: Louisiana State University Press, 2006.
Foucault, Michel. "Governmentality." In *The Foucault Effect: Studies in Governmentality*, edited by Graham Burchell, Colin Gordon, and Peter Miller, 87–104. Chicago: University of Chicago Press, 1991.
Franklin, John Hope, and Loren Schweninger. *Runaway Slaves: Rebels on the Plantation*. Oxford: Oxford University Press, 1999.
Freehling, William W. *Prelude to Civil War: The Nullification Controversy in South Carolina, 1816–1836*. New York: Harper & Row, 1966.
Frey, Sylvia R. *Water from the Rock: Black Resistance in a Revolutionary Age*. Princeton, NJ: Princeton University Press, 1993.
Gallay, Alan. *The Indian Slave Trade: The Rise of the English Empire in the American South*. New Haven, CT: Yale University Press, 2002.

Genovese, Eugene D. *Roll, Jordan, Roll: The World the Slaves Made*. New York: Vintage Books, 1976.
Gilroy, Paul. *The Black Atlantic: Modernity and Double Consciousness*. Cambridge, MA: Harvard University Press, 1993.
Glissant, Edouard. *Caribbean Discourse: Selected Essays*. Charlottesville: University of Virginia Press, 1991.
Godlewska, Anne, and Neil Smith, eds. *Geography and Empire*. Cambridge: Blackwell, 1994.
Gomez, Michael A. *Exchanging Our Country Marks: The Transformation of African Identities in the Colonial and Antebellum South*. Chapel Hill: University of North Carolina Press, 1998.
Goodrich, Carter. "Internal Improvements Reconsidered." *Journal of Economic History* 30, no. 2 (June 1970): 289–311.
——— . "The Revulsion against Internal Improvements." *Journal of Economic History* 10, no. 2 (November 1950): 145–69.
Gordon, Colin. "Governmental Rationality: An Introduction." In *The Foucault Effect: Studies in Governmentality*, edited by Graham Burchell, Colin Gordon, and Peter Miller, 1–52. Chicago: University of Chicago Press, 1991.
Graham, Richard. "Slavery and Economic Development: Brazil and the United States South in the Nineteenth Century." *Comparative Studies in Society and History* 23 (1981): 620–55.
Greene, Jack P. *The Quest for Power: The Lower Houses of Assembly in Southern Royal Colonies, 1689–1776*. Chapel Hill: University of North Carolina Press, 1963.
Gross, Robert A. "Forum: The Making of a Slave Conspiracy, Part I." *William and Mary Quarterly* 58, no. 4 (October 2001): 913–76.
——— . "Forum: The Making of a Slave Conspiracy, Part II." *William and Mary Quarterly* 59, no. 1 (January 2002): 135–202.
Guldi, Jo. *Roads to Power: Britain Invents the Infrastructure State*. Cambridge, MA: Harvard University Press, 2012.
Guthrie, Patricia. *Catching Sense: African American Communities on a South Carolina Sea Island*. Westport, CT: Greenwood, 1996.
Hadden, Salley E. *Slave Patrols: Law and Violence in Virginia and the Carolinas*. Cambridge, MA: Harvard University Press, 2001.
Hahn, Steven. *A Nation under Our Feet: Black Political Struggles in the Rural South from Slavery to the Great Migration*. Cambridge, MA: Harvard University Press, 2003.
Hall, Aaron. "Slaves of the State: Infrastructure and Governance through Slavery in the Antebellum South." Unpublished manuscript, shared with the author.
Hamer, Marguerite B. "The Fate of the Exiled Acadians in South Carolina." *Journal of Southern History* 4, no. 2 (May 1938): 199–208.
Hannah, Matthew G. *Governmentality and the Mastery of Territory in Nineteenth-Century America*. New York: 2000.
Harley, J. B. "Deconstructing the Map." *Cartographica* 26, no. 2 (Summer 1989): 1–20.

———. "Maps, Knowledge, and Power." In *The Iconography of Landscape: Essays on the Symbolic Representation, Design, and Use of Past Environments*, edited by Denis Cosgrove and Stephen Daniels, 277–312. Cambridge: Cambridge University Press, 1988.

Harrison, Lowell. "South Carolina's Educational System in 1822." *South Carolina Historical and Genealogical Magazine* 51, no. 1 (1950): 1–9.

Hartman, Saidiya V. *Scenes of Subjection: Terror, Slavery, and Self-Making in Nineteenth-Century America*. New York: Oxford University Press, 1997.

Harvey, David. *Justice, Nature, and the Geography of Difference*. Cambridge: Blackwell Publishers, 1996.

Hatley, Tom. *The Dividing Paths: Cherokees and South Carolinians through the Revolutionary Era*. New York: Oxford University Press, 1995.

Heath, Milton S. *Constructive Liberalism: The Role of the State in Economic Development in Georgia to 1860*. Cambridge, MA: Harvard University Press, 1954.

Henderson, George L. "South of the North, North of the South: Spatial Practice in the Chaneysville Incident." In *Keep Your Head to the Sky: Cosmology, Ethics, and the Making of African American Home Ground*, edited by Grey Gundaker, 113–44. Charlottesville: University Press of Virginia, 1998.

Henry, H. M. "The Police Control of the Slave in South Carolina." PhD diss., Vanderbilt University, 1914.

Heuman, Gad. *Out of the House of Bondage: Runaways, Resistance, and Maroonage in Africa and the New World*. London: Frank Cass, 1986.

Hewitt, Gary L. "Expansion and Improvement: Land, People, and Politics in South Carolina and Georgia, 1690–1745." PhD diss., Princeton University, 1996.

———. "The State in the Planters' Service: Politics and the Emergence of a Plantation Economy in South Carolina." In *Money, Trade, and Power: The Evolution of Colonial South Carolina's Plantation Society*, edited by Jack P. Greene, Rosemary Brana-Shute, and Randy J. Sparks, 49–73. Columbia: University of South Carolina Press, 2001.

Hilliard, Kathleen M. *Masters, Slaves, and Exchange: Power's Purchase in the Old South*. New York: Cambridge University Press, 2014.

Hodson, Christopher. "'A Bondage So Harsh': Acadian Labor in the French Caribbean, 1763–1766." *Early American Studies* 5, no. 1 (Spring 2007): 95–131.

Howe, Daniel Walker. *What Hath God Wrought: The Transformation of America, 1815–1848*. New York: Oxford University Press, 2009.

Hudson, Anglea Pulley. *Creek Paths and Federal Roads: Indians, Settlers, and Slaves in the Making of the American South*. Chapel Hill: University of North Carolina Press, 2010.

January, Alan F. "The South Carolina Association: An Agency for Race Control in Antebellum Charleston." *South Carolina Historical Magazine* 78, no. 3 (July 1977): 191–201.

Johnson, Michael P. "Denmark Vesey and His Co-Conspirators." *William and Mary Quarterly*, 3rd ser., 58, no. 4 (October 2001): 915–76.

Johnson, Walter. "A Nettlesome Classic Turns Twenty-Five." *Common-Place* 1, no. 4 (July 2001). Accessed May 17, 2010. http://www.common-place.org/vol-01/no-4/reviews/Johnson.shtml.
———. "On Agency." *Journal of Social History* 37, no. 1 (2003): 113–24.
———. *River of Dark Dreams: Slavery and Empire in the Cotton Kingdom*. Cambridge, MA: Harvard University Press, 2013.
———. *Soul by Soul: Life inside the Antebellum Slave Market*. Cambridge, MA: Harvard University Press, 1999.
Jordan, Winthrop. *White over Black: American Attitudes toward the Negro, 1550–1812*. Chapel Hill: University of North Carolina Press, 1968.
Joyce, Patrick. *The Rule of Freedom: Liberalism and the Modern City*. New York: Verso, 2003.
———. *The State of Freedom: A Social History of the British State since 1800*. New York: Cambridge University Press, 2013.
Joyce, Patrick, and Tony Bennett. "Material Powers." In *Material Powers: Cultural Studies, History and the Material Turn*, edited by Patrick Joyce and Tony Bennett, 1–22. New York: Routledge, 2010.
Joyner, Charles. *Down by the Riverside: A South Carolina Slave Community*. Champaign: University of Illinois Press, 1984.
Kantrowitz, Stephen. *Ben Tillman and the Reconstruction of White Supremacy*. Chapel Hill: University of North Carolina Press, 2000.
Kapsch, Robert. *Historic Canals and Waterways of South Carolina*. Columbia: University of South Carolina Press, 2010.
Kaye, Anthony E. *Joining Places: Slave Neighborhoods in the Old South*. Chapel Hill: University of North Carolina Press, 2007.
Kirkland, Thomas J., and Robert Macmillan Kennedy. *Historic Camden: Part One, Colonial and Revolutionary*. Columbia, SC: The State Company, 1905.
Klein, Rachel N. *Unification of a Slave State: The Rise of the Planter Class in the South Carolina Backcountry, 1760–1808*. Chapel Hill: University of North Carolina Press, 1990.
Kupperman, Karen Ordahl. "Fear of Hot Climates in the Anglo-American Colonial Experience." *William and Mary Quarterly* 41, no. 2 (April 1984): 213–40.
Lander, Ernest M. "The Iron Industry in Ante-Bellum South Carolina." *Journal of Southern History* 20, no. 3 (1954): 337–55.
Landers, Jane. "Africans and Native Americans on the Spanish Florida Frontier." In *Beyond Black and Red: African-Native Relations in Colonial Latin America*, edited by Matthew Restall, 53–80. Albuquerque: University of New Mexico Press, 2005.
Larson, John Lauritz. "'Bind the Republic Together': The National Union and the Struggle for a System of Internal Improvements." *Journal of American History* 74, no. 2 (September 1987): 363–87.
———. *Internal Improvement: National Public Works and the Promise of Popular Government in the Early United States*. Chapel Hill: University of North Carolina Press, 2001.

Lefebvre, Henri. *The Production of Space*. Cambridge: Blackwell, 1991.
———. "Space and the State." In *State, Space, World: Selected Essays*, edited by Neil Brenner and Stuart Elden, 223–53. Minneapolis: University of Minnesota Press, 2009.
Leone, Mark P. "A Historical Archaeology of Capitalism." *American Anthropologist* 97, no. 2 (June 1995): 251–68.
———, and Gladys-Marie Fry. "Conjuring in the Big House Kitchen: An Interpretation of African American Beliefs Based on the Uses of Archaeology and Folklore Sources." *Journal of American Folklore* 112, no. 445 (Summer 1999): 372–403.
Lichtenstein, Alex. " 'That Disposition to Theft, with Which They Have Been Branded': Moral Economy, Slave Management, and the Law." *Journal of Social History* 21, no. 3 (Spring 1988): 413–40.
———. *Twice the Work of Free Labor: The Political Economy of Convict Labor in the New South*. New York: Verso, 1996.
Liles, Justin S. "Thomas Sumter's Law: Slavery in the Southern Backcountry during the American Revolution." PhD diss., University of South Carolina, 2011.
Littlefield, Daniel C. *Rice and Slaves: Ethnicity and the Slave Trade in Colonial South Carolina*. Champaign: University of Illinois Press, 1981.
Livingstone, David N. *The Geographical Tradition: Episodes in the History of a Contested Enterprise*. Cambridge: Blackwell, 1993.
Lockley, Timothy J. *Lines in the Sand: Race and Class in Lowcountry Georgia, 1750–1860*. Athens: University of Georgia Press, 2001.
———, ed. *Maroon Communities in South Carolina: A Documentary Record*. Columbia: University of South Carolina Press, 2009.
Lowndes, Joseph, Julie Novkov, and Dorian Warren, eds. *Race and American Political Development*. New York: Routledge, 2008.
MacGaffey, Wyatt. *Religion and Society in Central Africa: The BaKongo of Lower Zaire*. Chicago: University of Chicago Press, 1986.
———. "Twins, Simbi Spirits, and Lwas in Kongo and Haiti." In *Central Africans and Cultural Transformations in the American Diaspora*, edited by Linda M. Heywood, 211–26. Cambridge: Cambridge University Press, 2002.
Maris-Wolf, Ted. *Family Bonds: Free Blacks and Re-Enslavement Law in Antebellum Virginia*. Chapel Hill: University of North Carolina Press, 2015.
Marrs, Aaron W. *Railroads in the Old South: Pursing Progress in a Slave Society*. Baltimore: Johns Hopkins University Press, 2009.
Marshall, Amini T. " 'They Are Supposed to Be Lurking about the City': Enslaved Women Runaways in Antebellum Charleston. *The South Carolina Historical Magazine*, no. 3 (July 2014): 188–212.
Martin, Jonathan D. *Divided Mastery: Slave Hiring in the American South*. Cambridge, MA: Harvard University Press, 2004.
Massey, Doreen. "Places and Their Pasts." *History Workshop Journal* 39 (Spring 1995): 182–92.

McCandless, Peter. *Slavery, Disease, and Suffering in the Southern Lowcountry.* New York: Cambridge University Press, 2014.
McCinnis, Maurie D. *The Politics of Taste in Antebellum Charleston.* Chapel Hill: University of North Carolina Press, 2005.
McCoy, Drew. *The Elusive Republic: Political Economy in Jeffersonian America.* Chapel Hill: University of North Carolina Press, 1980.
McCurry, Stephanie. *Confederate Reckoning: Power and Politics in the Civil War South.* Cambridge, MA: Harvard University Press, 2010.
———. *Masters of Small Worlds: Yeoman Households, Gender Relations, and the Political Culture of the Antebellum South Carolina Low Country.* New York: Oxford University Press, 1997.
McKittrick, Katherine. *Demonic Grounds: Black Women and the Cartographies of Struggle.* Minneapolis: University of Minnesota Press, 2006.
Meinig, D. W. *The Shaping of America: A Geographical Perspective on 500 Years of History.* Vol. 2, *Continental America, 1800–1867.* New Haven, CT: Yale University Press, 1993.
Mendenhall, Marjorie. "A History of Agriculture in South Carolina, 1790–1860." PhD diss., University of North Carolina at Chapel Hill, 1940.
Mercantini, Jonathan. *Who Shall Rule at Home? The Evolution of South Carolina Political Culture, 1748–1776.* Columbia: University of South Carolina Press, 2007.
Meriwether, Robert L. *The Expansion of South Carolina, 1729–1765.* Kingsport, TN: Southern Publishers, 1940.
Merrell, James H. *The Indians' New World: Catawbas and Their Neighbors from European Contact through the Era of Removal.* Chapel Hill: University of North Carolina Press, 1989.
Miller, Ivor L. *Voices of the Leopard: African Secret Societies and Cuba.* Oxford: University Press of Mississippi, 2009.
Mitchell, Timothy. "The Limits of the State: Beyond Statist Approaches and Their Critics." *American Political Science Review* 85, no. 1 (March 1991): 77–96.
———. "Society, Economy, and the State Effect." In *State/Culture: State-Formation after the Cultural Turn,* edited by George Steinmetz, 76–97. Ithaca, NY: Cornell University Press, 1999.
Morgan, Philip D. "Black Society in the Lowcountry, 1760–1810." In *Slavery and Freedom in the Age of the American Revolution,* edited by Ira Berlin and Ronald Hoffman, 83–142. Urbana: University of Illinois Press, 1983.
———. *Slave Counterpoint: Black Culture in the Eighteenth-Century Chesapeake and Lowcountry.* Chapel Hill: University of North Carolina Press, 1998.
Mukerji, Chandra. *Impossible Engineering: Technology and Territoriality on the Canal du Midi.* Princeton, NJ: Princeton University Press, 2009.
Myers, Amrita Chakrabarti. *Forging Freedom: Black Women and the Pursuit of Liberty in Antebellum Charleston.* Chapel Hill: University of North Carolina Press, 2014.
Novak, William J. "Beyond Stateless Democracy." *Tocqueville Review* 36, no. 1 (2015): 21–41.

———. *The People's Welfare: Law and Regulation in Nineteenth-Century America.* Chapel Hill: University of North Carolina Press, 1996.

Oatis, Steven J. *A Colonial Complex: South Carolina's Frontiers in the Era of the Yamasee War, 1680–1730.* Lincoln: University of Nebraska Press, 2004.

O'Brien, Michael. *Conjectures of Order: Intellectual Life and the American South, 1810–1860.* Vol. 1. Chapel Hill: University of North Carolina Press, 2004.

Olwell, Robert. "'Domestick Enemies': Slavery and Political Independence in South Carolina, May 1775–March 1776." *Journal of Southern History* 55, no. 1 (February 1989): 21–48.

———. *Masters, Slaves, and Subjects: The Culture of Power in the South Carolina Low Country, 1740–1790.* Ithaca, NY: Cornell University Press, 1998.

Otto, John S. "The Origins of Cattle-Ranching in Colonial South Carolina, 1670–1715." *South Carolina Historical Magazine* 87, no. 2 (April 1986): 117–24.

Paquette, Robert L. "From Rebellion to Revisionism: The Continuing Debate about the Denmark Vesey Affair." *Journal of the South Carolina Historical Society* 4, no. 3 (September 2004): 291–334.

———. "Jacobins of the Lowcountry: The Vesey Plot on Trial." *William and Mary Quarterly* 59, no. 1 (January 2002): 185–92.

Paquette, Robert L., and Douglas R. Egerton. "Of Facts and Fables: New Light on the Denmark Vesey Affair." *South Carolina Historical Magazine* 105, no. 1 (January 2004): 8–48.

Parrish, Susan Scott. *American Curiosity: Cultures of Natural History in the Colonial British Atlantic World.* Chapel Hill: University of North Carolina Press, 2006.

Pearson, Edward A. "'A Countryside Full of Flames': A Reconsideration of the Stono Rebellion and Slave Rebelliousness in the Early Eighteenth-Century South Carolina Lowcountry." *Slavery and Abolition* 17, no. 2 (1996): 22–50.

———, ed. *Designs against Charleston: The Trial Record of the Denmark Vesey Slave Conspiracy of 1822.* Chapel Hill: University of North Carolina Press, 1999.

Phillips, Ulrich Bonnell. *American Negro Slavery: A Survey of the Supply, Employment and Control of Negro Labor as Determined by the Plantation Regime.* New York: D. Appleton, 1918.

Piecuch, Jim. *Three Peoples, One King: Loyalists, Indians, and Slaves in the Revolutionary South, 1775–1782.* Columbia: University of South Carolina Press, 2008.

Pollitzer, William. *The Gullah People and Their African Heritage.* Athens: University of Georgia Press, 1999.

Powers, Bernard E. *Black Charlestonians: A Social History, 1822–1885.* Fayetteville: University of Arkansas Press, 1994.

Price, Richard, ed. *Maroon Societies: Rebel Slave Communities in the Americas.* Baltimore: Johns Hopkins University Press, 1996.

Quarles, Benjamin. *The Negro in the American Revolution.* Chapel Hill: University of North Carolina Press, 1961.

Quintana, Ryan. "Planners, Planters, and Slaves: Producing the State in Early National South Carolina." *Journal of Southern History* 81, no. 1 (February 2015): 79–116.

Raiford, Norman Gasque. "South Carolina and the Issue of Internal Improvement, 1775–1860." PhD diss., University of Virginia, 1974.
Ramsey, William L. *The Yamasee War: A Study of Culture, Economy, and Conflict in the Colonial South*. Lincoln: University of Nebraska Press, 2008.
Rao, Gautham. *National Duties: Custom Houses and the Making of the American State*. Chicago: University of Chicago Press, 2016.
Ristow, Walter W. *American Maps and Mapmakers: Commercial Cartography in the Nineteenth Century*. Detroit, MI: Wayne State University Press, 1985.
Rockman, Seth. *Scraping By: Wage Labor, Slavery, and Survival in Early Baltimore*. Baltimore: Johns Hopkins University Press, 2009.
———. "The Unfree Origins of American Capitalism." In *The Economy of Early America: Historical Perspectives and New Directions*, edited by Cathy Matson, 335–62. University Park: Pennsylvania State University Press, 2006.
Roper, L. H. *Conceiving Carolina: Proprietors, Planters and Plots, 1662–1729*. New York: Palgrave-Macmillan, 2004.
Rothman, Adam. *Slave Country: American Expansion and the Origins of the Deep South*. Cambridge, MA: Harvard University Press, 2005.
Rothman, Joshua D. *Flush Times and Fever Dreams: A Story of Capitalism and Slavery in the Age of Jackson*. Athens: University of Georgia Press, 2012.
Rucker, Walter C. *The River Flows On: Black Resistance, Culture, and Identity Formation in Early America*. Baton Rouge: Louisiana State University Press, 2006.
Said, Edward W. *Culture and Imperialism*. New York: Knopf, 1993.
———. *Orientalism*. New York: Vintage Books, 1979.
Saler, Bethel. *The Settlers' Empire: Colonialism and State Formation in America's Old Northwest*. Philadelphia: University of Pennsylvania Press, 2015.
Sanders, Albert E., and William D. Anderson Jr. *Natural History Investigations in South Carolina from Colonial Times to the Present*. Columbia: University of South Carolina Press, 1999.
Schermerhorn, Calvin. *Money over Mastery, Family over Freedom: Slavery in the Antebellum Upper South*. Baltimore: Johns Hopkins University Press, 2011.
Schweninger, Loren. "Slave Independence and Enterprise in South Carolina, 1780–1865." *South Carolina Historical Magazine* 93, no. 2 (April 1992): 101–25.
Scott, James C. *Seeing Like a State: How Certain Schemes to Improve the Human Condition Have Failed*. New Haven, CT: Yale University Press, 1998.
Sellers, Charles. *The Market Revolution: Jacksonian America, 1815–1846*. New York: Oxford University Press, 1994.
Shah, Nayan. *Contagious Divides: Epidemics and Race in San Francisco's Chinatown*. Berkeley: University of California Press, 2001.
Sheriff, Carol. *The Artificial River: The Erie Canal and the Paradox of Progress, 1817–1862*. New York: Oxford University Press, 1997.
Shugerman, Jed Handelsman. "The Louisiana Purchase and South Carolina's Reopening of the Slave Trade in 1803." *Journal of the Early Republic* 22, no. 2 (Summer 2002): 263–90.

Silver, Timothy. *A New Face on the Countryside: Indians, Colonists, and Slaves in South Atlantic Forests, 1500–1800*. Cambridge: Cambridge University Press, 1990.
Sinah, Manisha. *The Counterrevolution of Slavery: Politics and Ideology in Antebellum South Carolina*. Chapel Hill: University of North Carolina Press, 2000.
Singleton, Theresa A. "Slavery and Spatial Dialectics on Cuban Coffee Plantations." *World Archaeology* 33, no. 1 (June 2001): 98–114.
Slenes, Robert W. "The Great Porpoise-Skull Strike: Central African Water Spirits and Slave Identity in Early-Nineteenth-Century Rio de Janeiro." In *Central Africans and Cultural Transformations in the American Diaspora*, edited by Linda M. Heywood, 183–208. Cambridge: Cambridge University Press, 2002.
Smallwood, Stephanie E. *Saltwater Slavery: A Middle Passage from Africa to American Diaspora*. Cambridge, MA: Harvard University Press, 2007.
Smith, Alfred Glaze. *Economic Readjustment of an Old South Cotton State: South Carolina, 1820–1860*. Columbia: University of South Carolina Press, 1958.
Smith, Mark M., ed. *Stono: Documenting and Interpreting a Southern Slave Revolt*. Columbia: University of South Carolina Press, 2005.
Soja, Edward W. *Thirdspace: Journeys to Los Angeles and Other Real-and-Imagined Places*. Cambridge: Blackwell, 1996.
Sparke, Matthew. "Mapped Bodies and Disembodied Maps: (Dis)placing Cartographic Struggle in Colonial Canada." In *Places through the Body*, edited by Heidi J. Nast and Steve Pile, 306–66. New York: Routledge, 1998.
Spooner, Matthew. "Origins of the Old South: The Reconstitution of Southern Slavery, 1776–1800." PhD diss., Columbia University, 2015.
Stephens, Lester D. "The Literary and Philosophical Society of South Carolina: A Forum for Intellectual Progress in Antebellum Charleston." *South Carolina Historical Magazine* 104, no. 3 (July 2003): 154–75.
Stewart, Mart A. *"What Nature Suffers to Groe": Life, Labor, and Landscape on the Georgia Coast, 1680–1920*. Athens: University of Georgia Press, 1996.
St. John, Rachel. *A Line in the Sand: A History of the Western US-Mexico Border*. Princeton, NJ: Princeton University Press, 2010.
Sugrue, Thomas J. "The Reconfiguration of Political History." *Tocqueville Review* 36, no. 1 (2015): 11–20.
Sweet, James H. *Recreating Africa: Culture, Kinship, and Religion in the African-Portuguese World, 1441–1770*. Chapel Hill: University of North Carolina Press, 2003.
Tadman, Michael. *Speculators and Slaves: Masters, Traders, and Slaves in the Old South*. Madison: University of Wisconsin Press, 1989.
Taylor, George. *The Transportation Revolution*. New York: Routledge, 1951.
Thompson, Heather Ann. "Why Mass Incarceration Matters: Rethinking Crisis, Decline and Transformation in Postwar American History." *Journal of American History* 97, no. 3 (2010): 703–34.
Thompson, Michael D. *Working on the Dock of the Bay: Labor and Enterprise in an Antebellum Southern Port*. Columbia: University of South Carolina Press, 2015.

Thompson, Robert F. *Flash of the Spirit: African and Afro-American Art and Philosophy*. New York: Random House, 1983.
Thornton, John K. *African and Africans in the Making of the Atlantic World, 1400–1800*. Cambridge: Cambridge University Press, 1992.
———. "African Dimensions of the Stono Rebellion." *American Historical Review* 96, no. 4 (October 1991): 1100–1113.
Turnbull, Robert J. *Bibliography of South Carolina, 1563–1950*. Vol 2. Charlottesville: University of Virginia Press, 1956.
Vlach, John Michael. *Back of the Big House: The Architecture of Plantation Slavery*. Chapel Hill: University of North Carolina Press, 1993.
Waddell, Gene. "Robert Mills, Cartographer." In *Mills Atlas: Atlas of the State of South Carolina, by Robert Mills*, edited by Gene Waddell, i–xii. Greenville: South Carolina Historical Press, 1980.
Wade, Richard C. "The Vesey Plot: A Reconsideration." *Journal of Southern History* 30, no. 2 (May 1964): 143–61.
Wallace, David Duncan. *The History of South Carolina*. New York: American Historical Society, 1934.
———. *The Life of Henry Laurens, with a Sketch of the Life of Lieutenant-Colonel John Laurens*. New York: G. P. Putnam's Sons, 1915.
Waselkov, Gregory A. "Indian Maps of the Colonial Southeast." In *Powhatan's Mantle: Indians in the Colonial Southeast*. Vol. 2, edited by Gregory Waselkov, Peter H. Wood, and M. Thomas Hatley, 435–502. Lincoln: University of Nebraska Press, 2006.
Watts, Sheldon. *Epidemics and History: Disease, Power, and Imperialism*. New Haven, CT: Yale University Press, 1997.
Wax, Darold D. "'The Great Risque We Run': The Aftermath of Slave Rebellion at Stono, South Carolina, 1739–1745." *Journal of Negro History* 67, no. 2 (1982): 136–47.
Way, Peter. *Common Labor: Workers and the Digging of North American Canals, 1780–1860*. Baltimore: Johns Hopkins University Press, 1997.
Weir, Robert. *Colonial South Carolina: A History*. Columbia: University of South Carolina Press, 1997.
———. "'The Violent Spirit,' the Reestablishment of Order, and the Continuity of Leadership in Post-Revolutionary South Carolina." In *An Uncivil War: The Southern Backcountry during the American Revolution*, edited by Ronald Hoffman, 70–98. Charlottesville: University of Virginia Press, 1985.
White, Deborah Gray. *Ar'n't I a Woman? Female Slaves in the Plantation South*. New York: W. W. Norton, 1999.
Winichakul, Thongchai. *Siam Mapped: A History of the Geo-Body of the Nation*. Honolulu: University of Hawaii Press, 1994.
Withers, Charles W. J. "Geography, Natural History and the Eighteenth-Century Enlightenment: Putting the World in Place." *History Workshop Journal* 39 (Spring 1995): 136–63.
Wood, Peter H. *Black Majority: Negroes in Colonial South Carolina from 1670 through the Stono Rebellion*. New York: Alfred A. Knopf, 1975.

———. "The Changing Population of the Colonial South: An Overview by Race and Region, 1685–1790." In *Powhatan's Mantle: Indians in the Colonial Southeast*, edited by Gregory A. Waselkov, Peter H. Wood, and M. Thomas Hatley, 57–132. Lincoln: University of Nebraska Press, 2006.

Young, Jason R. *Rituals of Resistance: African Atlantic Religion in Kongo and the Lowcountry South in the Era of Slavery*. Baton Rouge: Louisiana State University Press, 2007.

Young, Jeffrey Robert. *Domesticating Slavery: The Master Class in Georgia and South Carolina, 1670–1837*. Chapel Hill: University of North Carolina Press, 1999.

Index

Abbeville District, 42
Abraham (slave), 121
Abram (slave), 144
Adams, John, 9
Æra Furnace, 55, 57
African Slave Trade, 97, 127, 132–33; Embargo, 48–49, 68, 73
Amos (slave), 121
Ancrum, William, 56
Anthony, Captain Hezekiah, 54
Ashepoo River, 45, 125
Ashley River, 125
Austin, George, 122

Baker, William, 43
Bakongo Cosmogram, 138
Ball, Elias, 80, 125
Ball, Elias, Jr., 79, 144
Ball, Issac, 101, 138
Bank of the United States, 152
Baptiste, Louis Antoine Jean, 54, 157
Barney (enslaved child), 81
Bartram, John, 47
Bartram, William, 93–94, 99
Beale, Othniel, 35, 36, 157
Beaufort, SC, 84
Beaufort District, 113
Belleisle Island, 82
Bennett, Thomas, 151
Bennett's Mill, 116, 170
Blackburn, George, 154–57, 161, 167, 170, 174
Black River, 99
Blackswamp Association, 109
Blake, Daniel, 124
Blanding, Abram, 159, 161, 162, 169, 172, 174, 175, 176, 182

Board of Public Works, 153, 158–62, 173–77
Bonus Bill, 152
Boundary Line: with Georgia, 84–87; with North Carolina, 45–46, 154
Bridgewater Canal, 68
Brindley, James, 68
British: capture of Savannah, 53, 83; enslaved troops and labor, 81; invasion of Charleston, 51, 53; invasion of Georgetown, 64; Loyalists, 58
Broad River, 72, 161
Brown, James, 75–76
Buford, Warham, 72
Bull, William, Jr., Lt. Gov., 15, 34, 35, 36, 81
Bull's Island, 74
Butler, Thomas, 81

Calhoun, John C., 152–53
Camden, SC, 96
Canal du Midi, 154
Cannon, Daniel, 43, 51
Capital Crime, 167
Cartography, 65–66, 153
Catawba (people), 45, 83–84, 105
Catawba Canal, 73
Catawba Company, 73–74, 158
Catawba River, 60, 73, 161
Cattle Ranges, 94, 120
Charleston: British siege, 55; commercial traffic, 76–78, 102, 122, 123; enslaved movement, 113, 118, 122, 123, 129–31, 141; security, 37, 48–49, 50–54; slave trade, 127
Charleston District, 109
Charleston-Hamburg Railroad, 131, 180
Charleston Neck, 78, 118, 128, 129

Charleston Turnpike and Bridge Company, 78, 158
Charlotte, NC, Courthouse, 63
Cherokee, 32, 84
Chloe (slave), 81
Clinton, Dewitt, 177
Colleton District, 109, 113, 122, 124, 148
Colleton Family, 95
Columbia, SC, 75–76, 144
Commissioners for the Reopening of Wall's Cut, 74–75
Commissioners of (High) Roads, 16, 17, 19–20, 22–23, 64–65, 70–71, 76–78, 161; contractors, 23; mandatory labor, 24
Commissioners of Columbia, South Carolina, 75–76
Commissioners of the Navy, 54
Committee of Forfeited Estates, 61
Committee on Inland Navigation, 59
Common Good, 17
Compensation for slave deaths, 42–44, 105–8
Confiscation, 56, 57, 61–62, 79–81
Congaree River, 27, 149
Congarees, 18
Constitutional Reform of 1808, 159
Cook, James, 65–66, 67
Cooper River, 65
Cordes, James, Jr., 39
Council of Safety, 43, 50
Courson, Benjamin, 144
Crafts, William, 163–64, 165, 166

Daniel (slave), 42–43
Daufuskie Island, 74
de Brahm, Ferdinand, 54
de Brahm, William Gerard, 17, 37, 44, 157
Deerskin Trade, 21–22
Deleiesseline, John, 147–48
Deliesseline, Thomas, 147–48
Denmark Vesey Conspiracy, 109, 170–72, 179, 181
Dido (slave), 80

Dillon, Robert, 63
Dinah (slave), 137
Drayton, Charles, 69, 99, 101, 103, 113, 122, 126, 139–41, 175; as road commissioner, 69; Cossawhatchie River, 90; Drayton Hall, 101; Bob Savannah, 101; Jehossee Island, 90, 100, 113, 122, 124, 139–40; Long Savannah, 113; multiple plantations, 89–90, 97; Sullivan's Island, 90; and Wateree Plantation, 89, 96–97
Drayton, John, 98, 111–12, 153
Dubose, Samuel, 81–82
Dubose, William, 179
Duc de Lauzun, 63
Dunmore (slave), 104–5

Edisto Canal, 175–76
Edisto Island, 122, 139, 140
Edisto River, 60, 122
Edwards, John, 44
Elliott, Bernard, 51
Elliott, Stephen, 153–54, 160
Elliott's Cut, 125
Engineers, 35, 36, 37, 44, 54, 64, 68, 157
Erie Canal, 177–78
Esther (slave), 96
Eutaw Springs, 134
Exeter (slave), 140–41

Farrow, Samuel, 151, 165
Ferguson, Thomas, 59
Ferries, 28
Floods. *See* Freshets
Ford, George, 147, 149
Forest Joe (slave), 3, 147, 149–50, 152, 166, 169, 171, 172, 174, 178–79, 181
Fort Congaree, 56
Fort Johnson, 35, 43
Fort Sullivan, 51
France: Fear of War with, 35; Revolutionary War, 63
Fraser, James, 128
Free Black Carolinians, 34, 180–82

Freer, Solomon, 140
Free School System, 164–65
French Acadians, 38
Freshets, 98–99, 128
Frogmore Manor, 137–38

Galliard, John, 61
Galliard, Peter, 77
Galliard, Theodore, 61
Geddes, John, 112, 167–68
George (slave), 63
Georgetown, 64, 81, 108, 118, 126
Georgetown District, 103, 109
Georgia: 1749 Invasion, 33–35; boundary dispute, 84–88; internal improvements, 161; Savannah River Maroons, 82–87
Gervais, John Lewis, 103
Gibbes, Ann, 124
Gibbes, John, 124
Gibson, Ebenezar, 107
Gilchrist, Adam, 72
Greene, Nathanael, 58, 61

Haitian Revolution, 142, 174
Hales, John J., 101
Hamilton, Paul, 160
Hampton, Wade, 57
Harriet (slave), 80
Harris, Samuel, 42
Harry (slave), 42
Hartstone, Joachim, 83
Hayne, Issac, 55, 57
Herbemont, Nicholas, 159, 165, 167, 171, 174, 182
Hercules (slave), 125
Heriot, Robert, 61, 80–81
Heyward, Nathaniel, 124
Hill, Col. William, 54–55, 58, 59
Hilton Head Island, 74
Hogg, Lewis, 113–14, 168
Horn, Alexander, 54
Horry, Elias, 131

Horry, Peter, 61
Horse Shoe Swamp, 104
Hort, William, 74–75
Hughes, Arthur, 125

Indian Slave Trade, 21–22
Inland Navigation, 19, 27–28, 59–60, 65–68, 71–72, 120–27
Insurrection Scare, 15–18, 106–7, 108, 141
Internal Improvements, 150, 151, 153–54, 157–65, 169

Jack (enslaved boatman), 126
Jack (slave), 149
Jackson, James, 83, 85
Jacksonboro, 47; as temporary capital, 56, 67
Jacob (enslaved driver), 138–39
Jefferson, Thomas, 159, 160
Jehossee Island, 90, 100, 113, 122, 124, 139–40, 147
Jemmy (slave), 44
Jenny (slave), 80
Jim (slave), 130
Johnson, William, 164
Jones, Robert, 75
Joyce, Patrick, 163
Joyner, John, 74
June (slave), 128

Keller v. Hogg, 113–14, 148, 168
Kershaw, Joseph, 59
Kimpasi, 134–35
Kongo spiritual practices, 133–34

Langley, William, 164, 165, 169
Latrobe, Benjamin Henry, 159–60
Laurens, Henry: plantation owner, 95, 96, 100, 102–3, 118, 121, 136–37; road service, 39–42, 52, 78
Laurens, Henry, Jr., 71
Laval, 130
Lawson, John, 18

Lee, Charles, 51
Lincoln, Benjamin, 53
Literary and Philosophical Society, 153–54
Lord, Anne, 56
Lowcountry, 1
Loyalists, 28, 57–58
Lunatic Asylum, 164–66

Maddy (slave), 131–32
Map of South Carolina, 65–66, 67, 154–57
Marion, Frances, 64, 79, 80
Marion, James, 41
Maroons: 1765 Pon Pon District, 45, 104–5; 1816 Pon Pon District, 104–5; Dutch Suriname, 86–87; Jamaica, 86–87; Savannah River, 82–88; Williamsburg District, 106–7
Martin, John, 62
Massey (slave), 71
Mathews, John, 58, 61, 64, 79
Mathis, Samuel, 96
Mayrant's Landing, 121
May River Neck, 74
Mazyckborough, 130
McCants, William, 42–43
McCauley, Hugh, 138–39, 142
McCord's Ferry, 149
McDowell, Davison, 119, 125
Mepkin Plantation, 40, 100
Merchant, Thomas, 139–40
Middleton, Arthur, 57
Middleton, Henry, 77
Midwife, 137
Militia, 83, 91, 104, 125, 154
Mills, Robert, 1–2, 85, 153, 159, 163; Asylum, 165, 166; as member of Board of Public Works, 159, 160, 164, 167, 173–77, 182; penitentiary, 160; state atlas, 155
Miscampbell, Robert, 61
Mitchell, Samuel, 177–78
Morris, George, 116–17

Moultrie, William, 51, 80, 89
Mouzon, Henry, 65–66
Mowby (slave), 104–5

Nanny (slave), 80
Negro Seaman Act, 180
Nella (slave), 139
New Cut, 92, 122, 123
North Carolina, 45, 144, 161

Ocra (slave), 136–37
Ogilvie, Charles, 62
Oglethorpe, James, 33
Old Peggy (enslaved midwife), 137
Orde, John, 80
Ordinance for the Procurement of Negroes for Public Service, 51–53
Overseers, 97, 101

Pass System, 91–92, 105–8, 110–15, 168
Paternalism, 109–10, 167–69
Patrol Act of 1740, 111
Pearl, Charles, 75
Peddlers, 123–27
Pee Dee River, 99, 138–39, 161
Penal Reform, 167–68
Penitentiary, 160
Philip (enslaved driver), 139–40
Pierre Louis (slave), 130
Pinckney, Charles Cotesworth, 48–49, 54
Pinckney, Thomas, 83, 85
Pineville Police Association, 109, 179
Plantation Complex: expansion, 24, 97–100, 124, 142–43; indigo plantations, 90, 94; inland swamp plantations, 99; necessity of enslaved mobility, 112, 122; tidewater plantations, 90, 97–100
Pompey (slave), 106–7
Pon Pon River, 104–5, 125
Pooshee Swamp, 134
Porcher, Samuel, 127–28
Poro, 134–35
Prioleau, Samuel, 38

Proctor, Richard, 74–75
Property Rights, 11, 17, 20–21, 41–43, 52–53, 108
Prosser, Gabriel, 142
Public Buildings, 162–64
Purry, Charles, 44
Purry, Sarah, 44
Purrysburg, SC, 82

Quacoo (slave), 101
Queen Anne's War, 21

Ramsay, David, 67, 98
Rantowles's Bridge, 78, 92, 126
Rantowles's Creek, 90
Ravenel, Daniel, 70
Ravenel, Henry, 70, 134
Regulator Movement, 28
Roads: Between Willtown and Charlestown, 15–16; heavy traffic, 76–78; King's Highway, 93–94; St. James Santee, 26; State Road, 149, 161, 178–79
Robin (slave), 44, 63, 81–82, 85
Robinson, George, 59
Rocky Mount Arsenal, 73
Rodgers, David L., 106–7
Rose, John, 62
Royal (enslaved boatman), 178, 179–80
Ruffin, Edmund, 134, 142
Runaway Slaves, 79–82, 104–5, 116–17, 125, 128, 130, 136–37, 144–47
Rush, Benjamin, 67
Rutledge, Edward, 57, 89
Rutledge, John, 53, 59, 65

Saby (slave), 80
St. Augustine, Florida, Invasion of, 33
St. George's Parish, 77
St. Helena Island, 21, 137
St. James Goose Creek, 76
St. James Santee Parish, 26, 126, 144
St. John's Berkeley Parish, 24, 39, 70, 77, 122
St. John's Island, 20

St. Luke's Parish, 77
St. Paul's Parish, 122, 123, 144
St. Stephen's Parish, 70–71, 142, 144
Salters, William, 106–7
Saluda Gap, 161
Sam (slave), 80
Sande, 134–35
Santee Canal Company, 65, 68, 72–73, 78, 82, 158
Santee-Cooper Canal, 59–60, 65–74, 82, 109, 128, 134, 157–58, 178–79
Santee River, 18, 65, 149, 157, 161
Santees, 18
Savage's Island, 74
Savannah, GA, 82
Savannah River, 42, 77, 82–87, 126, 161
Schad, Abraham, 121
Senf, Johann Christian, 64, 68, 70, 71, 74, 157
Seven Years' War, 21, 37
Sewees, 18
Simbi, 133
Simmons, Charles H., 80
Simpson (slave), 124
Sinkler, Peter, 70
Slave Code, 91, 110
Slave Patrol, 91–92, 105–8, 110–15, 125
Slaves: as boat hands, 90, 102–4, 107, 113, 117, 120–22; and illicit trade, 108, 113, 120–22, 123–26, 142; and King's Army, 81; as labor on fortifications, 34–39, 48–49, 50–54, 63, 64; as labor for private companies and contractors, 68–69, 70, 74, 75–76, 79; as labor on state roads, 24–26, 29–32, 70, 76–78, 79, 124; midwives, 137; as mobile laborers, 100–104, 137, 180; murder by, 139–41, 147–48; murder of, 167–68; as objects of informational exchanges, 30–32, 33–43, 63; owned by state, 57–63; as payment to South Carolina soldiers, 55–57; as plantation drivers, 90, 131; and religion, 132–36, 137–39; skilled labor, 101–2, 137

Smith, Josiah, 122
South Carolina College, 154, 164
Sovereignty, 85–88
Spanish, 32
Steamboat, 161
Stono Rebellion, 3, 15–16, 32, 35, 46, 104; Aftermath, 25, 189n3
Stono River, 92, 122
Strawberry Causeway, 25
Sugarees, 18
Sullivan's island, 43, 50
Sumter, Thomas, 56
Syfax (slave), 80

Taylor, John, 79–80, 144
Tenah (slave), 80
Tim (enslaved boatman), 92
Tom (slave), 125
Toney (slave), 119–20
Tony (slave), 44
Township System, 26, 33
Treaty of Beaufort (1787), 84
Tucker, Daniel, 61
Turamoush (enslaved boatman), 103
Turnpike, 76–78
Tuscarora War, 18, 21–22

Vesey, Denmark, 1; and conspiracy, 1, 109

Waccamaw Neck, 125
Waccamaw River, 99
Wall's Cut, 74
Wappoo Creek, 92, 123
Wappoo Cut, 113, 125, 128
War of Jenkins' Ear, 21
Washaws, 18
Watboo Estate, 95
Wateree River, 27, 161
Waterees, 18
Watt's Cut, 123
Wauney, 81–82, 85
Wayne, William, 80
Weber, Max, 3
West Africans, 128, 130, 131, 132–36; and secret societies, 134–35
West-Central Africans, 128, 132–36; and burial practices, 134; and secret societies, 134–35; and simbi spirits, 132–34
White, James, 44
Williams, David, 104, 128, 156
Williamsburg Township, 27
Willtown Road, 21
Wilson, John L., 155, 156, 157–58, 160
Winyaw Bay, 93, 99
Winyaws, 18

Yamasee War, 17, 18, 21–22
Yazoo Flood, 98–99
Youngblood, William, 104

www.ingramcontent.com/pod-product-compliance
Lightning Source LLC
Chambersburg PA
CBHW030538230426
43665CB00010B/945